The JEWISH
EXPERIENCE in America

This bibliography was conceived and compiled from the periodicals database of the American Bibliographical Center by editors at ABC-Clio Information Services, Inc.

Robert de V. Brunkow, Assistant Editor
Lance Klass, Assistant Editor
David J. Valiulis, Assistant Editor

Pamela Byrne, Associate Editor
Gail Schlachter, Vice President, Publications

The JEWISH EXPERIENCE in America

 A Historical Bibliography

ABC-Clio, Inc.
Santa Barbara, California
Oxford, England

US ISBN 0-87436-034-x

ABC-Clio, Inc.
2040 Alameda Padre Serra, Box 4397
Santa Barbara, California 93103

Clio Press Ltd.
Woodside House, Hinksey Hill
Oxford, OX1 5BE, England

Manufactured in the United States of America

American Bibliographical Center
ABC-Clio, Inc.

CONTENTS

LIST OF ABBREVIATIONS

A.	Author-prepared Abstract	*IHE*	Indice Historico Espanol
Acad.	Academy, Academie, Academia	*Illus.*	Illustrated, Illustration
Agric.	Agriculture, Agricultural	*Inst.*	Institute, Institut-.
AIA	Abstracts in Anthropology	*Int.*	International, Internacional,
Akad.	Akademie		Internationaal, Internationaux,
Am.	America, American		Internazionale
Ann.	Annals, Annales, Annual, Annali	*J.*	Journal, Journal-prepared Abstract
Anthrop.	Anthropology, Anthropological	*Lib.*	Library, Libraries
Arch.	Archives	*Mag.*	Magazine
Archaeol.	Archaeology, Archaeological	*Mus.*	Museum, Musee, Museo
Art.	Article	*Nac.*	Nacional
Assoc.	Association, Associate	*Natl.*	National, Nationale
Biblio.	Bibliography, Bibliographical	*Naz.*	Nazionale
Biog.	Biography, Biographical	*Phil.*	Philosophy, Philosophical
Bol.	Boletim, Boletin	*Photo.*	Photograph
Bull.	Bulletin	*Pol.*	Politics, Political, Politique, Politico
c.	century (in index)	*Pr.*	Press
ca.	circa	*Pres.*	President
Can.	Canada, Canadian, Canadien	*Pro.*	Proceedings
Cent.	Century	*Publ.*	Publishing, Publication
Coll.	College	*Q.*	Quarterly
Com.	Committee	*Rev.*	Review, Revue, Revista, Revised
Comm.	Commission	*Riv.*	Rivista
Comp.	Compiler	*Res.*	Research
DAI	Dissertation Abstracts	*RSA*	Romanian Scientific Abstracts
	International	*S.*	Staff-prepared Abstract
Dept.	Department	*Sci.*	Science, Scientific
Dir.	Director, Direktor	*Secy.*	Secretary
Econ.	Economy, Econom-.	*Soc.*	Society, Societe, Sociedad, Societa
Ed.	Editor, Edition	*Sociol.*	Sociology, Sociological
Educ.	Education, Educational	*Tr.*	Transactions
Geneal.	Genealogy, Genealogical,	*Transl.*	Translator, Translation
	Genealogique	*U.*	University, Universi-.
Grad.	Graduate	*Vol.*	Volume
Hist.	History, Hist-.	*Y.*	Yearbook

Abbreviations also apply to feminine and plural forms.
Abbreviations not noted above are based on *Webster's Third New International Dictionary*
and the *United States Government Printing Office Style Manual*.

INTRODUCTION

The Jewish community in North America has provided historians, social scientists, researchers, and scholars from many disciplines with a unique and absorbing subject of study. Thousands of scholarly works, their numbers increasing dramatically in recent years, have sought to investigate and understand the nature of the Jewish experience in the United States and Canada. This proliferation of scholarship, while contributing significantly to our understanding of Jewish life and history and of American and Canadian society, has led to an increasing demand by librarians, researchers, and academics for comprehensive bibliographic control which would bring the huge amount of recent scholarship within easy reach.

That control now exists with the publication of *The Jewish Experience in America: A Historical Bibliography,* a significant addition to Jewish scholarship and an essential reference work for individuals wishing to discover the rich body of scholarly literature on Jews in America. This annotated bibliography was created from the American Bibliographical Center's vast database—the largest history database in the world—and includes 827 article abstracts selected from more than 2,000 journals in 42 languages, published in nearly 90 countries. The abstracts, which cover journal literature from 1973 through 1979, were prepared by a worldwide network of scholars. Abstracts are arranged alphabetically by author. All non-English article titles have been translated into English, and all abstracts are written in English, thereby providing the student and scholar with access to scholarship from all over the world.

The scope of the present work is as extensive and varied as the nature of the Jewish experience itself. Articles relate to the entire history of the Jewish community in North America, from the early days of discovery and colonization through to the present. In the following pages the researcher will find intensive studies of intra-Jewish relationships (including, for example, the development and relations between the Sephardic and Ashkenazic communities), the interaction of Jews with the larger society (including Jewish contributions to literature, art, commerce, education, and politics), and the responses of the Jewish community to world affairs (for example, its responses to the Holocaust and to the Arab-Israeli conflict). Within these pages the reader will also find citations to

INTRODUCTION

biographies of Jews from all walks of life, from pioneers in the Old West to Supreme Court justices, and to articles covering topics as diverse as the organization of garment workers and Albert Einstein's views on Zionism.

A rapid review of the subject index will reveal the diversity of materials covered. Using the Subject Profile Index (ABC-SPIndex) developed by the American Bibliographic Center, editors select four to six key terms or phrases from each entry, and these descriptive terms are linked together to form a composite index entry that provides a complete subject profile of the journal article. Each set (or "string") of index terms is then rotated so that the entire profile is listed in the index under each of its composite terms. In this way, users will find a full subject profile of the entry at four or five access points in the index. Please refer to the explanatory note at the head of the index for further information on ABC-SPIndex.

A companion volume, *Religion and Society in North America: A Bibliography,* will deal more fully with the religious aspects of the Jewish experience in America and is scheduled for publication in early 1983.

THE JEWISH EXPERIENCE
IN AMERICA

1. Abella, Irving, ed. PORTRAIT OF A JEWISH PROFESSIONAL REVO-LUTIONARY: THE RECOLLECTIONS OF JOSHUA GERSHMAN. *Labour [Canada] 1977 2: 184-213.* Gershman came to Canada from Europe in 1921. He soon began his association with the labor movement. In 1923 he joined the Communist Party and remained a member for 54 years. His memoir provides insights on left-wing Jewish unionism, Zionism, cultural life, and Communist activity in Winnipeg, Toronto, Montreal, and Chicago. He left the CP because of differences on the Jewish and national questions. Introduction gives historical perspective and emphasizes uniqueness of Jewish labor movement because of its dominance in the garment industry and its support of "progressive candidates and causes." Based on interviews; 3 notes.   W. A. Kearns

2. Abrahams, Edward. THE PAST FAILURE OF FASCISM IN THE U.S.A. *Patterns of Prejudice [Great Britain] 1974 8(2): 23-27.* Discusses fascist organizations and leaders in the United States in the 1930's, emphasizing anti-Semitism.

3. Adler, Adam W. MY FATHER WAS BORN A JEW. *Western States Jewish Hist. Q. 1974 6(4): 255-259.* Lewis Adler (1820-96) was one of the first persons of Jewish descent to arrive in California. His father had converted to Christianity in Germany in 1829 but the family retained its ethnic identity. Adler worked as a journeyman cooper for William Heath Davis for eight months and then opened his own store in Sonoma in late 1847. By 1850, Lewis had acquired a small fortune and traveled to Germany to visit his mother. In 1855, he opened a wholesale business with Jacob Bloomingdale, and later expanded into the wholesale liquor business. Photo, 4 notes.   R. A. Garfinkle

4. Adler, Frank J. REVIEW ESSAY: *HARRY S. TRUMAN. Am. Jewish Hist. Q. 1973 62(4): 414-425.* Criticizes Margaret Truman's description of the Palestine issue in her biography of her father. The review focuses on the partition question (1946-47) and on the part played by Truman's Jewish friend Eddie Jacobson. Margaret Truman mentions only one White House interview with Jacobson but the presidential records show 24 appointments during this period. Margaret Truman's picture of her father's dispassionate stance on these issues is inaccurate. 47 notes.   F. Rosenthal

5. Adler, Selig. THE UNITED STATES AND THE HOLOCAUST. *Am. Jewish Hist. Q. 1974 64(1): 14-23.* The US government did less to mitigate the catastrophe that befell European Jews than it could have because 1) Washington initially made incorrect assumptions concerning the extent and possible alleviation of the holocaust, 2) measures taken lacked a sense of urgency because of low priority on the war timetable and the end of war political maneuvers, and 3) measures taken came too late to save any considerable number of Jews. Proofs for these points constitute a new approach to the entire question. 23 notes.   F. Rosenthal

6. Alpert, David B. THE MAN FROM KOVNO. *Am. Jewish Arch. 1977 29(2): 107-115.* Not all history is the history of the famous or well-known. This is especially true for the story of American Jewry—where the poor and unlettered played a vital role in its development. Rabbi Abraham Alpert does not rank among the names that have become legend to most American Jews. But to a segment of Boston Jewry, his many efforts to improve the lot of immigrant life earned him a kind of love and respect that the rich and famous could indeed envy.
J

7. Alschuler, Al. THE COLMANS AND OTHERS OF DEADWOOD, SOUTH DAKOTA. *Western States Jewish Hist. Q. 1977 9(4): 291-298.* Nathan Colman, a German Jewish immigrant, came to Deadwood, South Dakota, in 1877 and opened a tobacco store. He was appointed postmaster in 1878, elected justice of the peace, and active in local Republican politics. In 1911 Colman's daughter Blanche became the first woman admitted to the South Dakota Bar. For more than 50 years she was a practicing attorney. Other Jews settled in frontier Deadwood in the 1870's and became prominent in businesses and industries. The Jewish community has diminished with the rest of Deadwood's population; Blanche Colman is the only remaining member of the pioneer Jewish community. Based on newspapers, family records and secondary sources; 4 photos, 20 notes.
B. S. Porter

8. Alter, Robert. DEFAMING THE JEWS. *Commentary 1973 55(1): 77-82.* Examines the negative image of Jews in the film *Portnoy's Complaint* and other Jewish and non-Jewish fiction and humor since the late 1960's; contrasts useful satire with destructive stereotypes.

9. Alter, Robert. MANNERS & THE JEWISH INTELLECTUAL. *Commentary 1975 60(2): 58-64.* Reviews the revolutionary tradition in Jewish intellectual thought as examined by John Murray Cuddihy in *The Ordeal of Civility: Freud, Marx, Lévi-Strauss, and the Jewish Struggle with Modernity* (New York: Basic Books, 1974).
S

10. Alter, Robert. WHAT JEWISH STUDIES CAN DO. *Commentary 1974 58(4): 71-77.* Discusses the place of Jewish studies in American colleges and universities during the 1960's and 70's.
S

11. Anderson, Elaine. WILLIAM KRAUS AND THE JEWISH COMMUNITY. *Northwest Ohio Q. 1977 49(4): 127-162.* Chronicles the demise of William Kraus, a leading member of the Jewish community in Toledo, Ohio, during 1869-76. A few unpopular acts during his administration as the city's mayor, compounded by the closing of his bank, and shady real estate dealings, led to his exile in Canada.

12. Angel, Marc D. NOTES ON THE EARLY HISTORY OF SEATTLE'S SEPHARDIC COMMUNITY. *Western States Jewish Hist. Q. 1974 7(1): 22-30.* The first Sephardic Jews arrived in Seattle in 1906 and by 1912 there were about 800 located there. They had many problems getting themselves organized as a religious group and locating a suitable rabbi. Their problems were similar to those faced by Sephardic Jews in other American cities who held onto the customs and traditions of their homelands. Few of the immigrants became American citizens. 15 notes.
R. A. Garfinkle

13. Angel, Marc D. THE SEPHARDIC THEATER OF SEATTLE. *Am. Jewish Arch. 1973 25(2): 156-160.* "An account of how the Turkish immigrant Leon Behar and others developed a theater for the Seattle Sephardic community, particularly during the 1920's and 1930's." J

14. Appelbaum, Paul S. U.S. JEWS' REACTION TO SOVIET "ANTI-ZIONISM." *Patterns of Prejudice [Great Britain] 1978 12(2): 21-32.* Examines attitudes toward anti-Semitism and anti-Zionism in the USSR by Jews in the United States, 1948-78.

15. Applebaum, Phillip. THE JEWS OF IOSCO COUNTY, MICHIGAN. *Michigan Jewish Hist. 1976 16(1): 18-38.* Describes the settlement patterns of the Eastern European Jews, generally merchants and tailors, from 1866 to 1975.

16. Applebaum, Phillip. THE JEWS OF KALKASKA COUNTY, MICHIGAN. *Michigan Jewish Hist. 1979 19(1): 4-10.* Discusses Jewish settlers during 1870-1900.

17. Applebaum, Phillip. THE JEWS OF MONTMORENCY COUNTY, MICHIGAN. *Michigan Jewish Hist. 1978 18(1): 5-14.* Covers 1893-1970.

18. Arden, Sylvia Ann. SAN DIEGO PURIM BALL IN 1888. *Western States Jewish Hist. Q. 1974 7(1): 39-43.* Reprints text of article from *The Jewish Progress*, San Francisco, 9 March 1888. Relates who served on the various Purim Ball committees with short biographies of the people mentioned in the original article. Primary and secondary sources; 20 notes. R. A. Garfinkle

19. Aristides. A LITERARY MAFIA? *Am. Scholar 1975 44(2): 182-194.* Younger, less well-situated writers claim that there is a literary mafia, located in New York, predominantly Jewish, and largely comprised of older men and women, who control literature, divide up the spoils of fame, money, and power, and take care of their own. Its true seats of power are a handful of magazines. Discusses in detail *The End of Intelligent Writing*, by Richard Kostelanetz. Concludes that the notion of a literary mafia ignores all the difficult issues. E. P. Stickney

20. Arnold, A. J. THE EARLIEST JEWS IN WINNIPEG 1874-1882. *Beaver [Canada] 1974 305(2): 4-11.* Describes the settlement of Russian Jews in Winnipeg. Disappointed at first because most failed to receive land grants or find employment, many eventually moved out of the city to find or create employment opportunities. For those who stayed, the city offered closer ties with Jewish cultural institutions. 11 illus. D. Heermans

21. Arnold, A. J. JEWISH PIONEER SETTLEMENTS. *Beaver [Canada] 1975 306(2): 20-26.* A series of settlements of Russian Jews was started in the 1880's at the instigation of Sir Alexander Galt. Three bad crop years led to dissatisfaction; some of the Jews went to Manitoba, others began "peddling." Mentions other contemporary Jewish settlements, occupations, travel problems, family life, and relations with neighboring communities. Provides details on the family of Alter Kaplun of Wapella, who settled there in 1891 and whose descendants are still on the farm. 12 illus., map. D. Chaput

22.   Asher, Robert.   JEWISH UNIONS AND THE AMERICAN FEDERA-
TION OF LABOR POWER STRUCTURE 1903-1935.   *Am. Jewish Hist. Q.
1976 65(3): 215-227.* Jewish unions, those with a substantial number of Jewish
members and led by Jewish officers, until the 1930's were largely in, but not of,
the mainstream of the American labor movement. Recognizing their differences
with the AFL, the Jewish unions cooperated with the AFL when they could, but
went their own way politically in their attempt to build a welfare state through
union institutions and trade agreements with employers. By the late 1920's the
Jewish unions, especially the International Ladies' Garment Workers' Union, had
drifted slowly to the right and the American Federation of Labor had moved
toward the left, so that the Amalgamated Clothing Workers of America could
be admitted into the AFL, and the ILGWU could be allowed into the AFL power
structure (executive council and resolutions committee). The accomplishments of
the New Deal Democratic Party accelerated this process. 23 notes.
                                                                F. Rosenthal

23.   Ashton, Dore.   NO MORE THAN AN ACCIDENT?   *Critical Inquiry
1976 3(2): 235-249.* Examples ever since the Franco-Prussian War demonstrate
how in Europe and in the United States vulgar associations of Jews with art have
persisted.

24.   Astrachan, Anthony.   ON THE BROAD PRAIRIE: IN WINNIPEG,
MANITOBA: A JEWISH PHENOMENON.   *Present Tense 1975 2(4): 31-35.*
History and description of the flourishing Jewish community in Winnipeg,
Manitoba.   S

25.   Auerbach, Jerold S.   FROM RAGS TO ROBES: THE LEGAL PROFES-
SION, SOCIAL MOBILITY AND THE AMERICAN JEWISH EXPERI-
ENCE.   *Am. Jewish Hist. Q. 1976 65(2): 249-284.* The experiences of Jewish
lawyers since 1900 illuminate the struggle for success within a profession whose
elite members preferred to ostracize or exclude them. Retraces the route from
"ghetto shyster and collection lawyer" to Wall Street partner, Federal and Supreme Court Justice, and government lawyer ever since the New Deal. As a
result, in the 1970's Jewish lawyers have often become the spokesmen for the
establishment against more recent "minorities" and the defenders of professional-
ism. At the same time, Jews still are overrepresented on local and national boards
of civil rights organizations, to say nothing of the records of the four Jewish
Supreme Court Justices. 79 notes.   F. Rosenthal

26.   Axe, Ruth Frey.   SIGMUND FREY: LOS ANGELES JEWRY'S FIRST
PROFESSIONAL SOCIAL WORKER.   *Western States Jewish Hist. Q. 1976
8(4): 312-325.* Rabbi Sigmund Frey (1852-1930) came to Los Angeles to be the
superintendent for the Jewish Orphan's Home then located at Mission and Macy
streets. In 1910 a fire destroyed the home and in November 1912 the new Jewish
Orphan's Home was dedicated in Huntington Park, California. Rabbi Frey
became a well known author, scholar, journalist, bibliophile, and teacher. In
1921, he resigned as superintendent. Before his death in Los Angeles Rabbi Frey
and his wife Hermine traveled several times to Europe. Primary and secondary
sources; 4 photos, 5 notes.   R. A. Garfinkle

27. Bachmann, Lawrence P. JULIUS ROSENWALD. *Am. Jewish Hist. Q. 1976 66(1): 89-105.* Julius Rosenwald (1862-1932), vice president and treasurer of the world's largest retail company, Sears, Roebuck and Company, was at the same time one of the most generous philanthropists. Sketches his business career, emphasizing the business acumen which made his company a model organization, and details his philanthropic activities. From 1917-32 the Julius Rosenwald Foundation initiated the establishment of 5,357 public schools for blacks which raised the level of teaching and teaching instruction throughout the country. Contributions to the University of Chicago and to various Jewish philanthropies were on a similar scale.   F. Rosenthal

28. Banks, Dean. H. L. MENCKEN AND "HITLERISM," 1933-1941: A PATRICIAN LIBERTARIAN BESIEGED. *Maryland Hist. Mag. 1976 71(4): 498-515.* Charles Angoff's *H. L. Mencken: A Portrait from Memory* (1956) was a chief source of the charges of "Hitlerism" leveled at H. L. Mencken after 1933. The book "marshalled selected data" and stressed Mencken's insensitivity to anti-Semitism. In reality, Mencken had an attachment to liberty and freedom of speech which also carried with it the "right to refrain from expression, the right to judicious restraint or silence." Mencken's elitist distrust of public opinion and mass emotionalism restrained him from actively joining the anti-Hitler militants. While scorning political radicalism, he consistently championed the right of free speech for all American extremists. Mencken's growing anti-New Deal sentiments would have spurred much resentment among intellectuals after early 1933 anyway; but his consistent scorn for chauvinism and emotional group behavior of all sorts, his basic belief that Nazism was most akin to Ku Klux Klanism, and the memory of his World War I attitude toward the "dangerous hysterias of democracy," made him equally oppose Jewish nationalism, 100 percent Americanism, and German racialism during the 1930's. Primary and secondary materials; 89 notes.   G. J. Bobango

29. Barberis, Mary A. THE ARAB-ISRAELI BATTLE ON CAPITOL HILL. *Virginia Q. R. 1976 52(2): 203-223.* Insists that in the struggle for US support in the Middle East the Jewish lobby in Washington has been far more influential than Arab supporters. Pro-Israel lobbying, aimed at Congress, has "acted to strengthen pre-existing attitudes." Most influential has been the American Israel Public Affairs Committee (AIPAC). Fewer Arabs in the US, less well-organized lobbying, and American public opinion have weakened the Arab position, but that may be changing now.   O. H. Zabel

30. Barnes, Al. JULIUS H. STEINBERG, EARLY JEWISH PIONEER OF TRAVERSE CITY AND THE STEINBERG GRAND OPERA HOUSE. *Michigan Jewish Hist. 1974 14(2): 24-28.* Documents Julius H. Steinberg's activities in the 1890's in Michigan.   S

31. Barnett, Lincoln. HOW ALBERT EINSTEIN, A GENTLE, MODEST GENIUS BORN 100 YEARS AGO, FOUND SANCTUARY AND INSPIRATION IN PRINCETON. *Smithsonian 1979 9(11): 68-79.* Einstein decided to accept an appointment to the newly established Institute for Advanced Study in Princeton, New Jersey, in 1933 after observing with horror the Nazi assault on the intellect. He renounced his German citizenship while he was a visiting professor at Caltech, shortly after Hitler became chancellor of Germany. In 1939 he

wrote President Roosevelt a prophetic letter warning about the atomic bomb. It was a prologue to the Manhattan Project and Hiroshima. Illus.

E. P. Stickney

32. Baron, Salo W. INTRODUCTION: REFLECTIONS ON THE ACHIEVEMENTS AND PROSPECTS OF *JEWISH SOCIAL STUDIES. Jewish Social Studies 1979 41(1): 1-8.* The first issue of *Jewish Social Studies* was published in January 1939 under Managing Editor Koppel S. Pinson, with the Conference on Jewish Relatins providing financial and scholarly support. The journal was issued to some extent to provide a forum for examination of contemporary and historical Jewish issues in a manner different from other Jewish scholarly journals, emphasizing ancient and medieval Biblical exegesis. Those connected with the journal and with the conference engaged in important bibliograpical work on Jewish studies published in the journal and, after World War II, aided in the tracing and recovery of important Jewish artifacts lost during the Holocaust. Recently a monograph series has been started under the auspices of the journal. Based on personal observation and involvement. N. Lederer

33. Barron, Jerome A. LIBERTY OR EQUALITY? *Rhode Island Jewish Hist. Notes 1975 7(1): 5-11.* Discusses liberty and equality for Jews, centering on the court case which Marco De Funis brought against a Washington law school, charging that he had been discriminated against when less-qualified applicants were admitted because of their other-minority status.

34. Bauer, Yehuda. "ONKEL SALY": DIE VERHANDLUNGEN DES SALY MAYER ZUR RETTUNG DER JUDEN 1944/45 ["Uncle Saly": the negotiations of Saly Mayer to save Jews, 1944-45]. *Vierteljahrshefte für Zeitgeschichte [West Germany] 1977 25(2): 188-219.* Describes the negotiations of Saly Mayer (1882-1950), Swiss industrialist and chairman of the Union of Jewish Communities in Switzerland, with representatives of SS Chief Heinrich Himmler. The American Jewish Joint Distribution Committee and the US government authorized negotiations in order to gain time, but did not authorize the offer of dollars and goods desired by the Nazis. With very limited means Mayer was able to delay and finally to prevent the deaths of many thousands of Jews. Based on records at the Roosevelt Library and in British, Israeli, and US archives, published documents, memoirs, and secondary sources; 64 notes. D. Prowe

35. Beck, Nelson R. THE USE OF LIBRARY AND EDUCATIONAL FACILITIES BY RUSSIAN-JEWISH IMMIGRANTS IN NEW YORK CITY, 1880-1914: THE IMPACT OF CULTURE. *J. of Lib. Hist. 1977 12(2): 129-149.* Discusses use of the public library and its services by Russian-Jewish immigrants in New York City between 1880 and 1914, and the historic and cultural influences which caused these particular immigrants not to fit Michael Harris's revisionist interpretation of American library history. Covers Hebrew educational associations and libraries, and Jewish newspapers of the period. Primary and secondary sources; 124 notes. A. C. Dewees

36. Belakoui, Janice Monti. IMAGES OF ARABS AND ISRAELIS IN THE PRESTIGE PRESS, 1966-74. *Journalism Q. 1978 55(4): 732-738, 799.* Compares US public opinion toward Israel and the Arab states from 1967 to 1975 and press coverage, 1966-74, by three US news magazines and two New York newspa-

pers. The press presented a more generally favorable image of Arab leaders and spokesmen in 1973 than it had six years before, just as Gallup opinion polls showed a slight increase in the percentage of respondents who expressed sympathy for the Arabs. 11 notes. R. P. Sindermann, Jr.

37. Ben-Amos, Dan. THE "MYTH" OF JEWISH HUMOR. *Western Folklore 1973 32(2): 112-131.* Discusses current conceptions of Jewish humor as "self-critical" and attributes this attitude to Freud and other psychoanalysts. After examining Jewish humor, the author concludes that "joking in Jewish society does not involve mocking of self either directly or indirectly." Based on primary and secondary sources; 42 notes. S. L. Myres

38. Benkin,, Richard L. ETHNICITY AND ORGANIZATION: JEWISH COMMUNITIES IN EASTERN EUROPE AND THE UNITED STATES. *Sociol. Q. 1978 19(4): 614-625.* In most essential respects, the immigrant communities of American Jews (and the total American Jewish community) were a direct continuation of those which appeared in Eastern Europe prior to 1914. The author reconstructs the sociohistorical environment in which they appeared. The extensive communal organization which characterized both settings actually served the interests of societal demands. These institutions provided needed services to the community, but they also supported the out-group's status, as determined by the larger society. A clear picture emerges of the impact on the collective Jewish, and individual Jew's, adaptation to society within a highly developed and organized community. Based on archives, government reports, and texts. J

39. Berger, Elmer. MEMOIRS OF AN ANTI-ZIONIST JEW. *J. of Palestine Studies [Lebanon] 1975-76 5(1-2): 3-55.* Publishes the memoirs of Rabbi Elmer Berger, an American anti-Zionist, who for over 30 years has led an active opposition to Zionism, racism toward the Arabs, and US support for such policies.

40. Berger, Graenum. AMERICAN JEWISH COMMUNAL SERVICE 1776-1976: FROM TRADITIONAL SELF-HELP TO INCREASING DEPENDENCE ON GOVERNMENT SUPPORT. *Jewish Social Studies 1976 38(3-4): 225-246.* The Jewish tradition of communal self-help was imported to America with the arrival of the first Jewish immigrants; it contributed to the rise of private, voluntary, sectarian social welfare agencies amid the American Jewish community. Jews assumed a responsibility to help their fellows in times of trouble in a way similar to that undertaken by various Christian denominations. With the necessity for increased governmental intervention in the social welfare area since the Depression of the 1930's, Jewish agencies have assumed a semiofficial, quasi-governmental status with increasingly nonsectarian emphases in their social services. N. Lederer

41. Bergman, Elihu. THE AMERICAN JEWISH POPULATION EROSION. *Midstream 1977 23(8): 9-19.* Through a birth rate below replacement levels, assimilation (mainly through intermarriage), and lack of significant immigration, the Jewish population of the United States has declined since 1970, so that by the year 2076 this community, which once numbered six million, is likely to amount to no more than 944,000; such a drastic reduction would be, among

other things, a disaster for Israel, which has received much support from American Jewry.

42. Berman, Hyman. POLITICAL ANTISEMITISM IN MINNESOTA DURING THE GREAT DEPRESSION. *Jewish Social Studies 1976 38(3-4): 247-264.* Anti-Semitism was successfully used as a political weapon to unseat Minnesota Farmer-Labor Governor Elmer A. Benson in the campaign of 1938. Many of Benson's liberal political aides and associates were Jewish. They were libeled as radical Jewish elements seeking to import Marxism into the state by political opponents such as Hjalmar Petersen and Raymond Chase. Political anti-Semitism in Minnesota proved a valuable tool in the conservative effort to thwart further government intervention to assist the unemployed, the unions, and producer-cooperative farmer elements. Primary sources.   N. Lederer

43. Berman, Myron, ed. JOSEPH JOEL: MY RECOLLECTIONS AND EXPERIENCES OF RICHMOND, VIRGINIA, U. S. A., 1884-1892. *Virginia Mag. of Hist. and Biog. 1979 87(3): 344-356.* Joel, a Jewish jewelry merchant of Richmond, looks back on his childhood from the perspective of the 1950's. Joel's family, headed by his father, a small-scale jewelry merchant, lived in Richmond to 1884 and returned to the Ukraine from whence it came. The younger Joel came back to the United States and ultimately Richmond in 1914. The bulk of the memoir deals with the social history of Richmond Jews. The editor provides translation of many Yiddish terms used by Joel. 70 notes.   P. J. Woehrmann

44. Berman, Myron. RABBI EDWARD NATHAN CALISH AND THE DEBATE OVER ZIONISM IN RICHMOND, VIRGINIA. *Am. Jewish Hist. Q. 1973 62(3): 295-305.* Rabbi Calish, who served the Richmond Jewish community 1891-1945, was a consistent foe of the Zionist movement, and thus shared the position of many southern Jews of his time and generation. He was one of the original founders of the American Council for Judaism.   F. Rosenthal

45. Bernstein, Seth. THE ECONOMIC LIFE OF THE JEWS IN SAN FRANCISCO DURING THE 1860'S AS REFLECTED IN THE CITY DIRECTORIES. *Am. Jewish Arch. 1975 27(1): 70-77.*

46. Berrol, Selma C. EDUCATION AND SOCIAL MOBILITY: THE JEWISH EXPERIENCE IN NEW YORK CITY, 1880-1920. *Am. Jewish Hist. Q. 1976 65(3): 257-271.* The New York City public schools were totally unprepared to accommodate the large number of immigrant children pouring into the Lower East Side. Because city schools held an educational philosophy unfriendly to non-English backgrounds, most Jews until 1910 or so did not move up the economic ladder by taking advantage of New York's educational opportunities. Widespread utilization of secondary and higher education followed improvements in educational status, rather than the other way around. Primary and secondary sources; 33 notes.   F. Rosenthal

47. Berry, Hannah Shwayder. A COLORADO FAMILY HISTORY. *Western States Jewish Hist. Q. 1973 5(3): 158-165.* Chronicles the history of the Isaac and Rachel Shwayder family, from their emigration from Poland in 1865, to their successful business activities in Denver in 1916.

48. Best, Gary Dean. JACOB H. SCHIFF'S GALVESTON MOVEMENT: AN EXPERIMENT IN IMMIGRANT DEFLECTION, 1907-1914. *Am. Jewish Arch. 1978 30(1): 43-79.* Although the career of Jacob H. Schiff is usually associated with the world of high finance, he was also involved with a plan to send hundreds of thousands of immigrant Jews into the interior regions of the United States and Canada and away from the congested cities of America's east coast. The city of Galveston, Texas, would serve as the departure point for many of these Jews. The Galveston Plan, as it came to be known, necessitated complex political and financial maneuverings on the parts of Schiff, the American immigration authorities, and the English Territorialist, Israel Zangwill.   J

49. Betcherman, Lita-Rose. CANADA'S HUMAN RIGHTS AFTER THE QUEBEC ELECTIONS. *Patterns of Prejudice [Great Britain] 1977 11(3): 23-27.* The 1 April 1977 promulgation of the French Language Charter by the Parti Quebecois government of René Levesque disturbs the province's 116,000 Jews, who sense anti-Semitism is implied in the law, in a climate of extreme French-Canadian nationalism.

50. Betcherman, Lita-Rose. THE EARLY HISTORY OF CANADA'S AN-TI-DISCRIMINATION LAW. *Patterns of Prejudice [Great Britain] 1973 7(6): 19-23.* Discusses the passing of anti-discrimination legislation in Canada in the 1930's as a reaction against the anti-Semitism of Nazism.

51. Bingham, Richard D.; Frendreis, John P.; and Rhodes, James M. THE NOMINATING PROCESS IN NONPARTISAN ELECTIONS: PETITION SIGNING AS AN ACT OF SUPPORT. *J. of Pol. 1978 40(4): 1044-1053.* Arthur Jones was the candidate of the (Nazi) National Socialist White People's Party in the nonpartisan Milwaukee mayoral primary of 17 February 1976. Under the conditions of "minimal information" elections, interviews with registered voters who signed Jones' nominating petition indicated that most: were unaware of Jones' party affiliation, neither supported the Nazi party's principles nor shared Nazi millenarian views, and did not vote for Jones in the election. Primary and secondary sources, especially interviews; 3 tables, 8 notes.   A. W. Novitsky

52. Blayney, Michael S. HERBERT PELL, WAR CRIMES, AND THE JEWS. *Am. Jewish Hist. Q. 1976 65(4): 335-352.* Herbert Claiborne Pell, a Harvard classmate of Franklin D. Roosevelt, was one of Roosevelt's political appointees in various foreign service posts. Pell was an early and vigorous denouncer of Nazi policies; his letters to the President stand in marked contrast to the restrained style and attitude of the State Department. His 1943 appointment to the UN War Crimes Commission led almost from the beginning to increased conflict with the State Department, which did not agree with his definition of war crimes and atrocities. The question whether crimes against Jews, regardless of location and nationality, came within the jurisdiction of the commission was another issue that divided Pell and the Department. All of this led to his abrupt dismissal in 1945. 45 notes.   F. Rosenthal

53. Blu, Karen I. VARIETIES OF ETHNIC IDENTITY: ANGLO-SAX-ONS, BLACKS, INDIANS, AND JEWS IN A SOUTHERN COUNTY. *Ethnicity 1977 4(3): 263-286.* Analyzes concepts of group identity in Robeson

County, South Carolina, 1967-68, finding that each group studied (Negroes, Lumbee Indians, and Jews) identifies itself according to its relations to other minority-ethnic groups, the self-concept of each group, and stereotypes held by the greater Anglo-Saxon culture. Examines the bases for stereotypes and dimensions involved: concept of image, kind and depth of belief in the image, consensus on the image within outside social structure, and action related to the image.

G. A. Hewlett

54. Bluestein, Gene. *PORTNOY'S COMPLAINT*: THE JEW AS AMERICAN. *Can. R. of Am. Studies 1976 7(1): 66-76.* Cites reasons why a 1969 novel, *Portnoy's Complaint* by Philip Roth, is likely to attain critical recognition and high stature in the American literary tradition. Roth candidly treated themes and used language that long had been taboo in Jewish-American literature.

H. T. Lovin

55. Blumauer, Blanche. COUNCIL OF JEWISH WOMEN IN PORTLAND —1905. *Western States Jewish Hist. Q. 1976 9(1): 19-20.* Organized in 1895 for self-help and improvement, the Council of Jewish Women of Portland, Oregon, established a Neighborhood House in 1904. In 1905, 200 children took advantage of the various schools and activities provided by this project. Quoted from *The Jewish Times and Observer,* San Francisco, 17 February 1905.

B. S. Porter

56. Boxerman, Burton Alan. THE EDISON BROTHERS, SHOE MERCHANTS: THEIR GEORGIA YEARS. *Georgia Hist. Q. 1973 57(4): 511-525.* Traces the history of the retail shoe store ventures of five sons of a Russian Jewish emigrant in Georgia and their merger into the Edison Brothers Company that became the largest chain of women's shoe stores in the nation.   D. L. Smith

57. Boxerman, Burton Alan. KAHN OF CALIFORNIA. *California Hist. Q. 1976 55(4): 340-351.* Julius Kahn (1861-1924) was a 12 term Congressman from California whose career spanned the presidencies from Theodore Roosevelt to Calvin Coolidge. Born of German Jewish parents, Kahn came to California at age seven and grew up in San Francisco. After an initial career as an actor he became a lawyer. Elected to Congress in 1898, Kahn was continuously returned by his San Francisco constituents except for the 1902 election. Kahn generally followed the Republican Party position favoring free tolls for American ships through the Panama Canal, opposing Woodrow Wilson's Mexican policy and the League of Nations, and supporting the operation of Muscle Shoals by private enterprise. An advocate of military preparedness, Kahn crossed party lines to support Wilson's preparedness policy in 1917. He sponsored the first Selective Service Act and favored universal military training. While reflecting his constituents' opposition to Japanese immigration and naturalization, Kahn voted against laws designed to restrict European immigration. He died of a cerebral hemorrhage in 1924. Based on primary and secondary sources; photos, 48 notes.

A. Hoffman

58. Boxerman, Burton Alan. LOUIS PATRICK ALOE. *Missouri Hist. Soc. Bull. 1974 31(1): 41-54.* Louis Patrick Aloe (1867-1929), a St. Louis businessman, served the city of St. Louis in many public capacities, always seeking to make St. Louis a "progressive, dynamic" city second to none in the United States. In 1925,

Aloe ran for Mayor but lost the election. The embittered Aloe blamed his defeat upon anti-Semitism in the city. Based on newspaper sources; 43 notes.

H. T. Lovin

59.   Boxerman, Burton Alan.   LUCIUS NATHAN LITTAUER.   *Am. Jewish Hist. Q. 1977 66(4): 498-512.* Lucius Nathan Littauer (1859-1944) was the son of Nathan and Harriett Littauer of New York. After graduation from Harvard, he founded a flourishing glove factory and became a prominent businessman, active in Republican politics. He served 10 years in the House of Representatives and became one of the great philanthropists of the era. His gifts provided seed money for many educational, academic, medical, scientific, and civil activities. 41 notes.

F. Rosenthal

60.   Bradbury, Malcolm.   SAUL BELLOW AND THE NOBEL PRIZE. *J. of Am. Studies [Great Britain] 1977 11(1): 3-12.* Analyzes the novels and ideas of Saul Bellow (b. 1915) that earned him the 1976 Nobel Prize in literature. Earlier American recipients of that prize usually experienced a decline in their work and reputations following its receipt. Bellow may escape these troubles because he clearly is "a novelist of an urban, alien, stressed world" who has never "shirked" that world's "mass and pressure." 12 notes.

H. T. Lovin

61.   Brandes, Joseph.   FROM SWEATSHOP TO STABILITY: JEWISH LABOR BETWEEN TWO WORLD WARS.   *Yivo Ann. of Jewish Social Sci. 1976 (16): 1-149.* Traces the growth of the Jewish labor movement from its inception, with particular emphasis on the period between World War I and World War II. Stresses the uniqueness of the Jewish labor movement and puts particular emphasis on the growth of the Jewish labor movement within the garment industry. Describes the roles of such notable labor leaders as David Dubinsky and Sidney Hillquit. Particular stress is put on the International Ladies' Garment Workers' and the United Hebrew Trades' role in the development of Jewish labor in the 1920's-30's.

R. J. Wechman

62.   Braude, William G.   *EZRA:* A JOURNAL OF OPINION.   *Rhode Island Jewish Hist. Notes 1977 7(3): 432-436.* Short discussion on the aim, contents, and availability of a Jewish journal, *Ezra,* printed by the Order of Ezra, 1911-77, from Providence, Rhode Island.

63.   Braude, William G.   HARRY WOLFSON AS MENTOR.   *Rhode Island Jewish Hist. Notes 1975 7(1): 140-148.* Author relates events of his academic and rabbinical career which was aided and influenced by a Brown University professor, Harry Wolfson.

64.   Braude, William G.   SAMUEL BELKIN AT BROWN.   *Rhode Island Jewish Hist. Notes 1974 6(4): 610-613.* Reminiscences about Samuel Belkin, President of Yeshiva University, by Rabbi William G. Braude, his friend during their years at Brown University (1932-35).

S

65.   Breibart, Solomon.   THE SYNAGOGUES OF KAHAL KADOSH BETH ELOHIM, CHARLESTON.   *South Carolina Hist. Mag. 1979 80(3): 215-235.* Provides a brief history of Jews in South Carolina dating to 1695, and describes the synagogues of Kahal Kadosh Beth Elohim (Holy Congregation House of God), from 1749 until 1978, in Charleston; includes photographs and floor plans.

66. Brener, David A. LANCASTER'S FIRST JEWISH COMMUNITY, 1715-1804: THE ERA OF JOSEPH SIMON. *J. of the Lancaster County Hist. Soc. 1976 80(4): 211-321.* Examines the Jewish community in Lancaster County, begun by the first Jewish resident, Joseph Simon.

67. Broadbent, T. L. THE SUD-CALIFORNIA POST: A JEWISH EDITOR VIEWS THE NEWS. *Western States Jewish Hist. Q. 1973 6(1): 34-40.* Conrad Jacoby published the German-language newspaper *Die Sud-California Post* in Los Angeles, 1874-92. The paper ran until 1914 and served the large German-speaking population of southern California. 8 notes.
                                                                        R. A. Garfinkle

68. Brokhin, Yuri. FATHOMING THE FREE WORLD: OR: ADVENTURES OF SOVIET JEWISH EMIGRANTS. *Dissent 1974 21(4): 542-548.* Discusses conditions of Soviet Jews inside the USSR and the United States.

69. Bronstein, Phil. ELDRIDGE CLEAVER—REBORN. *Midstream 1977 23(1): 57-63.* Examines the hesitancy of Jews to support black activist Eldridge Cleaver because of his anti-Israeli stand as a member of the Black Panther Party in the 1960's; considers Cleaver's discovery of racism and the servitude of blacks in Arab States as the reason for his changing attitudes toward Jews and Zionism, 1968-70's.

70. Bronstein, Zelda and Kann, Kenneth. BASHA SINGERMAN, COMRADE OF PETALUMA. *California Hist. Q. 1977 56(1): 20-33.* Presents an interview with a resident of Petaluma, California, as part of an oral history project about the Petaluma Jewish chicken farmers. Names were changed to protect privacy. The interviewee, a socialist woman, left Minsk, Russia, to go to South Africa, Montreal, and finally California. In 1915 she and her husband bought land and began operating a chicken ranch. The work was hard but she preferred it to the big city sweatshops. Their neighbors were mainly Jewish socialists. In the 1920's, Petaluma's Jewish population grew to 100 families. The community prospered in the 1920's but suffered in the Depression. Eventually the subject had to sell her home. Now 83, she meets socially with a declining number of old friends, and the Socialist community is fading for a conservative suburban one. Photos.
                                                                        A. Hoffman

71. Burke, John C. THE BREAK IN. *Rhode Island Jewish Hist. Notes 1974 6(4): 532-541.* An account of the forcible reopening of the Touro Synagogue by the Jewish community of Newport, Rhode Island, as told by Judge John C. Burke, who aided in the 1902 struggle.   S

72. Busi, Frederick. THE DEFUNIS CASE REVEALS QUOTA PRACTICES IN U.S. HIGHER EDUCATION. *Patterns of Prejudice [Great Britain] 1974 8(4): 21-26.* Cites the legal case (1974) of Marco DeFunis, a Sephardic Jew who was denied admission to the graduate school of the University of Washington because he was not considered a member of a minority group.

73. Caditz, Judith. JEWISH LIBERALS IN TRANSITION: AMBIVALENCE TOWARD ETHNIC INTEGRATION. *Sociol. and Social Res. 1975 59(3): 274-287.* White liberals believing in ethnic integration were questioned on busing in schools, entrance of blacks into their occupations, blacks entering

predominantly white neighborhoods, quotas in colleges, apartment rentals to blacks, and hiring blacks. The Jewish portion of the sample responded to questions on black anti-Semitism. These interracial situations thrust Jewish liberals more often than their non-Jewish counterparts into belief dilemmas and role conflicts that they resolved by mechanisms redefining liberal roles. Although the sample is representative of only the upper range of statuses among Jews and non-Jews, it permits rigorous test of an ethnic identification hypothesis among those most committed to racial liberalism.   J

74. Carmichael, Joel. A JEWISH DISEASE. *Midstream 1975 21(5): 52-57.* The disease referred to in this article is the Jews' tendency to self-alienation, which expresses itself for instance in Noam Chomsky's anti-Israel stance, which sacrifices Jewish identity for "humanity."

75. Carosso, Vincent P. A FINANCIAL ELITE: NEW YORK'S GERMAN-JEWISH INVESTMENT BANKERS. *Am. Jewish Hist. Q. 1976 66(1): 67-88.* German Jewish bankers began to assume an important role in American finance in the 1830's when public and private borrowing to pay for internal improvement increased rapidly and significantly. Men such as August Belmont, Rothschild's agent, Philip Speyer, Jacob Schiff, the Seligmans, the Lehman brothers, Jules Bache, and Marcus Goldman are some of the people whose careers illustrate this financial elite. As was true of their non-Jewish counterparts, family, personal, and business connections, a reputation for honesty and integrity, ability, and a willingness to take calculated risks were essential to recruit capital from widely scattered sources. The contributions of these investment bankers to American and Jewish life and society have been continuous, many sided, and substantial for over a century. 55 notes.   F. Rosenthal

76. Carson, Herbert L. and Carson, Ada Lou. THE JEWS, ROYALL TYLER, AND AMERICA'S DIVIDED MIND. *Am. Jewish Arch. 1976 28(1): 79-84.* Discusses early American playwright and novelist Royall Tyler (1757-1826) as an example of America's divided attitudes of toleration and prejudice towards Jews.

77. Chiel, Arthur A. GEORGE ALEXANDER KOHUT AND THE JUDAICA COLLECTION IN THE YALE LIBRARY. *Yale U. Lib. Gazette 1979 53(4): 202-210.* George Alexander Kohut's (1874-1933) love for books was inspired by the scholarship of his father, Rabbi Alexander Kohut. The Hebraic bibliophile's interest in Yale was first expressed in an editorial published in the *Jewish Exponent* in November 1901; it culminated in the Alexander Kohut Memorial Collection of Judaica donated to Yale in 1915 by George Alexander Kohut. The original Kohut gift to Yale was supplemented by the establishment of a fellowship in 1919 and a later gift of Heinrich Heine material in 1930. 8 notes.
D. A. Yanchisin

78. Choynski, Isidor N. and Eckman, Julius. TWO LETTERS TO HARRIET CHOYNSKI. *Western States Jewish Hist. Q. 1974 7(1): 44-48.* Two letters addressed to Harriet Choynski written in 1863 and 1872 give a glimpse of life in the West at that time. Mrs. Choynski had five children, taught at a religious school in San Francisco for many years, and marched in San Francisco's first May Day parade. 19 notes.   R. A. Garfinkle

79. Churgin, Gershon A. RAV TZAIR'S VIEWS ON THE CULTURAL UNITY OF THE JEWISH PEOPLE. *Bitzaron 1974 65(6): 277-281.*

80. Chyet, Stanley F. AMERICAN JEWISH LITERARY PRODUCTIVITY: A SELECTED BICENTENNIAL BIBLIOGRAPHY. *Studies in Biblio. and Booklore 1976 11(1/2): 5-24.* Presents a bibliography of anthologies of literature dealing with the works of Jewish writers in the United States, published in the 1950's-70's.

81. Chyet, Stanley F. MOSES JACOB EZEKIEL: A CHILDHOOD IN RICHMOND. *Am. Jewish Hist. Q. 1973 62(3): 286-294.* The sculptor Moses Ezekiel (1844-1917) spent most of his adult life in Europe but never concealed his American background or his Jewishness. His *Autobiography* describes his early interest in art. His maternal grandmother, Hannah Waterman, was a strong influence on him. 2 photos, 16 notes.
F. Rosenthal

82. Clar, Reva. EARLY STOCKTON JEWRY AND ITS CANTOR-RABBI HERMAN DAVIDSON. *Western States Jewish Hist. Q. 1973 5(2): 63-86, (3): 166-187.* Part I. A biography of Herman Davidson (1846-1911) emphasizes his operatic career in Russia, his family life, and his work with Jews in Stockton, 1876-91. Part II. Chronicles the relationship between Davidson and Stockton Jews, and efforts to reform the Jewish congregation, 1893-1911.

83. Clar, Reva. PAVLOVA AND ME. *Western States Jewish Hist. Q. 1979 11(4): 350-353.* The author was a student at San Francisco's Hirsch-Arnold Ballet School in 1924 when Anna Pavlova (1885-1931) and her dance company came to the city to perform the ballet *Don Quixote.* The author and two or three other students volunteered to help as extras in the performance. Personal recollection; photo, 3 notes.
B. S. Porter

84. Clifford, Clark M. RECOGNIZING ISRAEL: THE 1948 STORY. *Am. Heritage 1977 28(3): 4-11.* Admitting that political considerations are a part of every major policy decision, the author defends Harry S. Truman against revisionist charges on the Palestine question. Suggests that Truman's position was consistent with his long-standing position of favoring the underdog. Serious internal opposition, spearheaded by the Office of Near Eastern and African Affairs in the State Department, hampered the formulation of US policies. 3 illus.
J. F. Paul

85. Coerver, Don M. and Hall, Linda B. NEIMAN-MARCUS: INNOVATORS IN FASHION AND MERCHANDISING. *Am. Jewish Hist. Q. 1976 66(1): 123-136.* As innovative merchants and merchandizers Neiman-Marcus of Dallas, Texas, revolutionized the Southwestern approach to fashion. Relates the story of the store, its founders, and its progress until the present. 44 notes.
F. Rosenthal

86. Coffee, Rudolph I. JEWISH CONDITIONS IN SAN FRANCISCO. *Western States Jewish Hist. Q. 1976 8(3): 251-256.* In this reprint of an article published in *The Menorah*, New York, September 1906, the author details the condition of Jews in San Francisco after the earthquake. His report covers the destruction and repair of several synagogues. The Home for Aged and Disabled Hebrews was destroyed, the Old People's Home was damaged, and the buildings

of the Eureka Benevolent Society and the Independent Order of B'nai B'rith were burned. Many Jews left the city and settled in Oakland. 11 notes.

                                                                    R. A. Garfinkle

87. Cohen, Blanche Klasmer. BENJAMIN KLASMER'S CONTRIBUTION TO BALTIMORE'S MUSICAL HISTORY. *Maryland Hist. Mag. 1977 72(2): 272-276.* Records the important role played by Benjamin Klasmer in bringing music to Baltimore for over 30 years, first as a cofounder of the Baltimore Symphony Orchestra, in 1916, and then as conductor of the Jewish Educational Alliance Symphony Orchestra in the 1920's. Throughout his career, Klasmer was the "leading musical director of pit orchestras" furnishing accompaniment to silent movies and vaudeville acts at the New Theater, the Garden and Rivoli Theaters, and the Hippodrome until his death in 1949. The tradition which he began is continued today by the Jewish Community Center and other groups. Perhaps his most popular renown, however, comes from his coauthorship of the theme song of the Baltimore Colts. 3 illus.   G. J. Bobango

88. Cohen, Michael J. AMERICAN INFLUENCE ON BRITISH POLICY IN THE MIDDLE EAST DURING WORLD WAR TWO: FIRST ATTEMPTS AT COORDINATING ALLIED POLICY ON PALESTINE. *Am. Jewish Hist. Q. 1977 67(1): 50-70.* US entry into Middle Eastern politics during World War II inevitably led to friction with Great Britain. The British feared a US challenge to their political, military, and economic hegemony. The United States suspected British imperialism would exploit American resources. The author examines problems blocking an Anglo-American consensus on the Palestine question, such as attitudes toward Zionism, immigration quotas, and the formation of a Jewish Army. Franklin D. Roosevelt's attempts to placate the British on these issues highlight the dilemma American policymakers faced. 63 notes.   F. Rosenthal

89. Cohen, Naomi W. PIONEERS OF AMERICAN JEWISH DEFENSE. *Am. Jewish Arch. 1977 29(2): 116-150.* In antebellum America, Jews did not enjoy the services of an organized, institutional response to anti-Jewish outrages both at home and abroad. Instead, protests against anti-Semitism and other anti-Jewish activities were delivered by three American Jewish periodicals of the time—*The Occident, The Asmonean,* and *The Israelite.* Analyzes the methods employed by these pioneers of American Jewish defense.   J

90. Cohen, Naomi W. SCHOOLS, RELIGION, AND GOVERNMENT: RECENT AMERICAN JEWISH OPINIONS. *Michael: On the Hist. of the Jews in the Diaspora [Israel] 1975 3: 340-392.* Reproduces 11 documents reflecting American Jewish views on the principle of separation of church and state with regard to state-supported education. On the issue of keeping religion out of public schools, American Jewish organizations energetically supported separation, although Jews in smaller communities may have been inhibited in expressing such an opinion. But on the issue of public aid to church schools the American Jewish consensus broke down. Orthodox and even non-Orthodox circles began to support such aid, long demanded by Catholic groups, as the Jewish day-school movement grew. Primary and secondary sources; 24 notes.   T. Sassoon

91. Cohen, Robert, ed. BIBLIOTHECA ROSENTHALIANA TE KOOP ENIGE BRIEVEN VAN MEIJER ROEST MZN. EN GEORGE ROSENTHAL AAN DR. B. FELSENTHAL IN DE VERENIGDE STATEN [The Bibliotheca Rosenthaliana for sale: some letters from Meyer Roest and George Rosenthal to Dr. B. Felsenthal in the United States]. *Studia Rosenthaliana [Netherlands] 1975 9(1): 90-102.* Reprints letters 1868-96, from George Rosenthal and Meyer Roest in Amsterdam to Rabbi Bernard Felsenthal in Chicago, Illinois, concerning the purchase of the late Rabbi Leeser Rosenthal's library by US buyers.

92. Coiner, Miles W., Jr. THE GRAND OPERA HOUSE AND THE GOLDEN AGE OF THE LEGITIMATE THEATER IN KANSAS CITY. *Missouri Hist. R. 1973 67(3): 407-423.* Relates the history of the Grand Opera House in Kansas City, Missouri. Built in 1891 by Abraham Judah and a partner, the Grand earned a national reputation, attracted great stars, and maintained popular prices. In 1916 it was sold and became a movie house until 1926, when it was turned into a parking garage. Based on contemporary newspaper reports and secondary sources; 9 illus., 3 photos, 48 notes.   N. J. Street

93. Cole, Sylvan. MEMORIES OF AN 1890'S POMONA BOYHOOD. *Western States Jewish Hist. Q. 1979 11(4): 327-331.* The author's father operated a dry goods and clothing store, known as the People's Store, in Pomona, California, 1886-1901. The author recalls working in his father's store, accepting cookies from the bakery next door, and playing with boys from a variety of ethnic and religious backgrounds. Personal recollections and published sources; 2 photos, 11 notes.   B. S. Porter

94. Cowan, Max P. MEMORIES OF THE JEWISH FARMERS AND RANCHERS OF COLORADO. *Western States Jewish Hist. Q. 1977 9(3): 218-225.* Two attempts to establish Jewish farm colonies in Colorado, in 1882 and 1884, failed, but many individual Jews were successful as farmers and ranchers. Young immigrants who came to Colorado as miners and railway laborers settled on the land and took up farming. Some who started out as cattle brokers acquired ranches and herds of their own. Most of the Jews who went into farming and ranching have passed away. Their children moved to the cities and their farms became part of large conglomerates. Based on personal recollection; 5 photos.   B. S. Porter

95. Cox, Oliver C. JEWISH SELF-INTEREST IN "BLACK PLURALISM." *Sociol. Q. 1974 15(2): 183-198.* From time immemorial Jewish tribal exclusiveness among dominant societal groups has resulted in various forms of conflict determined by the social situation. The critical force involved has been the group's peculiar resistance to social assimilation. Different social systems react differently to the persistence of this trait. The caste system of India, for example, would hardly notice it. But capitalist culture, which originated in the European medieval city, has constantly resisted it; that culture is basically assimilationist. American Negroes, in their opposition to racism have relied mainly on the ideology of assimilation. These two divergent tendencies have come into collision recently.   J

96. Cripps, Thomas. THE MOVIE JEW AS AN IMAGE OF ASSIMILA-TIONISM. *J. of Popular Film 1975 4(3): 190-207.* Discusses ethnic stereotypes in early cinema (1900's-20's) dealing specifically with immigrants and Jews.

97. Cronbach, Abraham. THE SPROUT THAT GREW. *Am. Jewish Arch. 1975 27(1): 51-60.* Points out the contributions of Isaac M. Wise to the Hebrew Union College in Cincinnati, 1870's-1900. S

98. D'Ancona, David Arnold. AN ANSWER TO ANTI-SEMITISM: SAN FRANCISCO 1883. *Western States Jewish Hist. Q. 1975 8(1): 59-64.* Reprint of a letter to the editor of the *San Francisco Call*, 26 January 1883, in response to anti-Semitic statements published in the San Francisco *Argonaut* by its editor, Frank M. Pixley. Pixley's remarks contained many untruths and misconceptions concerning Jewish religious ceremonies and life-styles. D'Ancona (1827-1908) clearly rebutted Pixley's statements. Pixley recognized his mistakes and ceased his anti-Semitic writings. R. A. Garfinkle

99. Daniels, Doris Groshen. COLONIAL JEWRY: RELIGION, DOMES-TIC AND SOCIAL RELATIONS. *Am. Jewish Hist. Q. 1977 66(3): 375-400.* Describes the activities of New York's colonial Jewry. Discusses social relations with Christian surroundings, the influx of Ashkenazi Jews until they outnumbered the Sephardim after 1720, inevitable intermarriages, the role of the synagogue, the nature of strong family bonds, and the problems of 18th-century schools. Abigail Franks, the best-known Jewish lady of the age, had much in common with Abigail Adams. 61 notes. F. Rosenthal

100. Davis, Moshe. FROM THE VANTAGE OF JERUSALEM. *Am. Jewish Hist. Q. 1974 63(4): 313-333.* Compares the Jewish studies program in Jerusalem to that which exists in the United States. One of nine related articles in this issue. S

101. Davis, Perry. CORRUPTION IN JEWISH LIFE. *Present Tense 1978 5(2): 19-24.* Investigates the growth of "white-collar" crime within the Jewish community, and opposition to such crimes, 1969-78.

102. Dawson, Nelson L. LOUIS D. BRANDEIS, FELIX FRANK-FURTER, AND FRANKLIN D. ROOSEVELT: THE ORIGINS OF A NEW DEAL RELATIONSHIP. *Am. Jewish Hist. 1978 68(1): 32-42.* The Brandeis-Frankfurter partnership influencing national political events began in 1917 (re the appointment of an economic "czar"). By the 1920's the extensive correspondence between them included politics, law, and Zionism. By 1933, Frankfurter acted as the intermediary between Brandeis and Roosevelt. The intellectual relation of these three men demonstrates the importance of personal contact as a source of political influence and the truth of their philosophy's central thesis: that the richest sources of a democracy are the individuals in public service. F. Rosenthal

103. DeMartini, Joseph R. STUDENT ACTIVISTS OF THE 1930S AND 1960S: A COMPARISON OF THE SOCIAL BASE OF TWO STUDENT MOVEMENTS. *Youth and Soc. 1975 6(4): 395-422.* Student activists at the University of Illinois in the 1930's were generally from professional families, urban, Jewish, arts and sciences majors, and unlikely to belong to campus orga-

nizations. Thus their social background was very similar to that of student activists of the 1960's. However, they differ from those of the 1960's in having followed the lead of parent political groups, developed a greater conservatism during their life as students, and in lacking the type and degree of cultural alienation of their later counterparts. Based on University of Illinois archives; primary and secondary sources; 9 tables, 4 notes, biblio.   J. H. Sweetland

104. Dershowitz, Alan M.; Silverglate, Harvey A.; and Baker, Jeanne. THE JDL MURDER CASE: "THE INFORMER WAS OUR OWN CLIENT." *Civil Liberties R. 1976 3(1): 43-60.* Civil rights questions were raised by the trial of Sheldon Seigel. Seigel, along with other members of the Jewish Defense League, was indicted for murder in the bombing of Sol Hurok's office in New York City. The authors, Seigel's lawyers, learned that Seigel was a government informer after they accepted his case. Subsequently, their focus on the 1972-73 case changed to investigating the legal and moral limits "of governmental intervention to prevent and prosecute the most serious kinds of crime," and to protecting the civil rights of informers.   S

105. Dester, Chester McArthur. INTRODUCTION. *Am. Jewish Hist. Q. 1976 66(1): 3-9.* This Bicentennial issue explores different aspects of the role that American Jewish business enterprise has played in the economy of the United States. The eight monographs range from essays on colonial trade and mid-19th century financiers to Neiman-Marcus and Jewish businesswomen of the past and present.   F. Rosenthal

106. Diamond, Sander A. *HOLOCAUST* FILM'S IMPACT ON AMERICANS. *Patterns of Prejudice [Great Britain] 1978 12(4): 1-9, 19.* Discusses American public opinion about the television miniseries, *Holocaust,* which appeared in 1978.

107. Dinnerstein, Leonard. ANTI-SEMITISM IN THE EIGHTIETH CONGRESS: THE DISPLACED PERSONS ACT OF 1948. *Capitol Studies 1978 6(2): 11-26.* The Displaced Persons Act (US, 1948), enacted to aid homeless victims of World War II, discriminated against Jews in favor of ethnic Germans who fled Eastern Europe.

108. Dinnerstein, Leonard. SOUTHERN JEWRY AND THE DESEGREGATION CRISIS, 1954-1970. *Am. Jewish Hist. Q. 1973 62(3): 231-241.* Despite the participation of many Jews in the civil rights movement, the level of commitment varied widely. Southern Jews, many of them merchants dependent upon the goodwill of their neighbors, were circumspect in their allegiance to equal rights, except in a few areas like Atlanta and among some college groups. In the early 1960's, perhaps six to 10 rabbis in the South worked for the cause, including Jacob Rothschild, Emmet Frank, Perry Nussbaum, and Charles Mantninband. Based on correspondence of southern rabbis at the American Jewish Archives; 32 notes.   F. Rosenthal

109. Dinnerstein, Leonard. THE U.S. ARMY AND THE JEWS: POLICIES TOWARD THE DISPLACED PERSONS AFTER WORLD WAR II. *Am. Jewish Hist. 1979 68(3): 353-366.* Forced to deal with the care and supervision of millions of displaced persons, the US Army did a generally creditable job. Unfortunately, subordinate military personnel often showed little awareness of

the particular difficulties of Jewish DP's, the remnants of the final solution. Earl G. Harrison's inspection of conditions in July 1945 led to orders by President Truman and General Eisenhower which abolished some of the worst abuses and provided better facilities and treatment for the survivors of the death camps. 28 notes. F. Rosenthal

110. Dobkowski, Michael N. ACCEPTANCE OR REJECTION: THE IM-AGE OF THE JEW IN AMERICAN SOCIETY. *Studies in Hist. and Soc. 1974 5(2): 61-65.* A review essay on the role of American Jews in American society, prompted by Leslie H. Carlson and George A. Colburn, eds., *In Their Place: White America Defines her Minorities* (New York: John Wiley and Sons, Inc., 1972), Rudolf Glanz's *The Jew in Early American Wit and Graphic Humor* (New York: KTAV Publishing House, 1973), Arthur A. Goren's *New York Jews and the Quest for Community* (New York: Columbia U. Pr., 1970), Michael Selzer's *"Kike!": A Documentary History of Anti-Semitism in America* (New York: World Publishing Co., 1972), and Robert G. Weisbrod and Arthur Stein's *Bitter-Sweet Encounter: The Afro American and the American Jew* (New York: Schrocken Books, 1972). These diverse works generally dispute the theory that American anti-Semitism has had economic rather than stereotypic causes. 7 notes. V. L. Human

111. Dobkowski, Michael N. AMERICAN ANTISEMITISM: A REIN-TERPRETATION. *Am. Q. 1977 29(2): 166-181.* Popular American literature and drama of the 19th and early 20th centuries presented unfavorable stereotypes of the Jews which contributed to a generation of anti-Semitism. Religious novels depicted Jews as bigots. Plays and popular novels included Jewish representations who were greedy and mercenary in business, amoral in social behavior, and generally unscrupulous. By the early 20th century, Jews were associated with radicalism and politically revolutionary movements in popular literature. Primary sources; 59 notes. N. Lederer

112. Dobkowski, Michael N. POPULIST ANTISEMITISM IN U.S. LITER-ATURE. *Patterns of Prejudice [Great Britain] 1976 10(3): 19-27.* Discusses anti-Semitism and racial stereotypes of Jews in US literature during the Populist era, including the influence of the Rothschild image and the theory of Jewish world conspiracy.

113. Dobkowski, Michael N. WHERE THE NEW WORLD ISN'T NEW: ROOTS OF U.S. ANTISEMITISM. *Patterns of Prejudice [Great Britain] 1975 9(4): 21-30.* Discusses the historiography of anti-Semitism in the United States from 1855 to the turn of the century, emphasizing ethnic stereotypes in popular novels and in Populism.

114. Dreier, Peter and Porter, Jack Nusan. JEWISH RADICALISM IN TRANSITION. *Society 1975 12(2): 34-43.* Chronicles the trend toward radical politics in theology, focusing on Jewish radicalism as a political and social indicator. S

115. Dreier, Peter. POLITICAL PLURALISM AND JEWISH LIBER-ALISM: BEYOND THE CLICHES. *J. of Ethnic Studies 1976 4(3): 85-94.* Reviews Henry L. Feingold's *Zion in America: The Jewish Experience from Colonial Times to the Present*, and Stephen D. Isaacs' *Jews and American*

Politics. The first is "solid social history, perhaps the most comprehensive and readable one-volume history of American Jewry to date," while Isaacs' work is an excellent documentation of political roles and behavior, but "weak on analysis and interpretation." The overall influence of the Jewish lobby and its control over American policy is overestimated. Assessing Jewish political behavior by focusing solely on cultural and psychological factors is of dubious merit. Jewish support for liberal politics and the Welfare State stems from the nature of their embourgeoisement: professional Jews rely on state spending to maintain occupational opportunities, while Jewish businessmen favor policies stimulating aggregate consumer demand. A cultural, or consensus, theory is an inadequate explanation which encourages "the myths of group pluralism and ethnic self-interest over class politics," and the current romanticization of the white ethnic obscures the dynamics of class society. Note.   G. J. Bobango

116. Dubrovsky, Gertrude.   FARMDALE, NEW JERSEY: A JEWISH FARM COMMUNITY.   *Am. Jewish Hist. Q. 1977 66(4): 485-497.* In 1919 the first Jewish farmer moved to Farmdale, New Jersey. He was aided by the Jewish Agricultural Society (JAS), which was helping immigrants to buy farms. Farming was supplemented by summer boarders. Within 10 years more than 50 Jewish families were attracted to the town. Most were assisted by the JAS, which also provided a loan for building a Jewish Community Center in 1930. A Yiddish school affiliated with the Sholem Aleichem Folk Institute provided instruction to the children. Acculturation and changing economic and social patterns at work gradually reduced the Jewish community to its present dwindling status.
                                                            F. Rosenthal

117. Eakin, Paul John.   ALFRED KAZIN'S BRIDGE TO AMERICA.   *South Atlantic Q. 1978 77(1): 39-53.* Alfred Kazin, Brooklyn-born Jew and author, has written three autobiographical works which underscore his belief in the continuities between private experience and a larger social reality. The rhythms of his Brooklyn experience found their way into *A Walker in the City* (1951), *On Native Grounds* (1956) and *Starting Out in the Thirties* (1965). All of his works have been devoted to the complex fate of the American artist, his problematical relation to his native land, and the working out of this common theme. Thus any account of Kazin's sense of America necessarily focuses on his autobiographies. Like Van Wyck Brooks, he believed that writers must be understood in relation to their native culture and its past. Based on Kazin's writings and criticism of his works; 18 notes.   H. M. Parker, Jr.

118. Eckardt, Alice L.   THE HOLOCAUST: CHRISTIAN AND JEWISH RESPONSES.   *J. of the Am. Acad. of Religion 1974 42(3): 453-469.* Surveys, with some analysis and evaluation, the writings of leading Jewish and Christian scholars who have offered responses to the slaughter of six million Jews by Hitler. While most agree that no solution can be considered adequate, some explanation must be attempted. Stresses the nature of this theological problem for Jews and Christians. 68 notes.   E. R. Lester

119. Edgar, Irving I.   BEGINNINGS OF DETROIT JEWISH WELFARE FEDERATION.   *Michigan Jewish Hist. 1975 15(2): 6-8.* Minutes of the 5 May 1926 organization meeting of the Jewish Welfare Federation of Detroit.   S

120. Edgar, Irving I.   DR. MAX BALLIN AND HARPER HOSPITAL OF DETROIT: PART III.   *Michigan Jewish Hist. 1978 18(2): 3-6.* Concluded from a previous article (see *Michigan Jewish History,* January 1970 and July 1971). Discusses the association of Max Ballin, surgeon of international reputation, with Harper Hospital in 1906-24, noting his involvement in the development of teaching techniques and facilities and in fostering progressive change.

121. Edgar, Irving I.   THE EARLY SITES AND BEGINNINGS OF CONGREGATION BETH EL: THE MICHIGAN GRAND AVENUE SYNAGOGUE, 1859-1861.   *Michigan Jewish Hist. 1973 13(1): 13-20.* Discusses the beginnings of Congregation Beth El in Detroit.   S

122. Edgar, Irving I.   PRESIDENT'S ANNUAL REPORT, JUNE 14, 1973. *Michigan Jewish Hist. 1974 14(1): 3-6.* Report of the 14 Annual Meeting of the Jewish Historical Society of Michigan.   S

123. Edgar, Irving I.   RABBI LEO M. FRANKLIN: THE OMAHA YEARS (1892-1899).   *Michigan Jewish Hist. 1976 16(2): 10-21.* Details the organizational abilities of Rabbi Leo M. Franklin in his work in Temple Israel in Omaha, Nebraska. 4 letters, 26 notes.

124. Eisendrath, Maurice N.   THE UNION OF AMERICAN HEBREW CONGREGATIONS: CENTENNIAL REFLECTIONS.   *Am. Jewish Hist. Q. 1973 63(2): 138-159.* Evaluates the 100-year existence of the Union of American Hebrew Congregations. From a small nucleus of 28 congregations it grew to become the authoritative spokesman for American Reform Judaism and a vital participant in virtually all cooperative Jewish concerns. Describes some alternative modes for synagogues of the future.   F. Rosenthal

125. Elazar, Daniel J.   CONTEMPORARY JEWISH CIVILIZATION ON THE AMERICAN CAMPUS: RESEARCH AND TEACHING: INTRODUCTION.   *Am. Jewish Hist. Q. 1974 63(4): 311-312.* Introduces a colloquium on the teaching of contemporary Jewish civilization held at the annual meeting of the Association for Jewish Studies, 1972.   S

126. Elazar, Daniel J.   THE PLACE OF JEWISH POLITICAL STUDIES ON THE CAMPUS.   *Am. Jewish Hist. Q. 1974 63(4): 334-339.* Discusses the development of Jewish political studies as one facet of Jewish studies programs. One of nine related articles in this issue.   S

127. Ellerin, Milton.   AMERICAN NAZI FACTIONS.   *Patterns of Prejudice [Great Britain] 1978 12(2): 16-20.* Delineates eight political factions established in the United States, 1950's-77, which have been associated with Nazism.

128. Ellman, Yisrael.   THE ETHNIC AWAKENING IN THE UNITED STATES AND ITS INFLUENCE ON JEWS.   *Ethnicity 1977 4(2): 133-155.* Ethnic consciousness, awakened largely by the emerging racial consciousness among American blacks, is examined as a largely economic force in social and occupational mobility among white ethnic groups. Statistics show a disproportionately high representation of Jews in high pay-high prestige positions in the United States. Statistics correspondingly show a greater fear among Jewish groups of affirmative action, which they view as a quota system against admission of Jews to elite positions in the social structure. Religiosity has been supplanted

by ethnicity among Jewish groups as a result, and growing concern with poor Jews and Zionism is a reflection of Jewish response to possible exclusion.

G. A. Hewlett

129.   Ellsworth, S. George, ed.   SIMON BAMBERGER: GOVERNOR OF UTAH.   *Western States Jewish Hist. Q. 1973 5(4): 231-242.* Simon Bamberger, a German, Jewish immigrant active in railroads and charity work, was elected the first non-Mormon, Democratic governor of Utah in 1916.

130.   Endelman, Judith E.   JUDAICA AMERICANA.   *Am. Jewish Hist. Q. 1975 64(3): 245-257.* An annotated bibliography of monographic and periodical literature published since 1960 and received in the library of the American Jewish Historical Society.   F. Rosenthal

131.   Endelman, Judith E.   JUDAICA AMERICANA.   *Am. Jewish Hist. Q. 1975 64(4): 344-357.* An annotated bibliography of monographic and periodical literature published since 1960 and received in the library of the American Jewish Historical Society.   F. Rosenthal

132.   Endelman, Judith E.   JUDAICA AMERICANA.   *Am. Jewish Hist. Q. 1974 64(1): 55-68.* Annotated bibliography of monographic and periodical literature published since 1960 and received in the library of the American Jewish Historical Society. Twelve topical headings are employed for this annotation (bibliography, biography, cultural life, etc.).   F. Rosenthal

133.   Engelbourg, Saul.   EDWARD A. FILENE: MERCHANT, CIVIC LEADER, AND JEW.   *Am. Jewish Hist. Q. 1976 66(1): 106-122.* Edward A. Filene (1860-1937), American-born son of German Jewish immigrants, became a millionaire several times over, and because of his business success he was able to obtain fame as a philanthropist and a civic leader in Boston. He is credited with the "Automatic Bargain Basement" as his most distinctive business innovation. Describes the controversy with his associate Louis Kirstein (1867-1942), his cooperation with Louis Brandeis, his share in the development of the Credit Union movement, the influence of his Twentieth Century Fund, his marginal interest in Jewish philanthropy, and the fight against anti-Semitism. 49 notes.

F. Rosenthal

134.   Engle, Paul.   "THOSE DAMN JEWS . . . "   *Am. Heritage 1978 30(1): 72-79.* The author tells of his introduction to Jews as a boy in Cedar Rapids, Iowa, and how his early fears changed to affection and sympathy for the plight of Jews, particularly in Germany. 5 illus.   J. F. Paul

135.   Epstein, Helen.   CHILDREN OF THE HOLOCAUST: SEARCHING FOR A PAST—AND A FUTURE.   *Present Tense 1976 3(4): 21-25.* Children of Holocaust survivors possess a legacy that Jews everywhere have sworn never to forget; some of the children have refused to cooperate in that effort, others have joined it, and still others have not decided how to assimilate these events into their own lives.

136.   Erens, Patricia.   GANGSTERS, VAMPIRES, AND J.A.P.'S: THE JEW SURFACES IN AMERICAN MOVIES.   *J. of Popular Film 1975 4(3): 208-222.* Discusses the way Jews have been portrayed in recent American films which have done much to dispel earlier stereotypes (1970's).

137. Erideres, James S. ATTITUDE AND BEHAVIOUR: PREJUDICE IN WESTERN CANADA. *Patterns of Prejudice [Great Britain] 1973 7(1): 17-22.* Summarizes research on Canadian anti-Semitism to the early 1960's and explores continued anti-Semitism, and its causes and its study. Active anti-Semitism continues in Canada; a large percentage of Canadians have strong anti-Semitic attitudes. Based on secondary sources and a study of 315 randomly selected households in an urban location; 2 tables, 36 notes. G. O. Gagnon

138. Eris, Alfred. ONE MAN'S WARS: AN ECHO OF 1967. *Midstream 1977 23(5): 56-65.* Personal account of the hysteria of New York City Jews and the near-nonchalance and courage of Israelis actually faced with the outbreak of the 1967 Six-Day War.

139. Eris, Alfred. PORTRAIT OF THE ARTIST AS A MASS-MURDERER. *Midstream 1976 22(2): 50-60.* Reviews anti-Semitism in 20th-century literature, including gentiles such as T. S. Eliot and Ezra Pound and Jews such as Philip Roth.

140. Eversole, Theodore W. THE CINCINNATI UNION BETHEL: THE COMING OF AGE OF THE SETTLEMENT IDEA IN CINCINNATI. *Cincinnati Hist. Soc. Bull. 1974 32(1-2): 47-59.* Outlines the history of social reform settlement houses in Cincinnati, Ohio, specifically the Jewish Cincinnati Union Bethel settlement house, 1838-1903.

141. Farb, Judith and Farb, Nathan. THEY CAN'T GO HOME AGAIN. *Present Tense 1973 1(1): 59-61.* Jewish deserters and exiles in Canada. S

142. Faur, José. INTRODUCING THE MATERIALS OF SEPHARDIC CULTURE TO CONTEMPORARY JEWISH STUDIES. *Am. Jewish Hist. Q. 1974 63(4): 340-349.* Discusses the teaching of Sephardic culture and intellectual tradition; one of nine related articles in this issue. S

143. Faust, Ray. DI TSIRKULATSIE FUN YIDDISHE BICHER IN DI NEW YORKER SHTUTISHE BIBLIOTEKEN UN DI LEINERSHAFT [The circulation of Yiddish books in the New York public libraries, and the readership]. *Yivo Bleter 1973 44: 283-285.* The author visited several libraries in the Bronx, Manhattan, and Brooklyn to conduct a survey of the number of Yiddish books circulated over the last decade and to observe the people who read these books. B. Klein

144. Fein, Helen. ATTITUDES IN THE U.S.A., 1933-1945: TOLERATION OF GENOCIDE. *Patterns of Prejudice [Great Britain] 1973 7(5): 22-28.* Alleges toleration of genocide by the Roosevelt administration in its refusal to aid Jewish refugees from Germany by amending US immigration laws, 1933-45.

145. Fein, Leonard J. LIBERALISM AND AMERICAN JEWS. *Midstream 1973 19(8): 3-18.*

146. Fein, Leonard J. THINKING ABOUT QUOTAS. *Midstream 1973 19(3): 13-17.* Jews should support quotas to end discrimination. S

147. Feingold, Henry. AMERICAN ZIONISM. *Midstream 1975 21(8): 70-72.* Reviews Melvin I. Urofsky's *American Zionism from Herzl to the Holocaust* (New York: Doubleday, 1975).   S

148. Feingold, Henry L. RESCUE THROUGH MASS RESETTLEMENT: SOME NEW DOCUMENTS, 1938-1943. *Michael: On the Hist. of the Jews in the Diaspora [Israel] 1975 3: 302-335.* Presents 12 documents from the James G. McDonald papers relating primarily to ideas for the resettlement of European Jews under Nazi control. McDonald (1886-1959) headed the President's Advisory Committee on Political Refugees. The documents reflect the unwillingness and inability of the United States and the other major powers to confront the Jewish refugee problem directly, and include plans for diverting the Jews to places like Brazilian rubber plantations (Henry Ford's scheme), Surinam, Angola, the Dominican Republic, the Philippines, British Guiana, and Alaska. Also included is a proto-Zionist scheme by an American Christian woman, and a letter from Valdimir Jabotinsky, leader of the Zionist Revisionists. 28 notes.
T. Sassoon

149. Feingold, Henry L. WHO SHALL BEAR GUILT FOR THE HOLOCAUST: THE HUMAN DILEMMA. *Am. Jewish Hist. 1979 68(3): 261-282.* Analyzes the inability to save Jewish lives during the Holocaust and indicts the Roosevelt administration, the Vatican, the British government, other governments, and American Jewry's leadership. Political and military priorities were compounded by the sheer impossibility for most Americans, including Jews, to absorb what was happening, even as late as December 1944.   F. Rosenthal

150. Feld, Bernard T. EINSTEIN AND THE POLITICS OF NUCLEAR WEAPONS. *Bull. of the Atomic Scientists 1979 35(3): 5-16.* Chronicles Albert Einstein's work on the creation of nuclear arms, 1939-42, which he believed to be a necessary deterrant because of his Zionism and his fear of Nazi Germany, and his efforts to control and discourage the further use of the weaponry, which was rooted in his basic pacifism, 1943-55.

151. Feldman, Egal. AMERICAN EDITORIAL REACTION TO THE DREYFUS CASE. *Michael: On the Hist. of the Jews in the Diaspora [Israel] 1975 3: 101-124.* The court-martial and public degradation in 1895 of Captain Alfred Dreyfus in France aroused little interest in the United States, but events in 1898 including Émile Zola's trial, conviction, and flight to England, made Dreyfus's retrial a conspicuous issue in the US press. Reproduces 11 US editorials, 1898-99, reflecting a cross section of public opinion on the case. Anti-Semitism was but one of the themes evoked by this affair, which forced the United States to consider the possibility of an American Dreyfus case. A 12th editorial, dated 1906, reflects the renewed if brief interest aroused by Dreyfus's exoneration. 13 notes.   T. Sassoon

152. Feuer, Leon I. THE BIRTH OF THE JEWISH LOBBY: A REMINISCENCE. *Am. Jewish Arch. 1976 28(2): 107-118.* Rabbi Feuer "was in at the beginning of [the] so-called Jewish Lobby" in Washington, D.C., "and in fact was the first lobbyist." His efforts on behalf of Zionism during the early 1940's contributed toward "building a substantial base of support for Israel in American public opinion."   J

153. Feuer, Lewis S. THE LEGEND OF THE SOCIALIST EAST SIDE. *Midstream 1978 24(2): 23-35.* The Jews of New York City during the early 20th century were primarily conservatives with traditional values of religion and property, not the radical socialists that myth has created.

154. Feuer, Lewis S. RECOLLECTIONS OF HARRY AUSTRYN WOLFSON. *Am. Jewish Arch. 1976 28(1): 25-50.* Presents a biography of the great Jewish scholar Harry Austryn Wolfson (1887-1974), including anecdotes about his teaching career, political philosophy, and religious beliefs.

155. Fine, David M. ABRAHAM CAHAN, STEPHEN CRANE AND THE ROMANTIC TENEMENT TALE OF THE NINETIES. *Am. Studies (Lawrence, KS) 1973 14(1): 95-108.* By the 1890's city slums had a proven marketability in American fiction. Reform journalism became fiction, which offered a radical departure from the genteel, Victorian drawing room. The result was a mixture of cynicism and sentimentality, with all the attention devoted to the moral implications of slum conditions. For Crane and Cahan, however, poverty was not ennobling—a defiance of the romantic tenement tale. This proved uncomfortable to genteel audiences. Based on primary and secondary sources; 21 notes.
J. Andrew

156. Fine, David M. ATTITUDES TOWARD ACCULTURATION IN THE ENGLISH FICTION OF THE JEWISH IMMIGRANT, 1900-1917. *Am. Jewish Hist. Q. 1973 63(1): 45-56.* Most immigrant novelists, such as Elias Tobenkin, Ezra Brudno, and Edward Steiner, regarded assimilation and accommodation with the dominant culture as the true expression of "Americanization" or the melting pot. In their novels the immigrant protagonist achieves acceptance and fulfillment by marriage to a gentile girl. Sidney Nyburg's *The Chosen People* (1917) and Abraham Cahan's *The Rise of David Levinsky* (1917) probe the shallowness of that situation. In both books the hero meets loneliness, ennui, and guilt at the end of the American dream because outward success by denial of the past produces only emptiness. Old World values and New World experience did not yet produce a symbiosis of the kind suggested by Horace Kallen's philosophy of pluralism.
F. Rosenthal

157. Fine, Henry and Fine, Lea. NORTH DAKOTA MEMORIES. *Western States Jewish Hist. Q. 1977 9(4): 331-340.* Like many other Jewish immigrants, the authors' grandparents came from eastern Europe in the 1870's. They homesteaded free farm land near Fargo, North Dakota, and later moved to town and opened a clothing store. Their children managed the first soda pop factory in North Dakota. Both subjects remember friendship and kindness from their neighbors in the gentile community. Edited from taped interviews with former North Dakota residents.
B. S. Porter

158. Fisher, Alan. CONTINUITY AND EROSION OF JEWISH LIBERALISM. *Am. Jewish Hist. Q. 1976 65(2): 322-348.* Attempts to document the attitudinal changes of American Jews by examining selected relevant voting studies and opinion polls over the last 20 years. Yet, if the data is trustworthy, continuity of Jewish liberalism is more deep-seated than its erosion. In attitudes toward integration, equal rights, welfare, and national health care, Jews are more liberal than they were in the 1950's; as to marijuana, abortion, and pollution, differences with non-Jews are considerable. 29 notes, 14 tables.
F. Rosenthal

159.   Fisher, Alan M.   REALIGNMENT OF THE JEWISH VOTE?   *Pol. Sci. Q. 1979 94(1): 97-116.* Tests some recent perceptions of party realignment among American Jews by examining different data sources for party affiliation and voting in national and local elections. He finds continued support among Jews for Democrats and a relatively constant difference with the non-Jewish vote for the last 30 years.

160.   Fisher, Alan M.   WHERE IS THE NEW JEWISH CONSERVATISM? *Society 1979 16(4): 5, 15-18.* Examines sociopolitical attitudes of US Jews, 1969-79, and concludes that their alleged growing conservatism is largely a myth.

161.   Fisher, Minnie.   THE YIDDISHE ARBEITEN UNIVERSITETT: AN ORAL HISTORY.   *Urban Rev. 1976 9(3): 201-204.* Presents the narrative of a 76 year old former garment worker from the young immigrant Jewish community in New York City's Lower East Side during the 1920's. Through the Universitett the eager new citizens learned English, studied modern political and economic systems, debated, and developed socially.   D. L. Smith

162.   Fishman, Joshua A.; Mosse, George L.; and Silberstein, Laurence J. DISCUSSANTS.   *Am. Jewish Hist. Q. 1974 63(4): 369-378.* Discussion on the relationship between Jewish studies and existing academic departments. One of nine related articles in this issue.   S

163.   Fogelson, George J., ed.   A CONVERSION AT SANTA CRUZ, CALIFORNIA, 1877.   *Western States Jewish Hist. Q. 1979 11(2): 138-144.* In December 1877, Emma Schlutius was officially accepted as a convert to Judaism in a ceremony at the St. Charles Hotel in Santa Cruz. Schlutius correctly answered questions regarding her motives and tenets of the faith. On her admission to the covenant, her name was changed to Esther. She was shortly afterwards married to Abe Rothschild. Based on an article published in the *Santa Cruz Sentinel* on 8 December 1877; photo, 6 notes.   B. S. Porter

164.   Foner, Philip S.   BLACK-JEWISH RELATIONS IN THE OPENING YEARS OF THE TWENTIETH CENTURY.   *Phylon 1975 36(4): 359-367.* Certain well-focused events in the early 20th century forced blacks to reconsider the view they had long entertained that Jews, who also had felt the sting of prejudice, were less antiblack than other Americans. The black press reacted bitterly to Jewish involvement in efforts to disenfranchise black voters in Maryland and to the indifference of the Jewish community toward racial discrimination once they had achieved greater acceptance for their own community. Based on newspaper accounts and secondary sources; 43 notes.   K. C. Snow

165.   Forrey, Robert.   THE "JEW" IN NORRIS' *THE OCTOPUS.   Western States Jewish Hist. Q. 1975 7(3): 201-209.* An analysis of the character S. Behrman in Frank Norris' (1870-1902) book *The Octopus* (1901) and the real life Jewish financier and possible secret railroad agent Marcus Pollasky. Pollasky helped establish a branch railroad line in the San Joaquin Valley in California and then turned it over to the hated Southern Pacific Railroad. The fictional character Behrman is a banker who squeezes the local farmers for every cent they have. There are many similarities in the lives of these two men, and Norris capitalized on the anti-Semitism of his time to create hatred for his character, S. Behrman. 14 notes.   R. A. Garfinkle

166. Forster, Arnold. THE ANTI-DEFAMATION LEAGUE. *Wiener Lib. Bull. [Great Britain] 1975 28(33/34): 52-58.* Describes the aims and work of the American Jewish defense organization, the Anti-Defamation League of B'nai B'rith (ADL), established in 1913 to stop the defamation of the Jewish people and to work to end discrimination against all citizens. To the chief (and continuing) American concern of the ADL, the exposure of racism and bigotry, the energies of the ADL and of other Jewish service organizations now have to be marshalled to defend the validity of the Jewish claim to Israel against attacks from Arab and pro-Arab quarters. J. P. Fox

167. Fox, Marvin. PHILOSOPHY AND CONTEMPORARY JEWISH STUDIES. *Am. Jewish Hist. Q. 1974 63(4): 350-355.* Philosophy, as taught in the university, does not include Jewish philosophy; therefore Jewish studies should encompass it. One of nine related articles in this issue. S

168. Fram, Harry. WRITINGS OF A FOUNDER OF ZIONISM IN LOS ANGELES. *Western States Jewish Hist. Q. 1977 9(3): 238-245.* Harry Fram (1877-1960), owner of a retail stationery store, was one of the founders of Zionism in Los Angeles. He helped establish the Nathan Straus Palestine Advancement Society (later known as the Nathan Straus Israel Society) and the Young Zionist Association of Los Angeles. Fram published two pamphlets in 1905 and 1944 which explained the reason for creating a homeland for Jews, and advocated the establishment of a national financial institution to administrate this great project. Reprints excerpts from Fram's speeches and writings. Primary and secondary sources; photo, 13 notes. B. S. Porter

169. Fram, Leon. DETROIT JEWRY'S FINEST HOUR. *Michigan Jewish Hist. 1978 18(2): 14-19.* The author reminisces about his leadership role in Detroit's League for Human Rights during 1930's-40's, boycotting Nazi goods and services, and organizing a campaign of resistance to Nazism.

170. Franck, Isaac. THE AMERICAN JEWISH EXPERIENCE. *Midstream 1976 22(3): 7-18.* Discusses the social history and culture of Jews in the United States from the 1950's-70's, emphasizing current Jewish concern about Israel, education, civil rights and ethnic intermarriage.

171. Frankel, Jonathan. THE JEWISH SOCIALISTS AND THE AMERICAN JEWISH CONGRESS MOVEMENT. *Yivo Ann. of Jewish Social Sci. 1976 (16): 202-341.* Studies the movement for an American Jewish Congress in the years 1914-18. Takes the position that this was essentially a movement of the nationalist forces in Jewish politics. Shows how it was initiated to a large extent by the nationalist wing of the socialist movement and how the American Jewish Committee with its philosophy of Americanization opposed the concept of a Jewish nationality and Jewish nationalism. R. J. Wechman

172. Franklin, Harvey B. MEMORIES OF A CALIFORNIA RABBI: STOCKTON, SAN JOSE AND LONG BEACH. *Western States Jewish Hist. Q. 1977 9(2): 122-128.* Rabbi Harvey B. Franklin (1889-1976) spent his rabbinical career at Stockton, 1916-18; Oakland, 1918-20; San Jose, 1920-28; and Long Beach, 1928-57. Early in his career he faced the necessity of developing a religious service that satisfied a mixed and mutually antagonistic congregation of Reform, Orthodox, and Conservative members. Relates several anecdotes, some humorous, of his experiences at each Jewish community. B. S. Porter

173.   Franklin, Lewis A. and Levey, Samson H., ed.   THE FIRST JEWISH SERMON IN THE WEST: YOM KIPPUR, 1850, SAN FRANCISCO. *Western States Jewish Hist. Q. 1977 10(1): 3-15.* Lewis Abraham Franklin (1820-79), an English Jew, arrived in San Francisco early in 1849. He opened a tent store in which religious services were conducted on High Holy Days. In 1851 Franklin moved to San Diego where he and his brother Maurice operated a general merchandise store and a hotel. He returned to England in 1860. The Yom Kippur sermon of 1850 centers on atonement and pleads for stricter observance of the Sabbath and a revival of religious (instead of monetary) goals. America provides a unique opportunity for spiritual freedom and self-identity for Jews. Quotes original text; 45 notes.   B. S. Porter

174.   Franzoni, Janet Brenner.   TROUBLED TIRADER: A PSYCHOBIO-GRAPHICAL STUDY OF TOM WATSON. *Georgia Hist. Q. 1973 57(4): 493-510.* Thomas E. Watson (1856-1922), prominent Georgia politician, legislator, congressman, and vice-presidential candidate, was an enigmatic figure. His colorful tirades and efforts ranged in extremes from pro- to anti-black, Catholic, and Jew. Psychological analysis may well hold the key to an understanding of his career. 79 notes.   D. L. Smith

175.   Freund, Paul A.   JUSTICE BRANDEIS: A LAW CLERK'S REMEM-BRANCE. *Am. Jewish Hist. 1978 68(1): 7-18.* The author who served as Supreme Court justice Louis D. Brandeis's law clerk in 1932-33, calls him a working justice, incisive moralist, observant host, and ardent Zionist. Brandeis' power derived from a harmonious fusion of biblical moral responsibility, classical restraint and proportion, and the common law tradition of rubbing against the hard face of experience.   F. Rosenthal

176.   Frideres, James S.   OFFSPRING OF JEWISH INTERMARRIAGE: A NOTE. *Jewish Social Studies 1973 35(2): 149-156.* In sociological investigation of a Jewish community in the Canadian Midwest, the author found that the incidence of intermarriage could be correlated with the size of the Jewish community, the previous pattern of intermarriage, and the availability of Jewish education. Based on primary and secondary sources; 21 notes.   P. E. Schoenberg

177.   Fried, Lewis.   JACOB RIIS AND THE JEWS: THE AMBIVALENT QUEST FOR COMMUNITY. *Am. Studies (Lawrence, KS) 1979 20(1): 5-24.* Examines Jacob Riis's treatment of Jews against his general beliefs in civil liberties and social freedom. His thought expressed the tensions between the promise of egalitarianism and the realities of American society, and to him the downtown Jews highlighted this disparity. Their attachment to European cultural traditions confused Riis's impulse for cultural unity and Christian endeavor. Primary and secondary sources; 2 illus., 59 notes.   J. A. Andrew

178.   Friedlander, Alice G.   A PORTLAND GIRL ON WOMEN'S RIGHTS —1893. *Western States Jewish Hist. Q. 1978 10(2): 146-150.* In 1893 Alice G. Friedlander said there should be no question about the fundamental principal of women's equality. Any profession—such as journalism, law, medicine, education —requiring intellectual rather than manual force, is open to women. Soon they will vote and hold office, and, though lacking in parliamentary finesse, no matter how hard they try, they cannot be more ignorant and stupid than some gentleman

legislators. These new skills and attainments do not conflict with women's duties in the home. Quoted from original speech at Portland (Oregon) Press Club; photo. B. S. Porter

179. Friedler, Egon et al. JEWS WITHOUT MONEY TODAY. *Present Tense 1975 2(2): 62-67.* Discusses Jews currently living in poverty in Uruguay, Canada, France, and Great Britain.

180. Friedman, Murray. BLACK ANTI-SEMITISM ON THE RISE. *Commentary 1979 68(4): 31-35.* Discusses the rise of political anti-Semitism among well-educated black leaders, including Jesse Jackson and Reverend Joseph Lowery, and in the black middle class as a whole in the United States since the mid-1960's.

181. Friedmann, Thomas. BACK TO THE EDGES, THE CENTER WILL NOT HOLD: ONE REASON FOR THE EMERGENCE OF A NEW CON-SCIOUSNESS IN AMERICAN JEWISH LITERATURE. *Am. Jewish Arch. 1978 30(2): 126-132.* American Jewish literature has usually been identified by its universalistic approach, where, according to the author, Jewish writers found it easier to write for all Americans "than to be Jewish writers for Jews." But the tide is turning with the current collapse of the "American [Jewish] dream." A new attitude has emerged within the discipline which reflects American Jewry's emphasis on self-protection and self-preservation. J

182. Gal, Allon. IN SEARCH OF A NEW ZION: NEW LIGHT ON BRANDEIS' ROAD TO ZIONISM. *Am. Jewish Hist. 1978 68(1): 19-31.* Louis D. Brandeis's conversion both to a more positive Judaism as well as Zionism had taken place by the end of 1910 after he had sought support for his progressive position from the Boston Jewish community and after his contacts with Jewish workers and employers in the New York garment strike. Another factor was his association with Aaron Aronsohn of the Jewish Agricultural Experiment Station in Palestine. He was deeply impressed by the morality of the pioneer Zionists. 32 notes. F. Rosenthal

183. Ganin, Zvi. THE LIMITS OF AMERICAN JEWISH POLITICAL POWER: AMERICA'S RETREAT FROM PARTITION, NOVEMBER 1947-MARCH 1948. *Jewish Social Studies 1977 39(1-2): 1-36.* Forces within the Truman administration sought to undo the US commitment to the United Nations' Partition of Palestine resolution of 29 November 1947. These oppositionists included important members of the State Department, Secretary of Defense James Forrestal and members of the National Security Council and Central Intelligence Agency. Outside the government important sources of opposition were represented by James Reston of the *New York Times* and Kermit Roosevelt. President Truman was irritated by the interference of the American Jewish community into foreign policy matters by injecting the issue into domestic politics. Domestic Jewish groups and individuals failed to stem the retreat from supporting partition because they were unable to persuade the American foreign policy elite that the creation of a Jewish state was in the national interest. The foreign policy elite was able to effectively counter the presumed great strength of domestic Jewish political pressure. N. Lederer

184.   Garnham, David.   FACTORS INFLUENCING CONGRESSIONAL SUPPORT FOR ISRAEL DURING THE 93RD CONGRESS.   *Jerusalem J. of Int. Relations [Israel] 1977 2(3): 23-45.* Presents a model designed to assess dependent and independent factors affecting attitudes of Congress toward foreign aid to Israel, 1973-74, concluding that because of economic and political ties, Arab-US relations have a great bearing on Israeli-US relations and that the executive branch tended to support the Arabs while the Congress tended to support Israel.

185.   Gartner, Lloyd P.   NAPHTALI HERZ IMBER, POPULIST.   *Michael: On the Hist. of the Jews in the Diaspora [Israel] 1975 3: 88-100.* Naphtali Herz Imber (1856-1909) was a minor Hebrew poet best known for his "Hatikvah" (The Hope), which became Israel's national anthem. Much less known is his pamphlet *The Fall of Jerusalem: Reflecting upon the Present Condition of America,* written shortly after his arrival in the United States in 1892 and reprinted here. It fabricates a myth of Biblical history paralleling the Populist myth of American history, exhorting Americans to heed the warning of Jewish experience and not allow their wealth to lead America to ruin. Primary and secondary sources; 5 notes.   T. Sassoon

186.   Gastwirt, Zvi.   KASHRUT AND THE LAW IN NEW YORK CITY.   *Michael: On the Hist. of the Jews in the Diaspora [Israel] 1975 3: 281-301.* Reproduces and analyses document found among the personal papers of Lewis J. Gribetz, legal counsel to the Kashruth Association of Greater New York in its struggle to control *kashrut* supervision in New York City's kosher poultry industry during the 1930's. Scandals revealed in the *shohatim* (slaughterers) union prompted New York Jews to encourage Mayor James J. Walker to investigate the kosher poultry industry. The document represents the report issued in 1931 by Walker's committee. Despite the report's recommendations, the Department of Markets retained responsibility for the enforcement of New York State's 1915 "Kosher Bill" and licensing was never implemented. Primary and secondary sources; 31 notes.   T. Sassoon

187.   Geffen, M. David.   DELAWARE JEWRY: THE FORMATIVE YEARS, 1872-1889.   *Delaware Hist. 1975 16(4): 269-297.* Although the climate in Delaware was not hostile to Jews, few settled there until the great Jewish migrations from Russia and Eastern Europe in the late 19th century. The Jewish population remained small, concentrated in Wilmington, mercantile in character. The Wilmington Jews met with a favorable reception. They worked hard, earned the respect of the community, and invested their energies in establishing worship services in the city. The Moses Montefiore Mutual Aid Society took the lead in maintaining community life and in providing social and educational services. It also worked hard to bring Jews together for religious purposes, and by its fundraising efforts helped to underwrite the building of a synagogue staffed by a resident rabbi. The Wilmington Jewish community was largely of German origin and lived in a small area near the business district. By the end of the 1880's the Wilmington Jews were receiving an increasing number of Jewish families from Eastern Europe and feeling the cultural distance separating them. Based on contemporary newspapers; 2 illus., 84 notes.   R. M. Miller

188. Gelfand, Mitchell B. JEWISH ECONOMIC AND RESIDENTIAL MOBILITY IN EARLY LOS ANGELES. *Western States Jewish Hist. Q. 1979 11(4): 332-347.* Jews settled in Los Angeles as early as the final Mexican years. By 1870 they were a stable part of the commercial, social, and political life of the city. The immigration boom of the 1880's increased their numbers but reduced their relative proportion of the population. They were primarily business and professional men with a large stake in the growth of the city, which explains their tendency to remain in the area. They resided in fashionable areas on the outskirts of the business district. Their economic mobility in excess of the general population is explained by their traditional (European) commercial background; business, social, and family ties that facilitated economic opportunities; and their possession of middle-class values that inspired recent immigrants—particularly the "low status" Polish Jews—to adopt German-Jewish and American culture. Based on census records, other primary and secondary sources; 32 notes.
                                                                        B. S. Porter

189. Geller, Stuart. WHY DID LOUIS BRANDEIS CHOOSE ZIONISM? *Am. Jewish Hist. Q. 1973 62(4): 383-400.* Opposes the thesis advanced by Yonathan Shapiro that Louis Dembitz Brandeis (1856-1941) became a Zionist in order to secure political advancement during the administration of Woodrow Wilson. That Brandeis in 1912 joined the small and then unpopular group of Zionists rather than the American Jewish Committee is proof that he acted out of convictions rather than opportunism. Brandeis had learned to accept the new Jewish immigrant who, he thought, could be Americanized by Zionism, which he identified with an oppressed minority. 35 notes.   F. Rosenthal

190. Gendler, Carol. THE FIRST SYNAGOGUE IN NEBRASKA: THE EARLY HISTORY OF THE CONGREGATION OF ISRAEL OF OMAHA. *Nebraska Hist. 1977 58(3): 323-341.* Examines the beginnings of a formal Jewish community in Omaha, from 1867 through the construction of Temple Israel, dedicated in 1908. Focuses on prominent members of the community, early rabbis who served it, and the tensions between reform and traditional groups.
                                                                        R. Lowitt

191. Gendler, Carol. THE JEWS OF OMAHA: THE FIRST SIXTY YEARS. *Western States Jewish Hist. Q. 1973 5(3): 205-224, (4): 288-305, 6(1): 58-71, 1974 6(2): 141-154, (3): 222-233, (4): 293-304.* Part I. Discusses the role of Jews in the settlement of Omaha, 1820's-30's. Part II. Chronicles the development of the Orthodox and Reform Jewish congregations, the tenures of rabbis, and the erection of synagogues, 1854-1904. Part III. The Jews in Omaha formed several charity and mutual aid societies in the late 1800's. The main social club, the Metropolitan Club, lasted until 1911. Several Jews became leaders in Omaha. Edward Rosewater (1841-1906) served in the state legislature and founded the Omaha *Bee*. He ran for the US Senate twice, but lost. Jonas L. Brandeis (1837-1903), a successful businessman, gave large sums of money to charities. Photo, 41 notes. Part IV. In the late 1880's, thousands of Jews fled from eastern Europe. Several Jewish organizations were set up to help the refugees find homes and jobs in America. The Jews in Omaha came to the aid of those Jews that came to Omaha and wanted to settle there. By 1880, enough Orthodox Jews had settled in Omaha to make it possible to hold orthodox prayer services. The congregations were organized according to the country of origin of the immigrants. A strong

Jewish community developed in Omaha. Based on primary and secondary sources; 46 notes. Part V. Because of a depression that hit Omaha in 1890, many wealthy citizens lost their fortunes and had to move elsewhere. Although several wealthy Jews were hard hit by the bad economic conditions, the Jewish population of Omaha continued to grow. This growth necessitated the formation of new organizations to serve the community. The Jews set up their own charities, fraternal groups, and hospital. The Jewish community was a mixture of Orthodox and Reformed Jews working together to take care of their needs. Based on primary and secondary sources; 41 notes. Part VI. The Jews of Omaha became leaders in the professions and politics. Harry B. Zimman served on the city council and was acting mayor when the regular mayor died in 1906. In 1889, the first of many Jewish political groups was founded. A controversy developed over who controlled the "Hebrew vote." The Omaha Jews were planning on building a community center when in 1913 a tornado destroyed the center of the Jewish residential area. The Jewish Relief Committee was established to aid the victims. By 1915, the Jews in Omaha were well established within the larger community, and were taking an active part in its development. Based on primary and secondary sources; photo, 30 notes.   R. A. Garfinkle/S

192. Genizi, Haim. AMERICAN NON-SECTARIAN REFUGEE RELIEF ORGANIZATIONS (1933-1945). *Yad Vashem Studies on the European Jewish Catastrophe and Resistance [Israel] 1976 11: 164-220.* Examines the activities and role of the American nonsectarian organizations in the general field of aid and relief to refugees from Nazi Germany. The creation of nonsectarian committees comprising Jews and Christians was designed to ensure the greatest possible public support for a task which also involved the fight against the rising wave of anti-Semitism in the United States. The establishment of nonsectarian committees also stemmed from the need to care for professional groups with specific problems. Based on archival and published sources; 185 notes.   J. P. Fox

193. Genizi, Haim. JAMES MCDONALD AND THE ROOSEVELT ADMINISTRATION. Artzi, Pinhas, ed. *Bar-Ilan Studies in History* (Ramat-Gan, Israel: Bar-Ilan U. Pr., 1978): 285-306. Assesses the career of James G. McDonald (1886-1964) and his assistance to Jewish refugees in the 1930's. In 1933, the League of Nations set up a High Commission for Refugees; America put McDonald forward as a candidate, although it wanted to remain isolationist. As High Commissioner, McDonald found little support in America; he resigned after the Nuremberg decrees in 1935. Franklin D. Roosevelt became more helpful to the Jews after the German annexation of Austria in 1938. He set up the President's Advisory Committee, with McDonald as chairman and as liaison between the State Department and the social services. Various countries were suggested for the Jewish national home, but many European consuls and the State Department objected. For his strenuous efforts on the Jews' behalf, he was awarded the Gottheil Medal for Services to American Jewry. Based on archive sources and secondary works; 114 notes.   A. Alcock

194. Geoll, Yohai. ALIYA IN THE ZIONISM OF AN AMERICAN OLEH: JUDAH L. MAGNES. *Am. Jewish Hist. Q. 1975 65(2): 99-120.* Judah L. Magnes (1877-1948) was one of the native-born and American-educated Jews who formed a significant element of the leadership during the first two decades of American Zionism. Once Magnes had gone to Palestine, he assumed vital

responsibilities there too, culminating in his service as president of the newly founded Hebrew University. Magnes' attitudes and his development as a Zionist are described on the basis of letters, diary entries, and excerpts from his many publications. 50 notes. F. Rosenthal

195. Gephart, Jerry C.; Siegel, Martin A.; and Fletcher, James E. A NOTE ON LIBERALISM AND ALIENATION IN JEWISH LIFE. *Jewish Social Studies 1974 36(3-4): 327-329.* A 1971 survey of the entire Jewish community of Salt Lake City indicated the willingness of the people to submerge their ideological differences in order to have one synagogue to serve the entire community instead of maintaining two separate synagogues, Reform and Conservative. Both groups saw a strengthening of a common Jewish identity but feared that the differences between Reform and Conservative Judaism would be lost through the union of the two synagogues. Primary and secondary sources; 5 notes.
P. E. Schoenberg

196. Ghosh, Partha Sarathy. PRESENT STATE OF AMERICAN ZIONISM AND THE MIDDLE EAST CRISES OF 1967. *Q. Rev. of Hist. Studies [India] 1975-76 15(3): 151-157.* Zionist-organized activities exert a great influence on American government policy. This results from the scores of Jewish legislative and legal assistants serving in government, and the threat of the Jewish vote. Although fewer American Jews claim to be Zionists, they believe Israel must be preserved because it gives American Jews a sense of ethnic identity, and as a moral matter. 38 notes. J. C. Holsinger

197. Gidwitz, Betsy. PROBLEMS OF ADJUSTMENT OF SOVIET JEWISH EMIGRES. *Soviet Jewish Affairs [Great Britain] 1976 6(1): 27-42.* Discusses problems of social and cultural assimilation of Soviet Jews emigrating to Israel and the United States, 1967-70's, including their difficulties in obtaining employment.

198. Gilbert, Philip J. THE MEMORABLE SHOLEM ALEICHEM RECEPTION IN DETROIT, MICHIGAN, MAY 15, 1915. *Michigan Jewish Hist. 1977 17(1): 11-16.* The Detroit Progressive Literary and Dramatic Club held a reception in the Jewish community for Jewish author Sholem Aleichem in 1915.

199. Gilson, Estelle. TRUDE'S A HOLY TERROR: SCHOLAR, CRITIC, REBEL, GADFLY. *Present Tense 1978 5(2): 33-37.* Chronicles the career of Trude Weiss-Rosmarin, editor of *The Jewish Spectator* but dedicated critic and adherent of the Jewish community, 1930's-78.

200. Gilson, Estelle. YIVO—WHERE YIDDISH SCHOLARSHIP LIVES: HISTORY AND MISSION ON FIFTH AVENUE. *Present Tense 1976 4(1): 57-65.* Traces the history of the Yidisher Visnshaftlekher Institut (YIVO) from its inception in Vilna, Lithuania to its present location in New York City. Describes the physical facilities of the Institute and discusses YIVO's historic purpose and goals. Primary and secondary sources; 5 photos. R. B. Mendel

201. Ginzberg, Eli. ROBERT SZOLD: AN AUTHENTIC AMERICAN. *Midstream 1979 25(9): 47-52.* Biographical sketch of Robert Szold, a New York City attorney and investor active in Zionism, 1920's-70's.

202.   Gitelle, Tobey B.   PRELIMINARY LIST AND SUBJECT INDEX OF *JEWISH SOCIAL STUDIES,* 1964 THROUGH 1978.   *Jewish Social Studies 1979 41(1): 9-22.* Lists every article, conference report, review article, communication, and obituary published in *Jewish Social Studies* during 1964-78. Excludes reviews and book notes. A total of 276 entries are sequentially numbered and arranged according to last name of author or other identifier within each of the above indicated groups. A subject index with cross references is included.

N. Lederer

203.   Gitelman, Zvi.   SOVIET JEWISH EMIGRANTS: WHY ARE THEY CHOOSING AMERICA?   *Soviet Jewish Affairs [Great Britain] 1977 7(1): 31-46.* Fewer Soviet Jews are emigrating to Israel, and those who are attracted by the democratic image of the United States also originate in areas such as the Ukraine and the Russian Republic, where Zionism is relatively weak.

204.   Glanz, David.   AN INTERPRETATION OF THE JEWISH COUNTERCULTURE.   *Jewish Social Studies 1977 39(1-2): 117-128.* A recent development among American Jewry has been the activist role of a minority of Jewish students in support of the state of Israel, agitation for the rights of Soviet Jewry, the position of women in Judaism, and the search for a Jewish self-identity through an exploration of Jewish belief and ritual. The creation of this Jewish counterculture was based partially on the severance of Jewish involvement from the civil rights movement and a subsequent return to work within the Jewish community. The impact of the Six Day War and the tangible threat to the continued existence of Israel embodied in the conflict also was a factor in generating Jewish self-consciousness among the young. Within the Jewish community the counterculture has been spurred along by the successful work of the United Synagogue Youth and the Ramah camp movements of Conservative Judaism. To some extent this new thrust represents a return of third-generation Jews to their roots.

N. Lederer

205.   Glanz, Rudolf.   FROM FUR RUSH TO GOLD RUSHES: ALASKAN JEWRY FROM THE LATE NINETEENTH TO THE EARLY TWENTIETH CENTURIES.   *Western States Jewish Hist. Q. 1975 7(2): 95-107.* The Jewish-owned Alaska Commercial Company, founded in 1868, obtained the fur trading concession from the federal government, giving the company a monopoly in Alaska. The company established 87 trading posts in the territory. When its concession expired in 1890, the company was able to survive because of its other activities. The gold rushes in Alaska attracted many Jews, many establishing small businesses in the gold areas. The first organized Jewish community was in Nome. The Nome Hebrew Benevolent Society was established in 1901. Rabbi Samuel Koch of Seattle conducted religious instruction by correspondence with Jewish children in Alaska, beginning in 1916. Primary and secondary sources; photo, 50 notes.

R. A. Garfinkle

206.   Glanz, Rudolf.   THE JEWS IN THE SANDWICH ISLANDS.   *Western States Jewish Hist. Q. 1974 6(3): 177-187.* During the 1850's-60's, many Jews left California to settle in the Sandwich Islands. Many set up prosperous businesses, and several became civic leaders. Some of the Jews mentioned in the article are; L. Cohen, Isaac Wormser, Paul Neumann, A. S. Grinbaum, Hirsch Rayman, Rabbi Rudolph Coffe, and Michael Phillips. Primary and secondary sources; 37 notes.

R. A. Garfinkle

207. Glanz, Rudolf. SOME REMARKS ON JEWISH LABOR AND AMERICAN PUBLIC OPINION IN THE PRE-WORLD WAR I ERA. *Yivo Ann. of Jewish Social Sci. 1976 (16): 178-202.* Shows how the Jewish labor movement influenced American and Jewish American public opinion about the popular conception of a Jew and how it influenced the entire American labor movement.　　　　　　　　　　　　　　　　　　　　　R. J. Wechman

208. Glanz, Rudolf. THE SPREAD OF JEWISH COMMUNITIES THROUGH AMERICA BEFORE THE CIVIL WAR. *Yivo Ann. of Jewish Social Sci. 1974 (15): 7-45.* Explores the spread of Jewish communities, especially the German-Jews, in the antebellum period. Studies the effects of American conditions on the founding of Jewish communities, quoting extensively from settlers' memoirs, and discussing the locations and economic determinants on the spread of the Jewish population. 239 notes.　　　　　　　　　R. J. Wechman

209. Glaser, Richard. THE GREEK JEWS IN BALTIMORE. *Jewish Social Studies 1976 38(3-4): 321-336.* A study of the 28 Greek Jews in Baltimore indicates that they constitute a unique entity in the Baltimore Jewish population. Some of their traditional holidays have been eliminated in order to conform with Ashkenazim customs of celebration, while others have been modified in their observance because of economic circumstances or a general lack of emphasis within the general Jewish community. Those holidays that have been retained from their Greek origins include a large amount of the traditional modes of celebration. The ethnic solidarity of the Baltimore Greek Jews is declining in strength because of the propensity of the young to marry within the Ashkenazim community and the exposure to other customs.　　　　　　　　N. Lederer

210. Glazer, Michele. THE DURKHEIMERS OF OREGON: A PICTURE STORY. *Western States Jewish Hist. Q. 1978 10(3): 202-209.* Kaufman Durkheimer brought his family from Philadelphia to Portland, Oregon, in 1862, where he opened a second-hand furniture store. In 1874 his son Julius moved to Baker City, Oregon where he opened a general mechandise store. Julius sold the store in 1887 and opened a new store in Prairie City. The next year he opened another store in Canyon City. With the expansion of his merchandising businesses to a third site, in Burns, Oregon, Julius sent for his brothers Moses, Sam, and Sigmund to help run the firm. Julius's wife, Delia, was not happy in the primitive, isolated small towns of eastern Oregon, so the family moved to Portland. In 1896 Julius purchased an interest in the wholesale grocery firm of Wadham and Company, the northwest distributor of Olympia beer. Under the management of Julius's son and grandson, the company—now, Bevhold, Inc.—continues to market Olympia beer. Primary and secondary sources; 5 photos, 3 notes.　　　　　B. S. Porter

211. Glazer, Nathan. THE EXPOSED AMERICAN JEW. *Commentary 1975 59(6): 25-30.* "American Jews ... are more vulnerable because they have been more fortunate than some other groups, and because they must ask from their fellow citizens heavy support for [Israel]."　　　　　　　　　　S

212. Glickstein, Gary A. RELIGION AND THE JEWISH NEW LEFT: 1960 TO DATE. *Am. Jewish Arch. 1974 26(1): 23-30.* "A rising Jewish consciousness and an inability to adopt an anti-Israel stance have led many young Jewish radicals to break with the general New Left movement and form 'what could legitimately be called the Jewish New Left.' "　　　　　　　　J

213. Goldberg, Arthur. THE JEW IN NORWICH, CONNECTICUT: A CENTURY OF JEWISH LIFE. *Rhode Island Jewish Hist. Notes 1975 7(1): 79-103.*

214. Goldberg, Gordon J. MEYER LONDON AND THE NATIONAL SOCIAL INSURANCE MOVEMENT, 1914-1922. *Am. Jewish Hist. Q. 1975 65(1): 59-73.* Meyer London as legal counsel for the International Ladies' Garment Workers Union (ILGWU) and other unions became the principal spokesman for the labor movement and the urban immigrant. As the only Socialist representative in the 64th, 65th and 67th Congresses, London presented his party's social insurance program and waged a vigorous fight for its adoption. Although the plan was defeated, he helped educate colleagues and the public about labor reform, helping to pave the way for the New Deal.

F. Rosenthal

215. Goldberg, Reuben. DER OFKUM UN DER UNTERGANG FUN GOLDFADEN'S NUYORKER YIDISHE ILUSTRIRTE TSAYTUNG (1887-1888) [The rise and decline of Goldfaden's *Nuyorker Yidishe Ilustrirte Tsaytung* (1887-1888)]. *Yivo Bleter 1973 44: 171-186.* Abraham Goldfaden's primary interest was always the theater. However, the cold reception given him in America compelled him to turn to journalism. Because he would not easily give up the idea of the theater he attempted to pursue both simultaneously. This was humanly impossible and the publication became the victim. There was also no room at the time for another newspaper in Yiddish; the competition, lack of funds, and a libel case contributed to cessation of publication. Primary and secondary sources; 40 notes.

B. Klein

216. Goldberg, Richard B. MICHAEL WORMSER, CAPITALIST. *Am. Jewish Arch. 1973 25(2): 161-206.* "French-born Wormser 'helped build Arizona. Above all, he embodied the spirit of frontier materialism.' When it came to business enterprise, 'his creative energy was unlimited.' "

J

217. Golden, Harry. BICENTENNIAL OUTLOOK: JEWISH IMMIGRANT TODAY, AMERICAN TOMORROW. *Hist. Preservation 1976 28(4): 30-35.* Jews are, "at present, more middle-class American than middle-class America. . . . America gave the Jews political freedom and economic freedom of opportunity. The Jews gave America complete devotion, as well as intellectual achievement in science, commerce, medicine, and the arts." 3 illus., 2 photos.

R. M. Frame, III

218. Goldman, Martin S. TEACHING THE HOLOCAUST: SOME SUGGESTIONS FOR COMPARATIVE ANALYSIS. *J. of Intergroup Relations 1977 6(2): 23-30.* Comparing historiography of the Nazi treatment of Jews and the discrimination against Negroes and Indians in the United States would increase cultural understanding and cure prejudice.

219. Goldowsky, Seebert J. LOCAL JEWISH HISTORY—THE RHODE ISLAND EXPERIENCE. *Rhode Island Jewish Hist. Notes 1974 6(4): 622-628.* Discusses the origin and activities of the Rhode Island Jewish Historical Association.

S

220. Goldowsky, Seebert J. NEWPORT AS ARARAT. *Rhode Island Jewish Hist. Notes 1974 6(4): 604-609.* An account of the attempts by Mordecai Manuel Noah to establish a Jewish colony, Ararat, first in New York, then successfully in Newport, Rhode Island (1813-21). S

221. Goldsmith, Steven R. SAM HAMBURG: WORLD'S FOREMOST JEWISH FARMER. *Western States Jewish Hist. Q. 1978 10(4): 330-342.* Sam Hamburg (1898-1976) came to the United States from Palestine in 1920 to study modern agricultural techniques at the University of California at Berkeley and Davis. In 1932, after several years of tenant-farming, he bought land near Los Banos in the San Joaquin Valley. "Sam Hamburg Farms" became a showplace of modern agriculture, producing melons, cotton, vegetables, and seed alfalfa. In 1952 he returned to Israel where he used his own money and his knowledge of desert farming to develop cotton as an export crop that grossed $100 million a year by 1976. He commuted between California and Israel, bringing new agricultural ideas and materials to Israel, and developing strong bonds of friendship with Israeli leaders. In 1965 Hamburg developed Guillaume-Barre disease which left him deaf and partially paralyzed. When he died, he was mourned by great political leaders and small farmers from around the world. Based on personal interviews with friends and family; 4 photos, 11 notes. B. S. Porter

222. Goldstein, Judith. ETHNIC POLITICS: THE AMERICAN JEWISH COMMITTEE AS LOBBYIST, 1915-1917. *Am. Jewish Hist. Q. 1975 65(1): 36-58.* During 1915-17 the American Jewish Committee engaged in extensive lobbying with the executive and legislative branches of the federal government with respect to foreign relations with Russia and the restrictive literacy test for immigrants. Concern for the persecuted Jews of Russia was the prime reason for these activities. F. Rosenthal

223. Goldstein, Sidney and Goldstein, Alice. THE DECLINING USE OF YIDDISH IN RHODE ISLAND. *Rhode Island Jewish Hist. Notes 1977 7(3): 401-409.* The declining use of Yiddish as a mother tongue during 1910-70 is indicative of changing generational status and residential patterns among Jews in Rhode Island.

224. Gordon, Dudley. CHARLES F. LUMMIS AND THE NEWMARKS OF LOS ANGELES. *Western States Jewish Hist. Q. 1974 7(1): 32-38.* The friendship of author-editor Charles F. Lummis and the Newmark brothers, leading merchants in Los Angeles, led to the preservation of several historical sites and a crusade for culture in Los Angeles. Lummis founded the Southwest Museum and edited *Land of Sunshine* for many years. He also wrote the foreword to Harris Newmark's *Sixty Years in Southern California*. R. A. Garfinkle

225. Gordon, Leonard. THE FRAGMENTATION OF LITERARY STEREOTYPES OF JEWS AND OF NEGROES AMONG COLLEGE STUDENTS. *Pacific Sociol. Rev. 1973 16(4): 411-425.*

226. Goren, Arthur A. MOTHER ROSIE HERTZ, THE SOCIAL EVIL, AND THE NEW YORK KEHILLAH. *Michael: On the Hist. of the Jews in the Diaspora [Israel] 1975 3: 188-210.* In 1912 the Jewish community of New York City launched its own anti-crime campaign, setting up a Bureau of Social Morals to gather eivdence and present it to the city's law-enforcement agencies

for action. Presents documents written by the Bureau's chief investigator, 21-year-old Abe Shoenfeld, concerning a Hungarian Jewish immigrant family, headed by Mrs. Rosie Hertz, who owned and managed a string of brothels on the Lower East Side for more than 30 years. Convicted on 4 February 1913 of running a disorderly resort, Mrs. Hertz was committed to prison two months later. Primary and secondary sources; 15 notes.   T. Sassoon

227. Gorni, Yosef. THE JEWISHNESS AND ZIONISM OF HAROLD LASKI. *Midstream 1977 23(9): 72-77.* Follows Harold Laski's career during 1910-46 and concludes that, despite his early claims to the contrary, Laski was always a Zionist at heart and always felt himself a part of the Jewish nation, although he viewed traditional Jewish religion as restrictive.

228. Gotlieb, Yosef. EINSTEIN THE ZIONIST. *Midstream 1979 25(6): 43-48.* Albert Einstein (1879-1955) had little sense of Jewish identity during his early years, but about 1911 he became acquainted with Zionism in Prague, although he tended toward internationalism and pacifism until 1919, a date which marked the beginning of his strong belief in Zionism and his association with Hebrew University in Tel Aviv.

229. Gottlieb, Moshe. BOYCOTT, RESCUE, AND RANSOM: THE THREEFOLD DILEMMA OF AMERICAN JEWRY IN 1938-1939. *Yivo Ann. of Jewish Social Sci. 1974 (15): 235-279.* Studies attempts to deal with the Jewish refugee problem and the work of American Jews in organizing boycott, rescue, and ransom procedures. 95 notes.   R. J. Wechman

230. Gradwohl, Rebecca J. THE JEWESS IN SAN FRANCISCO—1896. *Western States Jewish Hist. Q. 1974 6(4): 273-276.* The Jewish woman of San Francisco in 1896 was not only concerned with running her household but was also active in charities and other societies. A few of the outstanding Jewish women in the city were: Dr. Adele Solomons Jaffa, Natalie Selling, and Amelia Levinson in medicine; writers Emma Wolf and her sister, Alice Wolf; teacher Mary Prag; Rabbi Ray Frank; and musicians Meta Asher and Mrs. Noah Brandt. Reprinted from *The American Jewess*, New York, October 1896.
                                                            R. A. Garfinkle

231. Greenberg, Gershon. THE DIMENSIONS OF SAMUEL ADLER'S RELIGIOUS VIEW OF THE WORLD. *Hebrew Union Coll. Ann. 1975 46: 377-412.* Samuel Adler (1809-91) was a German-born reform-rabbi who spent the last 35 years of his life as rabbi of Temple Emanuel of New York. For him Judaism is a significant level in the growth of moral consciousness where morality is amplified into an ontological realm, identical to the idealized world of creation. *Wissenschaft* becomes the God-given methodology for achieving insights into the moral possibilities of all literature and history. 100 notes.   F. Rosenthal

232. Greenberg, Gershon. A GERMAN-JEWISH IMMIGRANT'S PERCEPTION OF AMERICA, 1853-54. *Am. Jewish Hist. Q. 1978 67(4): 307-341.* In 1857 a German-Jewish literary society published this anonymous report in German of experiences of a German Jew. The identity of that writer remains a mystery, but he seems to have been well-educated, both yeshivah and university, and of the upper class. The report is extremely critical of the New York City Jewry, charging them with hypocrisy, lack of charity, and pride. The report

ridicules the newly formed order of B'nai B'rith as the Jewish version of the American love for secret societies. 46 notes.   F. Rosenthal

233. Greenberg, Gershon. THE HISTORICAL ORIGINS OF GOD AND MAN: SAMUEL HIRSCH'S LUXEMBOURG WRITINGS. *Leo Baeck Inst. Year Book [Great Britain] 1975 20: 129-148.* Samuel Hirsch (1815-89) is significant in modern Jewish history for transplanting Reform Judaism to America. While his American publications are journalistic and pragmatic, concentrating on man and society, his writings during his stay in Luxembourg, 1843-66, concentrate on the theological problem of man and God in history. The contiguity between time and eternity unfolds in history out of which reason and revelation emerge. This refocusing of Hirsch's attention explains his ability to concentrate on the human aspects of religion in America and sublimate his philosophy into the pragmatic world of Reform Judaism's future. 81 notes.   F. Rosenthal

234. Greenberg, Gershon. SAMUEL HIRSCH'S AMERICAN JUDAISM. *Am. Jewish Hist. Q. 1973 62(4): 362-382.* Samuel Hirsch (1815-89), who served as rabbi in Philadelphia 1866-89, wrote extensively on the meaning of Reform Judaism in America. In the nonideological and essentially nontheological atmosphere of the New World, he emphasized the sociohistorical factors in the evolution of Scripture and religion. His articles appeared in *Der Zeitgeist, Die Deborah,* and *The Jewish Times.* 47 notes.   F. Rosenthal

235. Greenberg, Gershon. THE SIGNIFICANCE OF AMERICA IN DAVID EINHORN'S CONCEPTION OF HISTORY. *Am. Jewish Hist. Q. 1973 63(2): 160-184.* Einhorn (1809-79) served several congregations in America during his last 24 years. He was a prolific writer who described the role of Israel in the inevitable progress of history. His interpretation of America as the land where history would culminate and the messianic redemption would come is unique. Based on primary and secondary sources; 61 notes.   F. Rosenthal

236. Greene, Michael. THE HANNAH SCHLOSS OLD TIMERS. *Michigan Jewish Hist. 1975 15(2): 34-39.* History of the philanthropic group, the Hannah Schloss Old Timers, active in the United Jewish Charities, headquartered in Detroit, Michigan.   S

237. Greenwood, N. H. SOL BARTH: A JEWISH SETTLER ON THE ARIZONA FRONTIER. *J. of Arizona Hist. 1973 14(4): 363-378.* Solomon Barth (ca. 1843-1928) came to the United States from East Prussia in 1856 and crossed the plains that year with a Mormon handcart group. For 20 years he traveled in the Far West, dealing in cattle, farming, trading, and sometimes gambling. He specialized in the opportunity of the moment. In 1873 he won squatters' equities, water rights, thousands of head of sheep, and cash in a card game at a key point on the Little Colorado River, in east central Arizona, at the juncture of two developing trade routes. Consolidating his land titles, he established St. Johns. Barth's fortunes were enhanced when he permitted Mormon colonists to locate there. Mormon-Mexican conflicts, prominence in local politics and graft, and a prison term occupied Barth. His anti-Mormon inclinations were tempered by the years; in the end he requested his funeral to be conducted in the Mormon church. 3 illus., 30 notes.   D. L. Smith

238. Griessman, B. Eugene. PHILOSEMITISM AND PROTESTANT FUNDAMENTALISM: THE UNLIKELY ZIONISTS. *Phylon 1976 37(3): 197-211.* "Puritan respect for the Old Testament provided a basis for treating those few Jews who dwelt in the New England colonies in a humane manner." Several of the colonial leaders believed that the American Indians were the Ten Lost Tribes of Israel. This myth stirred missionary activity for converting Indians. A pro-Semitic interpretation of the Abrahamic covenant (Genesis 12) is standard fare in fundamentalist churches. Generally, the conservative and fundamentalist denominations have supported Zionism. The Jewish missions affirm that Jews eventually will accept the Messiah and that it is the duty of Christians to convert Jews to Christianity. 49 notes.   E. P. Stickney

239. Grobman, Alex. THE WARSAW GHETTO UPRISING IN THE AMERICAN JEWISH PRESS. *Wiener Lib. Bull. [Great Britain] 1976 29(37-38): 53-61.* To establish the response of American Jewry to the Warsaw Ghetto revolt (1943), suggests that it is necessary to determine if American Jewry knew what was happening in Poland and in the Warsaw Ghetto prior to the revolt, and their reaction. It is also essential to examine and critically analyze the type of information received about the uprising and investigate the response of the American Jewish community. Finds that there was a steady stream of accurate information about the deteriorating plight of the Jews in the Warsaw Ghetto long before the rebellion. Furthermore, there was little response to the news of the uprising. Based on primary sources; 56 notes.   J. P. Fox

240. Grobman, Alex. WHAT DID THEY KNOW? THE AMERICAN JEWISH PRESS AND THE HOLOCAUST, 1 SEPTEMBER 1939-17 DECEMBER 1942. *Am. Jewish Hist. 1979 68(3): 327-352.* Examination of more than 20 periodicals and newspapers for the period in question shows that, while details often were inaccurate or incomplete, a general idea of the Nazi concentration camps was available. By 1942, the full horror story was known and was continuously being published in the general American press and the Yiddish press. American Jews reacted with protest meetings, memorial services, and days of fasting. 142 notes.   F. Rosenthal

241. Gross, Barry. WHAT SHYLOCK FORGOT, OR MAKING IT AND LOSING IT IN AMERICA. *J. of Ethnic Studies 1974 2(3): 50-57.* Surveys Jewish-American writers and major works since 1917 when Abraham Cahan's *Rise of David Levinsky* began the tradition of "warning American Jews against the dangers of assimilation," and the evils of materialistic American values, while equating Jewishness with spirituality. The incompatibility of these two values was preached also in the early works of Henry Roth, Budd Schulberg, and Michael Gold. After World War II the pattern changed and the "failed successes" gave way to the anti-heroes of Saul Bellow's *The Victim* and Bernard Malamud's *The Assistant*, wherein "suffering, failure, defeat represent a moral victory" and help atone for the American Jews' guilt for not having really suffered along with European Jewry. The pattern today is "thinning out," and may have climaxed, with works such as Philip Roth's *Goodbye Columbus* and *Portnoy's Complaint*, the latter being called "a satire on the Jewish-American novel itself." In essence, though, the old values have life yet,""as Jewish youth now turns its back on its parents' Americanness!"   G. J. Bobango

242. Gruneir, Robert. THE HEBREW MISSION IN TORONTO. *Can. Ethnic Studies [Canada] 1977 9(1): 18-28.* Focuses primarily on the Presbyterian Church and the Protestant-supported Jewish mission founded in 1912. Examines efforts to convert immigrant Jews to Protestantism. Though presented as an aid to social assimilation, conversion (even the hybrid Hebrew-Protestant variety which allowed maintenance of ethnic identity), failed to attract large numbers of Jews. The movement faded after World War I. K. S. McDorman

243. Grunwald, Kurt. THREE CHAPTERS OF GERMAN-JEWISH BANKING HISTORY. *Leo Baeck Inst. Year Book [Great Britain] 1977 22: 191-208.* The combination of a relative lack of anti-Jewish prejudice and presence of material self-interest formed the basis of economic collaboration between the many German rulers and the Jews after 1648. Jews' ability to procure goods and services, dispose of war booty advantageously, and provide necessary funds made them indispensable to their masters. The history of early 19th-century commercial banking in the United States shows the great contributions of immigrants, mostly from southwestern Germany. Summarizes the banking history of Abraham S. Joseph (1827-92) of Michelstadt and his descendants in Germany and England. 3 illus., 40 notes. F. Rosenthal

244. Gutfeld, Arnon. "A RUSSIAN JEW NAMED LEVINE". *Michael: On the Hist. of the Jews in the Diaspora [Israel] 1975 3: 211-225.* On 7 February 1919, Chancellor Edward C. Elliott suspended Prof. Louis Levine (later Lewis Lorwin, d. 1971) from the faculty of Montana State University for insubordination and unprofessional conduct prejudicial to the welfare of the university. Levine had published a monograph entitled *The Taxation of Mines in Montana,* questioning the tax exemptions enjoyed by the state's omnipotent mining interests and thus incurring the wrath of the Anaconda Copper Mining Co. Reconstructs the affair, connecting it with the "red scare" of the time and with anti-Semitism. Primary and secondary sources; 20 notes, 3 appendixes. T. Sassoon

245. Gutwirth, Jacques. HASSIDIM ET JUDAÏCITÉ À MONTRÉAL [Hasidism and Judaicity in Montreal]. *Recherches Sociographiques 1973 14(3): 291-325.* The Hasidic groupings that established themselves in Montreal during 1941-52 have, through their sociocultural and religious presence, had a direct and salutary impact on the Jewish community of the city. This has become possible through common reference points of Judaism where institutional collaboration takes place. In turn, Montreal's Jewish faction has permitted the Hasidic groupings to implant themselves. Based on field research and secondary sources; 87 notes. A. E. LeBlanc

246. Hadda, Janet. DI HASHPAOH FUN AMERICA OIF DER YIDDISHER LITERATUR [The influence of America on Yiddish literature]. *Yivo Bleter 1973 44: 248-255.* In analyzing the influence of America upon the Yiddish writers the author discusses the role of the writer's experiences, his place of residence, and the varied literary influences. The journal *Shriften*, published in New York City during 1912-26, was a bridge between the literature of the new arrivals and those who already went to college in this country. In their writings Yiddish writers reflected their experiences in America. Based on primary sources. B. Klein

247. Halevy, Zvi. WERE THE JEWISH IMMIGRANTS TO THE UNITED STATES REPRESENTATIVE OF RUSSIAN JEWS? *Int. Migration [Netherlands] 1978 16(2): 60-73.* Considers whether the Jews who immigrated to the United States at the beginning of the 20th century were representative of the Jewish population in Russia. Despite their great social mobility and attainments, the Jewish immigrants were far from being representative, because for the most part they belonged to socially inferior classes. The middle classes were barely represented.   S/J

248. Hall, Linda. NEIMAN-MARCUS: THE BEGINNING. *Western States Jewish Hist. Q. 1975 7(2): 138-150.* On 10 September 1907 in Dallas, Texas, Herbert Marcus and Al and Carrie Neiman opened their first store, which specialized in fine clothes for women. They had operated a store in Atlanta for two years, but sold it to open their new store in Dallas. They developed new methods of merchandising ready-to-wear clothing. In 1913, the store was destroyed by a fire, after which it moved to larger quarters and continued to grow. The Neiman-Marcus Co. contributed greatly to the development of Dallas as the major fashion market in the Southwest. 36 notes.   R. A. Garfinkle

249. Halpern, Ben. THE "QUOTA" ISSUE. *Midstream 1973 19(3): 3-12.* Criticizes the use of quotas to end discrimination.   S

250. Halpern, Ben. THE ROOTS OF AMERICAN JEWISH LIBERALISM. *Am. Jewish Hist. Q. 1976 65(2): 190-214.* Examines the European and American antecedents that made a devout and conventional liberalism the most respectable Jewish position in the United States during the 20th century. Unites two disparate strands in the history of Jewish political attitudes: 1) the truly traditional policy of reliance on the constituted authorities (in America, constitutionally liberal) and 2) the more recent 19th-century Western European traditions of strongly stressed national patriotism. Since the Holocaust and the founding of Israel, the fact of ultimate Jewish isolation and therefore solidarity has modified the traditional Liberalism. 26 notes.   F. Rosenthal

251. Halpern, Sheldon. JEWISH FOLKLORE: A NEW IMAGE. *J. of Popular Culture 1974 8(2): 338-341.* Review article prompted by *The Folklore of the Jews,* originally published in 1937, by Angelo S. Rappoport (Detroit: Singing Tree Pr., 1972) and *In Praise of the Baal Shem Tov,* translated and edited by Dan Ben-Amos and Jerome R. Mintz (Indiana U. Pr., 1970). Places both books within the historical context of their publication dates. Discusses the books' importance to an understanding of Jewish folklore and its relevance for modern Westernized Jews in the United States and elsewhere.   A. E. Wiederrecht

252. Hamlin, David M. SWASTIKAS AND SURVIVORS: INSIDE THE SKOKIE-NAZI FREE SPEECH CASE. *Civil Liberties Rev. 1978 4(6): 8-33.* Denial of the right to peaceably assemble, enforced by the village of Skokie, Illinois, in 1977 against an attempted assembly of the National Socialist Party of America, brought the American Civil Liberties Union into the fight to guarantee freedom of speech and freedom of assembly to the Nazi group in that primarily Jewish Chicago suburb.

253. Handlin, Oscar. A TWENTY YEAR RETROSPECT OF AMERICAN JEWISH HISTORIOGRAPHY. *Am. Jewish Hist. Q. 1976 65(4): 295-309.* Compares his 1948 evaluation of writing of the American Jewish past with the progress made since then. Greater abundance of material and its availability coupled with professionalization of authors and the elimination of an apologetic approach has contributed to greater scholarship. Setting the Jewish experience in America in a comparative, often sociological relationship to the contemporary trends in other immigrant religions and community organizations leads to a better understanding of the story, even though the extent of leakage through intermarriage, conversion, and apathy has not yet been assessed. The history of American anti-Semitism, 1900-40, also still remains to be written. Delivered at the 73rd annual meeting of the American Jewish Historical Society, 4 May 1975. 43 notes.

F. Rosenthal

254. Harap, Louis. IRVING HOWE AND JEWISH AMERICA. *J. of Ethnic Studies 1977 4(4): 95-104.* Review article prompted by Irving Howe's *World of Our Fathers* (New York: Harcourt Brace Jovanovich, 1976). The book was written so that the receding culture of Yiddish America would be adequately chronicled for future generations in a single, readable work. A central theme is the role of the socialist and labor movements on New York City's East Side. An avowed "democratic socialist," Howe's chief criticisms of contemporary society are against those he regards as a false left, rather than the right. His "abstract, perfectionist approach to socialism" occasionally brings him to tactics of omission and emphasis which he would condemn in totalitarians. Howe's qualifications for writing this work, his treatment of Yiddish scholarship, theater, literature, the European *shtetl*, and the social and mutual benefit organizations of the *landsmanshaften* are compelling and readable. The book is a comprehensive account of the origin and life-course of the massive Jewish immigration. 13 notes.

G. J. Bobango

255. Harris, Ira L. A LOS ANGELES POPULAR MUSIC DIRECTOR. *Western States Jewish Hist. Q. 1977 10(1): 62-67.* Abraham Frankum Frankenstein (1873-1934) began his musical career in Chicago, came to Los Angeles in 1897 with the Grau Opera Company, and remained to form the first permanent theater orchestra. During the 1920's Frankenstein conducted the Orpheum Theater orchestra for such stars as Jack Benny, Fanny Brice, George Jessel, the Marx Brothers, and Sophie Tucker. He organized the bands of the Los Angeles Police and Fire Departments. He served on the Los Angeles Fire Commission for most of the 1913-27 period. In collaboration with F. B. Silverwood he wrote the song, "I Love You California," in 1913; it became the official state song in 1951. Based on personal knowledge and published sources; photo, 18 notes.

B. S. Porter

256. Harris, Victor. THE BEGINNING OF LOS ANGELES' FIRST JEWISH HOSPITAL. *Western States Jewish Hist. Q. 1976 8(2): 136-138.* A Jewish hospital to treat people with tuberculosis was first proposed by Jacob Schlesinger, president of the Hebrew Benevolent Society. On 21 September 1902, the Kaspare Chon Hospital was dedicated at 1443 Carroll Avenue, Los Angeles. The house used as the hospital was donated to the society by Kaspare Chon. A memorial fund drive was started to supply the hospital with necessary equipment and supplies. In 1930 the name of the hospital was changed to Cedars of Lebanon

Hospital. Reprints an article first published in *B'nai B'rith Messenger*, Los Angeles, 23 July 1909. R. A. Garfinkle

257. Harris, Victor. HONOLULU JEWRY IN 1919. *Western States Jewish Hist. Q. 1979 11(3): 279-282.* Honolulu's Jewish community in 1919 consisted of about 13 Jewish families and an equal number of mixed marriages. There was no congregation. The old Jewish cemetery had been abandoned. The active Jews on the island were the 100 or so Jews in the US Army. These men were interested in having a Jewish center where they could meet and offer mutual encouragement in this foreign place. Reprinted from *Emanu-El,* San Francisco, 25 July 1919; 4 notes. B. S. Porter

258. Hasson, Aron. THE SEPHARDIC JEWS OF RHODES IN LOS ANGELES. *Western States Jewish Hist. Q. 1974 6(4): 241-254.* During 1910-30, many Jews from Rhodes came to settle in Los Angeles. Rhodesli families have remained together and continue their unique Sephardic customs and life styles. In 1917 they formed their own congregation, the Peace and Progress Society, later changed to the Sephardic Hebrew Center. The immigrants spoke Ladino, and their language barrier forced them to take lower-paying jobs. Several immigrants went into the flower business, which became the most successful occupation of the Rhodeslis. Based on interviews and secondary sources; 4 photos, 21 notes. R. A. Garfinkle

259. Hattem, Maurice I. I. M. HATTEM AND HIS LOS ANGELES SUPERMARKET. *Western States Jewish Hist. Q. 1979 11(3): 243-251.* Hattem's Day and Night Drive-In Market, established in 1927, was the first of its kind in Los Angeles. Its owner, Isadore M. Hattem (1894-1966), was a cosmopolitan merchant, born in Constantinople, Turkey, and a world traveler by the time he was 20. He came to Los Angeles in 1913, found a job at a fruit stand, and expanded the business. His flair for showmanship was apparent in the Spanish mission style of his famous Drive-In Market. Hattem's career in the grocery business encompassed both the wholesale and retail outlets until his retirement in 1949. 4 photos. B. S. Porter

260. Hayes, Saul. CANADIAN JEWISH CULTURE: SOME OBSERVATIONS. *Queen's Q. [Canada] 1977 84(1): 80-88.* Canadian Jews have been affected by the broader culture and are heterogeneous, but their "all important propulsion is an *élan vital* of folk, group, [and] people." J. A. Casada

261. Helmreich, William B. JEWISH MARGINALITY AND THE STRUGGLE FOR EQUALITY: SOME HISTORICAL CAUSES AND CONSEQUENCES. *J. of Intergroup Relations 1976 5(3): 37-40.* Jews, always prominent in social causes, should approach their participation in human rights movements with greater respect for themselves as Jews if they are to retain the respect of others.

262. Henig, Gerald S. CALIFORNIA JEWRY AND THE MENDEL BEILISS AFFAIR, 1911-1913. *Western States Jewish Hist. Q. 1979 11(3): 220-230.* Mendel Beiliss was a Jewish laborer in a Russian brick factory, charged with murdering a Christian boy for religious purposes. The nature of the charges, with their anti-Semitic overtones, aroused worldwide protest. California Jews, and especially the Jewish newspapers, recognized that the prosecution of Beiliss was

an attempt to justify pogroms. Public rallies attended by Jews and Christians in San Francisco and Oakland condemned the Russian government's action. Beiliss was acquitted, but the jury ruled that the boy was murdered as a ritual victim, and the Jews, as a group, were blamed for his death. Secondary sources; 55 notes.

B. S. Porter

263. Henig, Gerald S. "HE DID NOT HAVE A FAIR TRIAL": CALIFORNIA PROGRESSIVES REACT TO THE LEO FRANK CASE. *California History 1979 58(2): 166-178.* Analyzes the reaction of California progressives to the Leo Frank case, 1913-15. Frank, a Jew, was convicted of the murder of a 13-year-old factory girl in Georgia in 1913. Evident violations of due process of law provoked criticism of the verdict, especially in California where progressives actively protested. Progressive newspapers and spokesmen commented on aspects of social injustice involved in the affair. On the other hand, except for California Jewish leaders, few progressives discussed the problems of capital punishment and anti-Semitism evoked by the trial. When the death sentence was commuted to life imprisonment in 1915, Californians praised the courage of Georgia's governor. Soon after, however, Frank was lynched by a mob. Progressives and conservatives alike united in condemning that act. Califiornia stood as a leader in the fight for justice for Frank, though its leadership failed to confront the deeper issues brought forth by the Frank case. Photo, 91 notes. A. Hoffman

264. Henry, Henry Abraham. A SAN FRANCISCO RABBI REPORTS ON A VISIT TO SACRAMENTO IN 1858. *Western States Jewish Hist. Q. 1978 11(1): 60-63.* A letter from Rabbi Henry Abraham Henry to Rabbi Samuel Meyer Issacs on 17 August 1858 described Rabbi Henry's recent visit to Sacramento, California. Rabbi Henry was invited to preach in the synagogue, and participated in the ceremonial placement of a monument on the grave of Mr. Julius S. Winehill. The president and trustees of the synagogue offered a gratuity for Rabbi Henry's services. Reprinted from the *Jewish Messenger,* New York, 24 September 1858. 2 notes. B. S. Porter

265. Henry, Marcus H. HENRY ABRAHAM HENRY: SAN FRANCISCO RABBI, 1857-1869. *Western States Jewish Hist. Q. 1977 10(1): 31-37.* Henry Abraham Henry (1806-79) came to the United States from England in 1849. He served congregations in Ohio and New York before coming to San Francisco in 1857. He was minister of San Francisco's Sherith Israel (Polish) synagogue, from 1857-69. A popular lecturer, he officiated at the consecration of many synagogues and the dedications of secular institutions. Rabbi Henry contributed many articles to American Jewish journals. He published his two-part *Synopsis of Jewish History* in 1859. In 1860 he started and edited the weekly *Pacific Messenger.* In 1864 he issued his volume of *Discourses on the Book of Genesis.* His religious views were conservative. He upheld the dignity of his profession to the admiration of both Jews and Christians. Photo. B. S. Porter

266. Hentoff, Nat. THE ACLU'S TRIAL BY SWASTIKA. *Social Policy 1978 8(4): 50-52.* The American Civil Liberties Union's defense of the right of Chicago-based Nazis to demonstrate in a mainly Jewish suburb, Skokie, stirred up controversy among ACLU members and supporters, 1977-78.

267. Hentoff, Nat. NEIGHBORHOODS: A SHTETL IN THE NEW WORLD. *Social Policy 1979 10(2): 58-60.* The author recalls his childhood in the close-knit Jewish ghetto of Roxbury, a part of Boston, in the 1930's.

268. Herscher, Uri D. HERMAN ROSENTHAL, *THE JEWISH FARMER. Michael: On the Hist. of the Jews in the Diaspora [Israel] 1975 3: 59-87.* Herman Rosenthal (1843-1917) came to the United States in 1881 from the Ukraine, as the agent of a group he had founded to transplant Russian Jews to other lands in socialist agricultural colonies. His efforts in southern New Jersey, Alliance (founded in 1882) and Woodbine (1891), were especially successful, largely due to their combination of agriculture and industry. Article reproduces seven excerpts, in Yiddish and English translation, from the Yiddish periodical Rosenthal edited in 1891-92, *Der Yudisher Farmer: Monatliche Isaytshrift fir Landvirtshaftliche Kolonizatsyan,* reporting on the colonies' progress. Biblio.

T. Sassoon

269. Herscher, Uri D. THE METROPOLIS OF GHETTOS. *J. of Ethnic Studies 1976 4(2): 33-47.* Portrays the "classic" and stereotypical days of the Jewish ghetto from 1890 to 1920, with its sights, smells, tenements, habitual impoverishment and insecurity, and the all-consuming task of earning a living. Despite the hardship and ugliness of life, the ghetto was a world, complete and self-sustaining, with drama, humor, and romance as well. Fever for secular schooling was high, along with an innate distrust for the public, non-Jewish charities and their agencies. Intellectual life thrived in the cafes of Canal Street, prostitutes in Allen Street, and Jewish theaters in the Bowery. The Judaism of Europe grew progressively weaker, but still coexisted with the culture of the new land. World War I saw the garment manufacturers move to 14th Street, and non-Jews begin to move into the Lower East Side; they were willing to pay the higher rents traditionally levied on non-Jews. With these changes, the good old days of the ghetto were numbered. Based largely on personal conversations by the author in 1972 with individuals of immigrant stock who grew up on New York's Lower East Side; 25 notes.

G. J. Bobango

270. Hershkowitz, Leo. SOME ASPECTS OF THE NEW YORK JEWISH MERCHANT AND COMMUNITY, 1654-1820. *Am. Jewish Hist. Q. 1976 66(1): 10-34.* The 160-year period under discussion saw New York City grow from a village to a community of 100,000 people, and its Jewish segment from 23 to some 2,000 people. Diversity of origin and of occupation, although trade remained preeminent, were characteristic traits of the Jewish community for the entire period. The right to trade, the acquisition of citizenship, the right to worship publicly, the right to vote and to be elected, resulted in court actions producing a wealth of statistical and legal data which are provided to illustrate these points. 68 notes, 3 appendixes.

F. Rosenthal

271. Hertz, Edwin. IDEOLOGICAL LIBERALS IN REFORM POLITICS: A NOTE ON THE BACKGROUND AND MOVEMENT OF POLITICAL OUTSIDERS INTO MAJOR PARTY POLITICS. *Int. J. of Contemporary Sociol. 1974 11(1): 1-11.* Discusses the political participation of working class Jews, Negroes, and Puerto Rican Americans as pressure groups in social reform and civil rights issues in New York City, 1963-70's.

272. Hertzberg, Arthur. THE AMERICAN JEWISH INTELLIGENTSIA. *Midstream 1977 23(2): 45-47.* Considers the scope of characteristics of Jewish intellectuals and academics as a social class, 1945-70's.

273. Hertzberg, Arthur. GROWING UP JEWISH IN AMERICA. *Midstream 1979 25(2): 51-54.* Arthur Hertzberg, author of *Being Jewish in America,* discusses the evolution of his ideas concerning Judaism since the 1940's.

274. Hertzberg, Steven. THE JEWISH COMMUNITY OF ATLANTA FROM THE END OF THE CIVIL WAR UNTIL THE END OF THE FRANK CASE. *Am. Jewish Hist. Q. 1973 62(3): 250-287.* Atlanta's Jewish community was by 1913 the largest in a South transformed by urbanization, industrialization, and Negro emancipation. There were more than 1,200 Jewish immigrants from Eastern Europe by 1910. Under the leadership of Rabbi David Marx (1872-1962) the established German Jews were led into classical Reform, while the East European and Levantine settlers maintained various forms of traditional Judaism. Thus two separate communities were created. Only in philanthropic activities did the two cooperate. In Atlanta and throughout the United States during this period, discrimination against even the established community of Western European Jews was increasing, setting the stage for the Leo M. Frank tragedy of 1913. 84 notes.　　　　　　　　　　　　　　　F. Rosenthal

275. Hertzberg, Steven. MAKING IT IN ATLANTA: ECONOMIC MOBILITY IN A SOUTHERN JEWISH COMMUNITY, 1870-1911. *Ann. of Jewish Social Sci. 1978 17: 185-216.* Studies the mobility of Atlanta's Jewish population during 1870-1911. The Jews more than any other group viewed America as the Promised Land. Therefore, a study of their mobility within a major southern city is of special significance.　　　　　　　　　R. J. Wechman

276. Hertzberg, Steven. UNSETTLED JEWS: GEOGRAPHIC MOBILITY IN A NINETEENTH CENTURY CITY. *Am. Jewish Hist. Q. 1977 67(2): 125-139.* Analyzes Jewish mobility in Atlanta, Georgia, between 1870 and 1896. Using institutional records, census schedules, city directories, and tax lists, seven tabulations are presented. Variables such as economic and marital status, and urban or rural background, are considered. It appears that Jews remained in Atlanta to a high degree (88% of Jewish immigrants v. 79% of gentile immigrants, or 71% vs. 50% as to upward social improvement) because of economic success, urban background, and advantages of living in an established center of Jewish activities. 7 tables, 16 notes.　　　　　　　　　　　F. Rosenthal

277. Hexter, Maurice B. HISTORICAL REMINISCENCE. *Am. Jewish Hist. 1978 68(2): 122-130.* The author (b. 1871) entered Jewish communal work with the United Jewish Charities in Cincinnati, Ohio, in 1912. His reminiscences of the days before social work went academic and psychological deal with the real problems of illness, desertion, adjustments of immigrants, Hebrew free loans, etc. Then as now the relationship between the social service organizations and the synagogues might be categorized as "mutual distrust tinged with apprehension."　　　　　　　　　　　　　　　　　　F. Rosenthal

278. Hicks, James L. and Vorspan, Albert. KIVIE KAPLAN: "AN INCREDIBLE MAN"—KIVIE KAPLAN: A BRIDGE BETWEEN BLACKS AND JEWS—HIS SMILE AND DEEDS WILL NEVER DIE. *Crisis 1975*

82(7): 231-233. Kivie Kaplan devoted his life to eliminating man's inhumanity to man. He was chairman of the committee for Life Membership of the NAACP. Even with a pacemaker he preached brotherhood all over the country and handed out cards that asked people to "Keep Smiling." He symbolized the cooperation between Jews and Negroes. He preferred to burn out rather than rust out, and died 5 May 1975 en route from one meeting to another.   A. G. Belles

279.   Himmelfarb, Harold S.   THE INTERACTION EFFECTS OF PARENTS, SPOUSE AND SCHOOLING: COMPARING THE IMPACT OF JEWISH AND CATHOLIC SCHOOLS.   *Sociol. Q. 1977 18(4): 468-477.* Discusses the literature on the long-range impact of schooling and the types of effects that schools have shown. It compares data on the impact of Jewish schooling on adult religiosity with similar data from a study of Catholic schooling. Like previous studies on other types of schools, the main effect of Jewish schooling seems to be an accentuation of parental influences. This effect is diminished substantially if not supported by marriage to a religious spouse. However, on some types of religiosity, extensive Jewish schooling produces "conversion" effects which persisted even when pre-school and post-school supports were lacking.   J

280.   Himmelfarb, Milton.   ON LEO STRAUSS.   *Commentary 1974 58(2): 60-67.*

281.   Hindus, Milton.   EDWARD SMITH KING AND THE OLD EAST SIDE.   *Am. Jewish Hist. Q. 1975 64(4): 321-330.* American-born Edward Smith King (1848-96), author of the novel *Joseph Zalmonah*, and Scottish-born Edward Smith King (1846-1922), organizer of the Central Labor Union in New York in 1883, are often confused by later writers. This essay deals with the novelist and the background for his above-mentioned novel.   F. Rosenthal

282.   Hoffmann, Banesh.   ALBERT EINSTEIN.   *Leo Baeck Inst. Year Book [Great Britain] 1976 20: 279-288.* Reinterprets Albert Einstein's (1879-1955) life with emphasis on his religious and artistic sides. His writings and his major scientific achievements show the lucidity of his mind and his genius to see even the most complicated matters simply and artistically. The last 30 years of his life were devoted to furthering peace and strengthening human freedom. Einstein, the nonreligious Jew, shared the full burden of his Jewishness since he felt responsible for his people and their fate. 22 notes.   F. Rosenthal

283.   Holmes, William F.   WHITECAPPING: ANTI-SEMITISM IN THE POPULIST ERA.   *Am. Jewish Hist. Q. 1974 63(3): 244-261.* Whitecapping, a dirt farmer movement that became widespread in southwestern Mississippi during the early 1890's, espoused an anti-Semitic and anti-Negro ideology. It succeeded in driving black laborers off lands owned by merchants—mostly Jewish —and lumber companies, until forceful and courageous action by some local judges restored respect for law. In the counties wracked by whitecapping the Populist movement gained considerable support, but the two cannot be equated, even though some men may have belonged to both organizations. The two movements sprang from some of the same causes, however, and this study contributes an additional dimension to our knowledge of agrarian protest. 60 notes.
        F. Rosenthal

284. Hook, Sidney. ANTI-SEMITISM IN THE ACADEMY: SOME PAGES OF THE PAST. *Midstream 1979 25(1): 49-54.* Personal account chronicling the growth of Jewish faculty members, including Lionel Trilling, and the anti-Semitism they encountered at Columbia University, New York City, 1920's-70's.

285. Hook, Sidney. MORRIS COHEN: FIFTY YEARS LATER. *Am. Scholar 1976 45(3): 426-436.* Discusses Morris R. Cohen of the College of the City of New York, as a philosophy teacher. He early resorted to the Socratic method with devastating and sometimes cruel effects, which he termed a "logical disinfectant." Although he might appear negative, his great wisdom overshadowed his often personal pettiness. His wisdom combined a basic liberalism with his philosophic pluralism and doctrine of polarity which made him a "dominant figure in the cultural life of New York City." R. V. Ritter

286. Horn, Michiel. KEEPING CANADA "CANADIAN": ANTI-COMMUNISM AND CANADIANISM IN TORONTO, 1928-29. *Canada 1975 3(1): 34-47.* Discusses the role of immigration and national self-image in anti-Communist movements and anti-Semitism in Toronto, Ontario, in 1928-29, emphasizing freedom of speech issues.

287. Hornbein, Marjorie. DR. CHARLES SPIVAK OF DENVER: PHYSICIAN, SOCIAL WORKER, YIDDISH AUTHOR. *Western States Jewish Hist. Q. 1979 11(3): 195-211.* Dr. Charles Spivak (1861-1927) was a founder of Denver, Colorado's, Jewish Consumptives' relief society sanatorium (J.C.R.S.) in 1904. The J.C.R.S., in contrast with the National Jewish Hospital, accepted patients in the advanced stages of tuberculosis. Rivalry between the hospitals was part of the schism in the city's Jewish community. A specialist in gastrointestinal diseases, Dr. Spivak taught at the Medical School of the University of Denver, and also found time to write essays on medicine and Judaism. His best known literary work was a Yiddish dictionary, published in 1911. In 1920 Dr. Spivak was part of a team of medical experts, sponsored by the US Army, sent to Europe to study and report on sanitary and medical conditions in Poland. Dr. Spivak was not actively religious until late in life, but his fortitude and serenity helped him accept his fate as a victim of cancer. One of his final requests was that his body be given to a medical school. Primary and secondary sources; 2 photos, 59 notes. B. S. Porter

288. Horvitz, Eleanor F. THE JEWISH WOMAN LIBERATED: A HISTORY OF THE LADIES' HEBREW FREE LOAN ASSOCIATION. *Rhode Island Jewish Hist. Notes 1978 7(4): 501-512.* The Ladies' Hebrew Free Loan Association (LHFLA), which was established in 1931 to provide a loan fund for Jewish women in Providence, Rhode Island, to match the Hebrew Free Loan Association established in 1903 for male Jews, enabled Jewish women to maintain some element of independence; the LHFLA, no longer needed, disbanded in 1965.

289. Horvitz, Eleanor F. JEWS AND THE BOY SCOUT MOVEMENT IN RHODE ISLAND. *Rhode Island Jewish Hist. Notes 1977 7(3): 341-384.* Chronicles the participation of Rhode Island Jewish boys in the Boy Scouts of America, 1910-76.

290. Horvitz, Eleanor F. OLD BOTTLES, RAGS, JUNK! THE STORY OF THE JEWS IN SOUTH PROVIDENCE. *Rhode Island Jewish Hist. Notes 1976 7(2): 189-257.* Discusses the settlement of southern Providence by large numbers of Jews, 1900-12; includes attention to famous local personalities, religion, and daily life.

291. Horvitz, Eleanor F. THE OUTLET COMPANY STORY AND THE SAMUELS BROTHERS. *Rhode Island Jewish Hist. Notes 1974 6(4): 489-531.* Chronicles the establishment of the Outlet Company Store in Providence, Rhode Island.   S

292. Horvitz, Eleanor F. THE YEARS OF THE JEWISH WOMAN. *Rhode Island Jewish Hist. Notes 1975 7(1): 152-170.* Discusses the various benevolent organizations in Rhode Island established by Jewish women, ca. 1877-1975.

293. Howe, Irving. THE IMMIGRANT GLORY. *Midstream 1976 22(1): 16-26.* Studies the intellectual and cultural ferment of immigrant Jews in the US in the late 19th and early 20th centuries.

294. Howe, Irving. JEWISH IMMIGRANT ARTISTS. *Am. Scholar 1976 45(2): 241-252.* Since 1900 Jewish artists and sculptors have worked with devotion and success. With Jews who have become great artists, the qualities of individualism and universalism have predominated. Their art has lost its Jewishness and can be described under the inclusive category of modernism.
F. F. Harling

295. Hudson, Michael C. POLITIQUE INTÉRIEURE ET POLITIQUE EXTÉRIEURE AMÉRICAINE DANS SES RAPPORTS AVEC LE CONFLIT ISRAÉLO-ARABE [American foreign and domestic policy as affected by the Israeli-Arab conflict]. *Pol. Étrangère [France] 1974 39(6): 641-658.* As a result of the Israeli-Arab conflict of the 1970's, various pressure groups act on the Congress and American public opinion, thereby limiting the kind of foreign policy initiatives a president is able to take.

296. Hurvitz, Nathan. BLACKS AND JEWS IN AMERICAN FOLKLORE. *Western Folklore 1974 33(4): 301-325.* Examines "white Christian American" folklore about Negroes and Jews. Recounts jokes, stories, and folksayings to bear out the thesis that the two minority groups are frequently coupled together in folklore and "are deprecated and rejected individually and jointly by members of the dominant Christian society."
S. L. Myres

297. Ibrahim, Saad. AMERICAN DOMESTIC FACTORS AND THE OCTOBER WAR. *J. of Palestine Studies [Lebanon] 1974 4(1): 55-81.* Examines the impact of economic conditions, traditional loyalties, the mass media, the oil embargo, and pro-Zionist lobbies on the formation of US public opinion toward Arab-Israeli relations and the Six-Day War and the October War, 1967 and 1973.

298. Inge, M. Thomas. THE ETHNIC EXPERIENCE AND AESTHETICS IN LITERATURE: MALAMUD'S *THE ASSISTANT* AND ROTH'S *CALL IT SLEEP.* *J. of Ethnic Studies 1974 1(4): 45-50.* Taking Bernard Malamud's *The Assistant* and Henry Roth's *Call it Sleep* as examples, argues for a greater place for "ethnic literature" in college curricula. There is a need to re-evaluate

the traditional standards by which literature is judged, and as much can be gained from Roth's particularistic treatment of minority experience as can from Malamud's "very studied imitation of the majority-oriented classic American novel." 10 notes.   T. W. Smith

299. Isaacs, Stephen D. SO WHO HAS THE POWER?: HOW HARD DARE YOU PUSH IN FOREIGN POLICY? *Present Tense 1974 1(4): 24-28.* Jewish influence in United States politics and foreign policy.   S

300. Jacobson, Daniel. LANSING'S JEWISH COMMUNITY: THE BEGINNINGS. *Michigan Jewish Hist. 1976 16(1): 5-17.* Traces the settlement of Jews from Henry Lederer in 1850 to the establishment of a formal community numbering 450 in 1918.

301. Jacoby, Susan. WORLD OF OUR MOTHERS: IMMIGRANT WOMEN, IMMIGRANT DAUGHTERS. *Present Tense 1979 6(3): 48-51.* Discusses the lack of literature on the accomplishments of women immigrants to the United States since the late 19th century, here examining Jewish women immigrants in particular, concluding that second generation immigrant daughters growing up with new attitudes, will be more successful in transcending women's traditional sex roles.

302. Jaffe, Grace. FROM SAN JOSE TO HOLLYWOOD: THE RISE OF JESSE L. LASKY. *Western States Jewish Hist. Q. 1978 11(1): 20-24.* Jesse L. Lasky, vice-president of Paramount-Publix Corporation, started his career as a cornet player in San Francisco. He left the music business temporarily for newspaper reporting and gold mining in Alaska. On his return to San Francisco he performed in vaudeville. Later he formed a partnership with B. A. Rolfe to manage as many as 20 traveling vaudeville acts. Lasky met Cecil B. deMille and wrote several operettas with him, with great financial success. In 1912 Lasky opened a motion picture studio in Hollywood, a pioneer venture that eventually became Paramount enterprises. Reprinted from *Emanu-El,* San Francisco, 3 October 1930. 3 notes.   B. S. Porter

303. James, Janet Wilson. WOMEN AND RELIGION: AN INTRODUCTION. *Am. Q. 1978 30(5): 579-581.* The series of essays in this issue explores various facets and expressions of the place of women in religion as seen in Protestantism, Catholicism, and Judaism. The whole is set against two constants: women usually outnumber men and men exercise the authority. The paradox revealed is one of a religious heritage imparting hopes of freedom, but at the same time blocking women's way.   R. V. Ritter

304. Jeser, Beth. THE JEWS. *Hist. J. of Western Massachusetts 1976 (Supplement): 61-66.* Jews participated in the American Revolution as soldiers and as politicians. Many Jews fought in the war with the militia and the Continental Army. Haym Solomon played a major role in financing the war effort. Notes.
                                                                          W. H. Mulligan, Jr.

305. Jordan, Vernon E., Jr. TOGETHER! *Crisis 1974 81(8): 281-284.* Discusses the relations between Jews and Negroes during the 1960's-70's.   S

306. Joselit, Jenna Weissman. WITHOUT GHETTOISM: A HISTORY OF THE INTERCOLLEGIATE MENORAH ASSOCIATION, 1906-1930. *Am. Jewish Arch. 1978 30(2): 133-154.* The Intercollegiate Menorah Association was the first national organization which catered to the diversified needs of Jewish students at American colleges and universities. The author charts the rise, decline, and dissolution of this legendary institution which greatly influenced a whole generation of Jewish students in America with the genius of its aims and ideals.   J

307. Kabakov, Yaakov. MIKHTAVIM MI-YISRAEL ZINBERG LE-YIS-RAEL DAVIDZON [Letters from Israel Zinberg to Israel Davidson]. *Shvut [Israel] 1975 3: 128-130.* Reproduces four letters, 1925-37, from Israel Zinberg to Israel Davidson (1870-1939) concerning the American publication of the latter's *History of Jewish Literature.* Discusses five of the 12 volumes, published in English, 1972-74. Based on the Davidson Archive, Jewish Theological Seminary, New York; 23 notes.   T. Sassoon

308. Kabakov, Yaakov. TE'UDOT MITOKH "OSEF DEINARD" [Documents from the Deinard Collection]. *Michael: On the Hist. of the Jews in the Diaspora [Israel] 1975 3: 15-40.* Ephraim Deinard (1846-1930) immigrated from Eastern Europe to the United States in 1888, despite his conviction that Jews should immigrate to Palestine rather than America. He authored some 50 works, including bibliographies, and edited several newspapers, including the short-lived Hebrew weekly *Haleumi* (1889). Later he collaborated in Ze'ev Shur's weekly, *Hapisgah.* Active in the Hibbat Zion movement, he dreamt of establishing a center of Hebrew literature and culture in America, which would strengthen American Jewry's ties with Palestine. Important American libraries acquired Hebrew books which Deinard collected on his European and Middle Eastern travels. Presents five documents from his extensive archive, including a letter to Moshe Leib Lillienblum. Primary and secondary sources; 73 notes.
                                                                                      T. Sassoon

309. Kaganoff, Nathan M. THE BUSINESS CAREER OF HAYM SALOMON AS REFLECTED IN HIS NEWSPAPER ADVERTISEMENTS. *Am. Jewish Hist. Q. 1976 66(1): 35-49.* Haym Salomon's career and importance as a businessman, apart from his role in financing the American Revolution, can be measured by the large number of advertisements he placed in the newspapers during 1777-85. Some 1,085 ads appearing in 14 papers (seven each in Philadelphia and New York) have been located which would indicate that Solomon was one of the first businessmen to exploit this potential fully (e.g., his use of French and German, or the meticulous enumeration of merchandise). 31 notes, 24 examples of ads, appendix.   F. Rosenthal

310. Kaganoff, Nathan M. and Katz-Hyman, Martha B. JUDAICA AMERICANA. *Am. Jewish Hist. 1979 68(4): 534-551.* An annotated Bibliography of monographic and periodical literature published since 1960 and received in the Library of the American Jewish Historical Society. Covers general works and special studies.   S

311. Kaganoff, Nathan M. JUDAICA AMERICANA. *Am. Jewish Hist. Q. 1976 65(4): 353-367.* An annotated bibliography of monographical and periodical literature published since 1960 and received in the Library of the American Jewish Historical Society. The current section contains works published in 1974 and 1975.   F. Rosenthal

312. Kaganoff, Nathan M. and Katz-Hyman, Martha B. JUDAICA AMERICANA. *Am. Jewish Hist. Q. 1977 66(4): 513-537.* An annotated bibliography of monographic and periodical literature published since 1960 and received in the library of the American Jewish Historical Society.
                                                                    F. Rosenthal

313. Kaganoff, Nathan M. and Endelman, Judith E. JUDAICA AMERICANA. *Am. Jewish Hist Q. 1973 62(4): 401-413.* An annotated bibliography of monographic and periodical literature published since 1960 and received in the library of the American Jewish Historical Society.
                                                                    F. Rosenthal

314. Kaganoff, Nathan M. and Katz-Hyman, Martha B. JUDAICA AMERICANA. *Am. Jewish Hist. 1978 68(2): 213-230.* Annotated bibliography of new monographic and periodical literature published since 1960 as received in the Library of the American Jewish Historical Society.
                                                                    F. Rosenthal

315. Kaganoff, Nathan M. and Katz-Hyman, Martha B. JUDAICA AMERICANA. *Am. Jewish Hist. Q. 1978 67(4): 363-377.* An annotated bibliography of monographic and periodical literature published since 1960 and received in the library of the American Jewish Historical Society.
                                                                    F. Rosenthal

316. Kahane, Libby. MORDECAI MANUEL NOAH IN HEBREW PERIODICAL LITERATURE AND IN ISRAEL. *Am. Jewish Hist. Q. 1978 67(3): 260-265.* Tabulates 11 articles and six Mordecai Manuel Noah (1785-1851) manuscripts found in Israel. This listing is a supplement to the 1937 bibliographic essay by Jacob Kabakoff.   F. Rosenthal

317. Kallison, Frances Rosenthal. WAS IT A DUEL OR A MURDER: A STUDY IN TEXAS ASSIMILATION. *Am. Jewish Hist. Q. 1973 62(3): 314-320.* In 1857, the merchant Siegmund Feinberg died after a quarrel with Benedict Schwartz, a Jewish immigrant from Russia. Whether he was murdered by Schwartz or was shot accidentally has never been established. A Hebrew poem on his tombstone implies that he was murdered. Schwartz was killed in his pawnshop in 1882. The incident indicates the rapidity with which immigrant Jews assimilated to the surrounding society. 20 notes.   F. Rosenthal

318. Kalter, Bella Briansky. A JEWISH COMMUNITY THAT WAS: ANSONVILLE, ONTARIO, CANADA. *Am. Jewish Arch. 1978 30(2): 107-125.* "Oh, it was lovely, lonely, lighted with snow in the wintertime. . . ." So begins the author's poignant memoir of Jewish life in the harsh climate of Canada's northern Ontario province. There are glimpses in her recollection of an existence which many North American Jews have forgotten or never experienced: a sense of community, traditional in nature, which put its emphasis upon sharing and

caring; a life of hardship modified by the celebration of simple joys; a sense of continuity, uninterrupted by the geographic rootlessness of our time.   J

319.   Kaplan, Lawrence J.   THE DILEMMA OF CONSERVATIVE JUDA-ISM.   *Commentary 1976 62(5): 44-47.* During the 20 years after World War II Conservative Judaism became the most popular religious movement among American Jews. There has been a crisis in Conservative Judaism in recent years, giving rise to a split between the right and left wings of the movement. The former tend toward Orthodoxy; the latter approach the Reform movement. The left wing argues for religious change through legislation rather than interpretation; the right wing contends that limits on change and liberalization must be maintained. The conflict reflects the most basic issue facing the modern Jewish community: how can Judaism exist in the modern world, while maintaining its distinct identity? Primary and secondary sources.   S. R. Herstein

320.   Kaplan, Marilyn.   THE JEWISH MERCHANTS OF NEWPORT, 1740-1790.   *Rhode Island Jewish Hist. Notes 1975 7(1): 12-32.*

321.   Kaplan, Michael.   THE JOKER IN THE REPUBLICAN DECK: THE POLITICAL CAREER OF OTTO MEARS 1881-1889.   *Western States Jewish Hist. Q. 1975 7(4): 287-302.* Otto Mears was very influential in Colorado politics in the late 19th century. By 1876 he was an important Republican Party boss. He was elected to the state legislature in 1882 and served for one term. While a legislator he discovered that lobbyists held the real power to get laws passed. He began to lobby for laws that were favorable to his railroad business. In 1884 and 1886, he backed German-born William Meyer for governor. In 1889, Governor Job Cooper appointed Mears to the committee to build a state capitol building. 2 photos, 54 notes.   R. A. Garfinkle

322.   Kaplan, Michael D.   THE TOLLROAD BUILDING CAREER OF OTTO MEARS.   *Colorado Mag. 1975 52(2): 153-170.* Mostly during 1881-87 Mears built a network of approximately 450 miles of tollroads in the San Juan mining area of southwest Colorado. Cheap, efficient transportation was the basis for the growth of the area. Later he turned to railroads and automobile roads, but his tollroads remain the basis of the highway system in the San Juan. Mainly primary sources; 4 illus., 3 maps, table, 51 notes.   O. H. Zabel

323.   Kardonne, Rick.   MONTREAL, QUEBEC.   *Present Tense 1975 2(2): 50-55.* Discusses the social and religious life of the Jews of Montreal, Quebec during the 1970's and the problems presented by the emigration of Jews from Morocco in the 1960's.

324.   Karp, Abraham J.   FROM TERCENTENARY TO BICENTENNIAL. *Am. Jewish Hist. Q. 1974 64(1): 3-14.* Summarizes the changes in the developing self-image of the American Jewish community. Proposes a Center for the Study of Jewish Life and Institutions to achieve clarification and consistency. If, as sociologists suggest, America's new image is ethnic assimilation but religious differentiation, or "America as mosaic," the American Jew will need to know more about himself and his community, past and present, so that he can intelligently plan his future in response to his own personal need and in service to the nation. A Center would become an indispensable tool in the fashioning of this new community. 2 appendixes.   F. Rosenthal

325. Karp, Abraham J. IDEOLOGY AND IDENTITY IN JEWISH GROUP SURVIVAL IN AMERICA. *Am. Jewish Hist. Q. 1976 65(4): 310-334.* As a result of enlightenment and emancipation in the early 19th century, the Jews of Western Europe adopted the thesis "Judaism qua Religion"; their brethren in Eastern Europe countered with the antithesis, "Judaism qua nationalism." The American Jews, comprised of and influenced by both communities and by the realities of America, were working out the synthesis of "Religion plus Nationalism." Only in such a way could the threat of the melting pot, total assimilation, be countered. The insight of Horace M. Kallen and of Mordecai Kaplan substantiated the dual image identity—both religious as well as ethnic community—and provides the most creatively viable response to the challenge of Jewish group survival today. 41 notes.   F. Rosenthal

326. Karsh, Audrey R. MANNASSE CHICO: ENLIGHTENED MERCHANT OF SAN DIEGO. *Western States Jewish Hist. Q. 1975 8(1): 45-54.* In 1853, Joseph Samuel Mannasse (1831-97) moved to San Diego, California, from New York. He started in the merchandising business and then purchased several rancheros along with his partner and brother-in-law Marcus Schiller. They were very successful until an 1870 drought ruined the ranches and a fire in 1872 destroyed their store. The partnership soon broke up. Mannasse served on the San Diego city council and was very active in civic affairs until his death. 2 photos, 45 notes.   R. A. Garfinkle

327. Katz, Irving I. THE JEWISH PRESS IN DETROIT: AN HISTORICAL ACCOUNT ON THE OCCASION OF THE 150TH ANNIVERSARY OF THE JEWISH PRESS IN THE UNITED STATES. *Michigan Jewish Hist. 1974 14(1): 18-23.*

328. Katz, Irving I. RABBI KAUFMANN KOHLER BEGAN HIS DETROIT MINISTRY IN 1869. *Michigan Jewish Hist. 1979 19(1): 11-15.* Kaufmann Kohler (1843-1926) was a rabbi in Detroit; discusses his extensive influence in Reform Judaism in America, 1869-1926.

329. Katz, Jacob. EMANCIPATION AND JEWISH STUDIES. *Commentary 1974 57(4): 60-65.* Discusses assimilation and Jewish emancipation and Jewish studies since the 18th century.   S

330. Katz-Hyman, Martha B. A NOTE ON RABBI MOSES ZISKIND FINESILVER, 1847-1922. *Rhode Island Jewish Hist. Notes 1977 7(3): 430-431.* Note offers documentation of the fact that Moses Ziskind Finesilver was the Congregation Sons of Zion's (Providence, Rhode Island) first hazzan (cantor) and shohet (ritual slaughterer), not Eliasar Lipshitz as previously stated; covers 1880-83.

331. Kaufman, Menachem. 'ATIDAH SHEL SHE'ERIT HAPLEIṬAH BE-SHE'ELAT ERETS YIŚRAEL BE'EINEI HA-IRGUNIM HALO-TSIYONIIM BE-ARTSOT HABRIT BISHNAT 1945 [The future of the Holocaust survivors and the Palestine problem in the eyes of the non-Zionist Jewish organizations in the US]. *Yalkut Moreshet Periodical [Israel] 1976 21: 181-198.* Non-Zionist Jewish organizations in the US began to link the need for a home for the survivors of the Nazi Holocaust with the creation of a Jewish state in Palestine only when the US Government did so in late 1945.

332.   Kayfetz, Ben.   NEO-NAZIS IN CANADA.   *Patterns of Prejudice [Great Britain] 1979 13(1): 29-31, 34.* Since 1963 a rash of neo-Nazi organizations have been formed, especially in the Toronto area, and they have engaged in the publication of Hitlerite material and antisemitic acts of destruction, for some of which the participants have been caught, tried and sentenced according to the provisions of Canada's new (1970) "anti-hate" law.

333.   Keenan, Jerry.   MAX LITTMANN: IMMIGRANT SOLDIER IN THE WAGON BOX FIGHT.   *Western States Jewish Hist. Q. 1974 6(2): 111-119.* Max Littmann was a German immigrant to the United States in the mid-1860's. He joined the US Army in 1866 and became a hero in the Wagon Box Fight in 1867. He saved the lives of several of his fellow soldiers and killed several Indians. He was discharged in 1869 and became a highly successful businessman in St. Louis. He died in 1921. Secondary sources; illus., photo, 4 notes.
R. A. Garfinkle

334.   Keller, Allan.   THOSE SHREWD YANKEE PEDDLERS.   *Am. Hist. Illus. 1978 13(6): 8-16.* Selling goods from combs to stoves and later books and medicines, first in tinboxes, trunks, packs and later wagons, the Yankee peddlers were communication links from the east to the backcountry. Tycoons who started their businesses in this manner include: Moses Cone (textiles); Meyer Guggenheim (copper); Collis P. Huntington (railroads); Levi Strauss (levis); and B. T. Babbitt (soap).
D. Dodd

335.   Kerman, Julius C.   ADVENTURES IN AMERICA AND THE HOLY LAND.   *Am. Jewish Arch. 1976 28(2): 126-141.* "In my forty-three years in the rabbinate I served several communities, enjoying everywhere happy relationships with young and old. The thought that I have influenced some persons to think and live more Jewishly makes me happy." Byelorussian-born Rabbi Kerman also saw service in the Jewish Legion during World War I.
J

336.   Kessler-Harris, Alice and Yans-McLaughlin, Virginia.   EUROPEAN IMMIGRANT GROUPS.   Sowell, Thomas, ed. *Essays and Data on American Ethnic Groups* (Washington, D.C.: Urban Inst. Pr., 1978): 107-137. Analyzes the differences in social mobility patterns among the Irish, Italians, and Jews. Between 1820 and 1950, 4.5 million Irish, 5 million Italians, and 3 million Russians, mostly Jews, entered the United States. The Irish and Jews viewed their immigration as permanent, whereas the Italians often came to the New World to accumulate money to buy land in the old. Arriving when the United States had a largely agrarian economy, the Irish generally were unskilled laborers. The Italians and Jews, arriving later, moved into more professional occupations. Relative living conditions, community cohesion, politics, intermarriage, family structure, and education are discussed, as is discrimination in housing and employment. Primary and secondary sources; 2 tables, 86 notes.
K. A. Talley

337.   Kessler-Harris, Alice.   ORGANIZING THE UNORGANIZABLE: THREE JEWISH WOMEN AND THEIR UNION.   *Labor Hist. 1976 17(1): 5-23.* Surveys the lives and work of Pauline Newman, Fannia Cohn, and Rose Pesotta of the International Ladies' Garment Workers' Union. Their experience as women and their tasks as union officers persistently conflicted, but their class consciousness took precedence over their identification as women. Based upon the Pesotta, Schneiderman, and Cohn papers; 84 notes.
L. L. Athey

338. Kessner, Carole S. JEWISH-AMERICAN IMMIGRANT FICTION WRITTEN IN ENGLISH BETWEEN 1867 AND 1920: AN ANNOTATED BIBLIOGRAPHY. *Bull. of Res. in the Humanities 1978 81(4): 406-430.* Annotated bibliography of English-language works by Jewish Americans 1867-1920 covers bibliography, reference works, history, sociology, literary surveys and criticism, autobiography, and novels which relate the immigrant experience.

339. Kinsey, Stephen D. THE DEVELOPMENT OF THE JEWISH COMMUNITY OF SAN JOSE, CALIFORNIA, 1850-1900. *Western States Jewish Hist. Q. 1974 7(1): 70-87, (2): 163-182, (3): 264-273.* Part I. Jews began to arrive in San Jose, California, in the 1850's. In 1861, they established Congregation Bickur Cholim, with Jacob Levy as the first president. There were 35 members in 1869 and the congregation purchased land to construct a synagogue. On 21 August 1870, the synagogue was dedicated. The first ordained rabbi to serve the congregation was Dr. Myer Sol Levy. By 1916 the congregation was a mixture of orthodox and reform Jews. Based on primary sources; 3 photos, 79 notes. Part II. The development of the Jewish community in San Jose depended upon merchants who could give their time and money for Jewish activities. Many of these individuals held offices in Jewish community organizations, Congregation Bickur Cholim, Ariel Lodge, B'nai B'rith, and other community groups. Short biographies are included in the article. Based on primary and secondary sources; 5 photos, 108 notes. Part III. Established in 1857, the Beth Olam Cemetery was the first Jewish communal organization in San Jose. Other Jewish community organizations were the Hebrew Ladies Benevolent Society (established 1869), the Hebrew Young Men's Benevolent Association of San Jose (established 1872), and Ariel Lodge No. 248 of B'nai B'rith (established 1875). Even with these few organizations, Congregation Bickur Cholim remained the center of the Jewish community in early San Jose. Based on primary sources; photo, 32 notes.

R. A. Garfinkle

340. Kislov, A. K. BELYI DOM I SIONISTSKOE LOBBI [The White House and the Zionist lobby]. *Voprosy Istorii [USSR] 1973 (1): 48-61.* The author discloses the interrelations between the White House and the Zionist lobby over the past fifty years, tracing the influence exerted by the Zionists on the political life of the United States. Considerable attention is devoted in the article to the causes of this influence which becomes especially pronounced during election campaigns, as well as to the methods employed by the Zionists. The Zionists' ability to gain their objectives is limited. In the final analysis the decision to further one or another concrete course of action remains the prerogative of the US authorities which express the interests of the capitalist class as a whole. Consequently international Zionism has been forced to adapt itself to American interests.

J/S

341. Kislov, A. K. "LIGA ZASHCHITY EVREEV"—ORUDIE KRAINEI REAKTSII [The Jewish Defense League: an instrument of extreme reaction]. *Sovetskoe Gosudarstvo i Pravo [USSR] 1975 (6): 97-104.* Discusses the creation, methods and main directions of the Jewish Defense League which stands on the extreme right flank of Zionism. The most essential part of the League's strategy is to aggravate in every possible way international tension and especially Soviet-American relations. As a rule special activity in this respect is displayed by the League on the eve of summit meetings. At the same time the League does not

spare efforts to whip up nationalistic, chauvinistic feelings among Americans of the Jewish origin. The article gives characteristics of the leader of the League, Rabbi Meir Kahane, data on the organizational structure of the League, its membership and social structure. The author dwells on the League's relations with other Jewish and reactionary organizations in the United States, some of which take anti-Semitic positions and are openly gangster organizations.   J

342.   Kislov, A. K.   "LIGA ZASHCHITY EVREEV"—ORUDIE KRAINEI REAKTSII   [The Jewish Defense League: an instrument of extreme reaction]. *Sovetskoe Gosudarstvo i Pravo [USSR] 1975 (6): 97-104.* Discusses the creation, methods and main directions of the Jewish Defense League which stands on the extreme right flank of Zionism. The most essential part of the league's strategy is to aggravate in every possible way international tension and especially Soviet-American relations. As a rule special activity in this respect is displayed by the league on the eve of summit meetings. At the same time the league does not spare efforts to whip up nationalistic, chauvinistic feelings among Americans of Jewish origin. The article gives characteristics of the leader of the league, Rabbi Meir Kahane, data on the organizational structure of the league, its membership and social structure. The author dwells on the league's relations with other Jewish and reactionary organizations in the United States, some of which take anti-Semitic positions and are openly gangster organizations.   J

343.   Klaidman, Stephen.   THE NAZI HUNTERS: JUSTICE, NOT VENGEANCE.   *Present Tense 1977 4(2): 21-26.* Examines the motivations and activities of Nazi hunters (1947-77), including Shirley Korman, Vincent A. Schiano, Anthony DeVito, Wayne Perlmutter, Bessy Pupko, Charles R. Allen, Jr. Discusses litigation against suspected Nazi war criminals. Reviews the policies and actions of the US Immigration and Naturalization Service, US Department of Justice, US Congress, National Council of Churches, World Jewish Congress, Concerned Jewish Youth, Yad Vashem (Israel), etc. Primary and secondary sources; 5 photos.   R. B. Mendel

344.   Klein, Jeffrey.   ARMIES OF THE PLANET: A COMPARATIVE ANALYSIS OF NORMAN MAILER'S AND SAUL BELLOW'S POLITICAL VISIONS.   *Soundings 1975 58(1): 69-83.* The politicized worlds created by Norman Mailer in *The Armies of the Night* and by Saul Bellow in *Mr. Sammler's Planet* reveal both authors to be essentially Jewish in their obsession with the moral meaning of events. Mailer's espousal of the idea that what feels good is good along with his anticipation of apocalyptic orgasm, attacks on corporate WASP authoritarianism, and hatred of familial bondage is juxtaposed to Bellow's Arthur Sammler, who fears the coming holocaust because of the breakdown of civil order with youth as the leading edge of the problem.

N. Lederer

345.   Klein, Walter E.   THE JEWISH COMMUNITY COUNCIL OF METROPOLITAN DETROIT: THE ORGANIZING YEARS.   *Michigan Jewish Hist. 1978 18(1): 20-32.* The Jewish Community Council of Metropolitan Detroit was founded in 1937 after several meetings of prominent Jewish groups, formation of an organizing committee in 1935, and aid from the American Jewish Congress.

346. Knee, Stuart E. [ETHNIC ANTI-ZIONISM, 1917-41].
ETHNIC ANTI-ZIONISM IN U.S.A., 1917-1941. *Patterns of Prejudice [Great Britain] 1977 11(5): 30-33.* Greek, Irish, Polish, Negro, and Arab groups expressed varying degrees of anti-Zionism during the interwar period.
AMERICAN ARABS AND PALESTINE. *Patterns of Prejudice [Great Britain] 1977 11(6): 25-31, 34.* Reviews Arab American anti-Zionist movements and organizations (e.g., Dr. E. G. Tabet's Syria-Mt. Lebanon League of Liberation, Dr. Fuad Shatara's Palestine Anti-Zionism Society, etc.) during 1912-41, and finds that some groups became not only anti-Zionist but anti-Jewish and Fascist.

347. Knee, Stuart E. FROM CONTROVERSY TO CONVERSION: LIBERAL JUDAISM IN AMERICA AND THE ZIONIST MOVEMENT, 1917-1941. *Ann. of Jewish Social Sci. 1978 17: 260-289.* Deals with the gradual change within US Reform Judaism from firm anti-Zionism to reluctant acceptance of Zionism and gradually to pro-Zionism. The chief catalyst in this change was the advent to power of Adolf Hitler in Germany and the spread of Nazism.

R. J. Wechman

348. Knee, Stuart E. THE IMPACT OF ZIONISM ON BLACK AND ARAB AMERICANS. *Patterns of Prejudice [Great Britain] 1976 10(2): 21-28.* Discusses the impact of Zionism on black and Arab Americans from 1941 to the present, showing the Six-Day War (1967) as a turning point in the formation of the Third World.

349. Knee, Stuart E. JEWISH NON-ZIONISM IN AMERICA AND PALESTINE COMMITMENT 1917-1941. *Jewish Social Studies 1977 39(3): 209-226.* The non-Zionist element within American Jewry played a major role in shaping the destiny of Zionism; a role in fact equal to that exerted on the movement by American Zionists and anti-Zionists. Non-Zionists opposed the creation of a Jewish state but supported Jewish immigration to Palestine, economic development of the region, and a revival of religiocultural Judaism. The American Jewish Committee was the principal non-Zionist gathering place. Louis Marshall and, following his death, Felix Warburg and Cyrus Adler, were prominent in non-Zionist leadership. The involved efforts of these men and their adherents to follow a middle path in regard to Palestine and its future led to their participation in a series of conferences in the interwar period resulting in the bankruptcy of non-Zionism as a viable philosophy of action. By 1941 non-Zionism had been absorbed into the Zionist camp, largely through the medium of the Jewish Agency and its increasing commitment to a Jewish Palestine.

N. Lederer

350. Knee, Stuart E. JEWISH SOCIALISTS IN AMERICA: THE DEBATE ON ZIONISM. *Wiener Lib. Bull. [Great Britain] 1975 28(33-34): 13-24.* Surveys the changing nature of the debate on Zionism among American Jewish socialists from World War I to World War II with particular reference to the issue of Jewish nationalism in Palestine. Emphasizes the influence of Jewish European immigrants and through them the views of the *Bund*, the European Jewish labor organization. Bundists emphasized revisionist socialism; the Zionists the establishment of a Jewish national home in Palestine. Despite periods of

apparent modification, Jewish socialists remained opposed to the pro-capitalist and anti-Palestinian Arab views of the Zionists. Also discusses the anti-Zionist views of the American Communists in the 1930's against the background of international developments and Comintern directives. Based on private papers, interviews, and published sources; 62 notes.	J. P. Fox

351. Knee, Stuart E. THE KING-CRANE COMMISSION OF 1919: THE ARTICULATION OF POLITICAL ANTI-ZIONISM. *Am. Jewish Arch. 1977 29(1): 22-52.* The [US] anti-Zionist King-Crane Report of 1919 [on Palestine] owed much to the Christian missionary goals of its authors. It did not reflect the wishes of the Middle East's Moslem majority, but deserves to be recalled as a pro-Christian document.	J

352. Korn, Bertram W. AN AMERICAN JEWISH RELIGIOUS LEADER IN 1860 VOICES HIS FRUSTRATION. *Michael: On the Hist. of the Jews in the Diaspora [Israel] 1975 3: 42-47.* Though some American rabbis in the 1860's were men of stature who helped reorient Judaism and the Jew toward the conditions and demands of their new environment, most were minor religious functionaries who lacked any other specialized training. One such figure was Henry Loewenthal of Macon, Georgia, who reached the United States from England in 1854. Prints an 1860 letter he wrote to Rabbi Isaac Leeser of Philadelphia, complaining of ill treatment by members of his congregation and the poor Jewish example they present to their children. Primary and secondary sources; 12 notes.	T. Sassoon

353. Kozłowski, Józef. "TKACZE" G. HAUPTMANNA NA SCENIE ŻYDOWSKIEJ NA PRZEŁOMIE XIX I XX W [G. Hauptmann's *The Weavers* on the Jewish stages at the turn of the century]. *Biuletyn Zydowskiego Inst. Hist. w Polsce [Poland] 1976 (4): 95-101.* The sociopolitical conflict expressed by Gerhart Hauptmann in his famous tragedy *The Weavers* aroused interest and vivid response among the Jewish working class in Poland. The first performance of *The Weavers* in Poland took place on the Jewish workers' stage and in Yiddish in Warsaw in 1899. In the Austrian Partition the tragedy was put on stage by the association Briderlichkeit in 1901. A year later the tragedy was put on stage in New York by a Jewish amateur troupe working at the Polish Socialist Party's Help Union. The drama of the 1840's deeply touched the spectators, and the revolutionary fight of the Silesian weavers was associated with actual working-class problems.	J

354. Kramer, Will. BEANS TO BULLION. *Westways 1976 68(10): 18-21, 77.* Discusses the business career of Achille Levy (1853-1922), a native of France who immigrated to the United States in 1871 and moved in 1874 from San Francisco to Ventura County where he began raising beans, and eventually founded the Bank of A. Levy, 1905.	G. A. Hewlett

355. Kramer, William M. DANIEL CAVE: SOUTHERN CALIFORNIA PIONEER DENTIST, CIVIC LEADER AND MASONIC DIGNITARY. *Western States Jewish Hist. Q. 1977 9(2): 99-121.* Daniel Cave (1841-1936) had practiced dentistry in Vienna, Austria, before coming to America in 1873 to improve his skills. He established a practice in San Diego, California, later moving to Los Angeles. As founder of the Dental Society of San Diego he

emphasized that dentistry was a scientific medical profession. He was named a special clinician at the University of Southern California Dental School in 1897, attended every conference in his profession, and had a special interest in new equipment and techniques. Active participation in San Diego civic and political organizations was an important responsibility to Cave, who was a library trustee, president of the San Diego Water Company, an officer of the Society for the Prevention of Cruelty to Animals, and Republican candidate for alderman in 1889. Cave was also a leader of Masonic lodges in San Diego and Los Angeles. Based on interviews, personal correspondence and published material; 3 photos, 68 notes. B. S. Porter

356. Kramer, William M. and Clar, Reva. EMANUEL SCHREIBER: LOS ANGELES' FIRST REFORM RABBI, 1885-1889. *Western States Jewish Hist. Q. 1977 9(4): 354-370; 1977 10(1): 38-55.* Part I. Emanuel Schreiber left his native Germany in 1881. After serving synagogues in Mobile (Alabama) and Denver (Colorado) he was invited to Los Angeles' Congregation B'nai B'rith in 1885. Some of the traditionalists were offended by Schreiber's radical-Reform policies but the majority of the congregation supported him. He was active in community affairs; most significant was his role in the formation of the Associated Charities which developed into the present United Crusade. San Francisco journalist Isidore N. Choynski criticized Rabbi Schreiber's accumulation of wealth from astute land speculation. Based on newspapers and other published primary and secondary sources; 68 notes. Part II. Religious and social activities at Congregation B'nai B'rith were enhanced by the participation of the rabbi's wife. Reform-Orthodox tensions decreased as Rabbi Schreiber impressed the Jewish community with his considerable knowledge of religious phenomena. Schreiber's relations with the gentile community were excellent; Christian ministers appreciated his learning and invited him to speak to their congregations. Despite his esteemed position in Los Angeles, Schreiber's ambitions caused him to leave. He served at synagogues in Arkansas, Washington, Ohio, and Illinois, 1889-99. He was minister to Chicago's Congregation Emanu-El from 1899 to 1906 when he moved to the east coast. In 1920 he returned to Los Angeles, where he remained until his death in 1932. Based on newspapers and other published primary and secondary sources; illus., 65 notes. B. S. Porter

357. Kramer, William M. THE EMERGENCE OF OAKLAND JEWRY. *Western States Jewish Hist. Q. 1978 10(2): 99-125, (3): 238-259, (4): 353-373; 11(1): 69-86; 1979 11(2): 173-186, (3): 265-278.* Part I. Jewish families were among the pioneers of Oakland, California, in the 1850's. In the early years, the Oakland Hebrew Benevolent Society, founded in 1862, was the religious, social, and charitable center of the community. Later, the first synagogue, founded in 1875, took over the religious and burial functions. Jews from Poland or Prussian-occupied Poland predominated in the community, and most of them worked in some aspect of the clothing industry. David Solis-Cohen, the noted author, was a leader in the Oakland Jewish community in the 1870's. Primary and secondary sources; 3 photos, 111 notes. Part II. In 1879 Oakland's growing Jewish community organized a second congregation, a strictly orthodox group, Poel Zedek. Women's religious organizations flourished, their charitable services extending to needy gentiles as well as Jews. Jewish participants in civic and political affairs included David S. Hirshberg, who served in several Alameda County offices, and

Henry Levy, commander of the Oakland Guard militia organization. Oakland Jewry was part of the greater San Francisco community, yet maintained its own charm and character. Primary and secondary sources; 88 notes. Part III. On 6 July 1881 the First Hebrew Congregation of Oakland, California, elected Myer Solomon Levy as its rabbi. The London-born Levy practiced traditional Judaism. In 1884 the community faced the need of finding a larger, more fashionably located synagogue. The Israel Ladies Relief Society held a fair and raised $4,000 for the new building. On 17 June 1885 the First Hebrew's synagogue burned, increasing the urgency for a new building. Construction of the new synagogue began in May 1886 and was completed by September. Primary and secondary sources; 68 notes. Part IV. Oakland's Jews attended excellent schools, both secular and religious. Fannie Bernstein was the first Jewess to graduate from the University of California at Berkeley, in 1883. First Hebrew Congregation sponsored a Sabbath school which had 75 children in 1887. One of the pupils, Meyer Lissner, was a bright youngster whose letters were published in the Jewish press. The Jewish children of Oakland had an active social life with school events, birthday parties, and Bar Mitzvahs. The contract of the popular Rabbi Myer S. Levy was renewed for five years, from 1888 to 1893. Primary and secondary sources; 66 notes. Part V. Oakland Jewry was active in public affairs and charitable projects in the 1880's. Rabbi Myer S. Levy was chaplain to the state legislature in 1885, and was invited several times to speak to the congregation of the Unitarian Hamiltonian Church. The Daughters of Israel Relief Society continued its good works both inside and outside the Jewish community. Beth Jacob, the traditional congregation of Old World Polish Jews, continued its separate religious practices while it maintained friendly relations with the members of the first Hebrew Congregation. Primary and secondary sources; 44 notes. Part VI. Oakland's Jewish community had able social and political leadership in David Samuel Hirshberg. Until 1886 he was an officer in the Grand Lodge of B'nai B'rith. He served as Under Sheriff of Alameda County in 1883 and was active in Democratic Party political affairs. In 1885 he was appointed Chief Clerk of the US Mint in San Francisco. As a politician, he had detractors who accused him of using his position in B'nai B'rith to foster his political career. Primary and secondary sources; 56 notes. Part VII. In 1891 Rabbi Myer S. Levy moved to a new position in San Francisco's Congregation Beth Israel, bringing to a close this era of Oakland's Jewish history. Based on published sources; 21 notes.

B. S. Porter

358. Kramer, William M. and Stern, Norton B. A JEWISH HISTORY OF OAKLAND: A REVIEW ESSAY. *Western States Jewish Hist. Q. 1977 9(4): 371-377.* Review article prompted by Fred Rosenbaum's book, *Free to Choose: The Making of a Jewish Community in the American West,* subtitled, "The Jews of Oakland, California, from the Gold Rush to the Present Day" (Berkeley: Judah L. Magnes Memorial Museum, 1976). The title is misleading as it mainly covers the 1920's to the present. The book has numerous errors and omissions, as Rosenbaum's research was confined primarily to personal interviews and not documented from primary sources. He selected subjects poorly, discussing several people who had little or no effect on Oakland Jewry, and one person who was a "bad example" to the community.   B. S. Porter

359. Kramer, William M. and Stern, Norton B. A. LEVY OF THE BANK: FROM BEANS TO BANKS IN VENTURA COUNTY. *Western States Jewish Hist. Q. 1975 7(2): 118-137.* Achille Levy (1853-1922) came to California in 1871 from France. In 1874, he settled in Hueneme, where he opened a general merchandise store. In 1881, he returned to France to visit his family and met Lucy Levy, a distant cousin. They were married in 1882, and returned to Hueneme. Levy went into business buying and selling farm products and supplies. By extending credit to the farmers he slowly became a banker, expanding his business ventures into many areas until he became a multimillionaire. Provides brief biographies of his children and his business partners. Primary and secondary sources; 3 photos, 76 notes.   R. A. Garfinkle

360. Kramer, William M. LOS ANGELES JEWRY'S FIRST PRESIDENT. *Western States Jewish Hist. Q. 1975 7(2): 151-152.* Samuel K. Labatt served as the first president of the first Jewish organization in Los Angeles, the Hebrew Benevolent Society, which was formed in July 1854. Labatt had worked for Jewish organizations in his hometown of New Orleans before he came to California in 1853. His brother Henry J. Labatt was elected secretary of the First Hebrew Benevolent Society in San Francisco on 29 May 1853. 6 notes.
R. A. Garfinkle

361. Kramer, William M. and Stern, Norton B. NATHAN NEWMARK: FIRST VALEDICTORIAN OF THE UNIVERSITY OF CALIFORNIA. *Western States Jewish Hist. Q. 1977 9(4): 341-349.* Nathan Newmark (3 June 1853-15 June 1928) was a poor but brilliant San Francisco schoolboy whose accomplishments brought him to the attention of Joseph P. Newmark (no relation). The elder Newmark helped Nathan attend the new University of California, and later, law school. After graduation Nathan opened a law office in San Francisco but was principally occupied as a journalist for the leading western Jewish weekly, *The Hebrew.* He was an active member and officer of the Young Men's Hebrew Association. Some friends and contemporaries viewed Newmark's career as a failure because he lacked the "combative spirit" required for financial success. Others claimed that his success was in legal scholarship and journalism although these pursuits were not financially rewarding. Based on recollections of contemporaries, private correspondence, published primary and secondary sources; photo, 32 notes.   B. S. Porter

362. Kramer, William M. and Clar, Reva. RABBI SIGMUND HECHT: A MAN WHO BRIDGED THE CENTURIES. *Western States Jewish Hist. Q. 1975 7(4): 356-375, 8(1): 72-90.* Part I. Sigmund Hecht (b. 1849) emigrated to New York from Hungary with his parents. He completed his rabbinical studies at Temple Emanu-El's Theological School, New York. He soon became the leader of the temple's Sabbath school. In 1877, he became the Rabbi for Congregation Kahl Montgomery (Montgomery, Alabama). In 1885, he helped to establish and then served as the first treasurer of the Conference of Southern Rabbis. In 1888, he was appointed the Rabbi for Congregation Emanu-El, Milwaukee. He was active in many civic and religious groups. Based on primary and secondary sources; 2 photos, 68 notes. Part II. Rabbi Hecht left Milwaukee for Los Angeles in 1899 to become the rabbi at Temple B'nai B'rith. He found the congregation there very disunited. To reunite the congregation he started several new Jewish charitable organizations. In 1911, these separate groups united to form the Los

Angeles Federation of Jewish Charities. He fought against movie censorship and anti-Semitism. Includes excerpts from several sermons. Photo, 65 notes. Article to be continued.
R. A. Garfinkle

363. Kramer, William M. and Clar, Reva. RABBI SIGMUND HECHT: A MAN WHO BRIDGED THE CENTURIES (PART III). *Western States Jewish Hist. Q. 1976 8(2): 169-186.* Continued from a previous article. Rabbi Sigmund Hecht remained neutral toward Zionism. He was appointed to the board of directors of the Los Angeles public library by Mayor Meredith P. Snyder. He backed Mayor Snyder for reelection, but Snyder lost to Owen McAleer. Mayor McAleer appointed George N. Black, a Jewish friend of Hecht, to replace Hecht. Black refused the appointment so McAleer chose another Jew; patronage was strong in Los Angeles then. In 1914, Congregation B'nai B'rith hired Dr. Edgar Fogel Magnin to serve as an associate Rabbi for Rabbi Hecht. Rabbi Hecht died in 1925 after a long and distinguished career. He left many volumes of writings and had been active in many civic and Jewish community groups. 51 notes.
R. A. Garfinkle

364. Kramer, William M. and Stern, Norton B. SAN FRANCISCO'S FIGHTING JEW. *California Hist. Q. 1974 53(4): 333-346.* Joe Choynski (1868-1943) was American Jewry's first international sports figure. A professional boxer from San Francisco, Choynski contradicted the stereotype which excluded Jews from competitive sports. He fought 77 bouts, winning 50 of them during his 20-year career. Six of his opponents were or later became world champions, including Jim Corbett, Jim Jeffries, John L. Sullivan, and Jack Johnson. Known as a "scientific" boxer, Choynski fought at a time when matches could be declared illegal and the participants arrested. Bouts lasted for dozens of rounds and fighters used bare fists or two-ounce gloves. The sports press of the period praised Choynski's abilities, and his opponents held him in high esteem. Based on interviews, newspapers, and published works; photos, 73 notes.
A. Hoffman

365. Kramer, William M. and Stern, Norton B. A SEARCH FOR THE FIRST SYNAGOGUE IN THE GOLDEN WEST. *Western States Jewish Hist. Q. 1974 7(1): 3-20.* In 1851, the rivalry between German and Polish Jews in San Francisco led to the founding of two separate synagogues within the city. The German synagogue is Temple Emanu-El and the Polish is Temple Sherith Israel. In 1900, Rabbi Jacob Voorsanger of Emanu-El tried to prove that his temple was the first, but he used a misdated lease as his main proof. Research shows that both congregations were founded on 6 April 1851. Primary and secondary sources; photo, 56 notes.
R. A. Garfinkle

366. Kramer, William M. THE STINGIEST MAN IN SAN FRANCISCO. *Western States Jewish Hist. Q. 1973 5(4): 257-269.* Humorous tales of the miserly attitudes and actions of one of the wealthiest Jews in San Francisco, Michael Reese, 1850-78.

367. Krause, Allen. THE ENIGMATIC JUDAH BENJAMIN. *Midstream 1978 24(8): 17-20.* Although Judah Benjamin was an important civilian during the Confederacy and was tried with Jefferson Davis and Robert E. Lee in 1868, he has received little historical attention because of his Jewish background.

368. Krause, Corinne Azen. URBANIZATION WITHOUT BREAK-DOWN: ITALIAN, JEWISH, AND SLAVIC IMMIGRANT WOMEN IN PITTSBURGH, 1900-1945. *J. of Urban Hist. 1978 4(3): 291-306.* Most immigrant women adjusted to the cultural shock of immigration without serious or lasting problems. In part this was due to general human resiliency, but in Pittsburgh it was also due to the existence of immigrant neighborhoods and other bridges to the old world. Based on oral histories; fig., 41 notes.   T. W. Smith

369. Krausz, Ernest. THE RELIGIOUS FACTOR IN JEWISH IDENTIFI-CATION. *Int. Social Sci. J. [France] 1977 29(2): 250-260.* Examines the interconnections between religious and secular life for Jews, concluding that where religion is upheld, the ethnic factor is strong and that where shift in emphasis favors secularization, these will compensate for loss of religious identity; differentiates between Israeli and American Jews, 1957-77.

370. Kreader, J. Lee. ISAAC MAX RUBINOW: PIONEERING SPECIAL-IST IN SOCIAL INSURANCE. *Social Service Rev. 1976 50(3): 402-425.* Provides a biography of Isaac Max Rubinow (1875-1936), a ground-breaking theorist and tireless fighter for American social insurance during the Progressive era.

371. Kriegel, Annie. JEWS AND BLACKS. *Jerusalem Q. [Israel] 1978 (7): 22-33.* Compares the American Negro and the Jewish experience of slavery, ghettos, and emancipation, 15th-20th centuries.

372. Kruger, Arnd. "FAIR PLAY FOR AMERICAN ATHLETES": A STUDY IN ANTI-SEMITISM. *Can. J. of Hist. of Sport and Physical Educ. [Canada] 1978 9(1): 42-57.* In his 1935 pamphlet "Fair Play for American Athletes" and elsewhere, American Olympic Committee President Avery Brundage, in opposing the proposed boycott of the 1936 Olympic Games to be held in Berlin, indulged in anti-Semitism.

373. Kusinitz, Bernard and Kosch, Samuel. A HALF CENTURY OF JUDAH TOURO LODGE NO. 998 INDEPENDENT ORDER OF B'NAI B'RITH. *Rhode Island Jewish Hist. Notes 1975 7(1): 73-78.*

374. Kusinitz, Bernard. THE 1902 SIT-IN AT TOURO SYNAGOGUE. *Rhode Island Jewish Hist. Notes 1975 7(1): 42-72.* Discusses a disagreement between members of the Newport, Rhode Island, Touro Synagogue and the congregation Shearith Israel in New York City (who, for legal reasons were official trustees of the Touro Synagogue) which led to the 1902 take-over of Touro Synagogue by the Newport members.

375. Kuznets, Simon. IMMIGRATION OF RUSSIAN JEWS TO THE UNITED STATES: BACKGROUND AND STRUCTURE. *Perspectives in Am. Hist. 1975 9: 35-124.* From 1881 to 1914 1.5 million Russian Jews emigrated to the United States. Many of the forces motivating their emigration were common to most mass movements from Europe during the 19th century: the pressures of industrialization and new technology, and the dislocation of people from the land. Russian Jews, however, were also affected by factors not so common to other groups. Restrictions imposed by the Czarist Empire on Jews' residence, vocation, and education encouraged them to emigrate. Jewish immigrants were

more likely to be family-oriented and to remain in their new homeland. 14 tables, 34 notes. W. A. Wiegand

376. Lacks, Roslyn. TRYING TO MAKE IT IN THE U.S.A.: NEW EMIGRES, NEW PROBLEMS. *Present Tense 1976 3(4): 45-49.* Of the more than 100,000 Jews who have left the USSR since 1971 (more than one half from the Ukraine, nearly a third from Moscow and Leningrad, and smaller groups from Georgia, Moldavia, Byelorussia, Latvia, Estonia, and Lithuania), at least one in 10 has settled in the United States (almost half in New York City). Groups such as the New York Association for New Americans and the Hebrew Immigrant Aid Society have been attempting to find employment for the new immigrants, who frequently are reluctant to take lower-level jobs because they are not accustomed to the American concept of upward mobility, while professionals such as physicians and dentists face formidable examinations before they can receive licenses to practice in the USA. C. Moody

377. Lamb, Blaine. JEWS IN EARLY PHOENIX, 1870-1920. *J. of Arizona Hist. 1977 18(3): 299-318.* Jews who came to Phoenix in the 1870's and 1880's were primarily of German and Polish extraction. By 1900 they were generally of Russian and East European origin. Though a small minority, Jews played a vital role in the maturing of Phoenix in its crucial 1870-1920 years. 5 illus., 50 notes. D. L. Smith

378. Landau, Francine. SOLOMON LAZARD OF LOS ANGELES. *Western States Jewish Hist. Q. 1973 5(3): 141-157.* Solomon Lazard (1826-1916) was an innovator in his work with charities, other Jews, and civic associations.

379. Lander, Clara. SASKATCHEWAN MEMORIES OR HOW TO START A JEWISH CEMETERY. *Am. Jewish Arch. 1975 27(1): 5-7.*

380. Lapides, Abe. HISTORY OF THE JEWISH COMMUNITY OF PONTIAC, MICHIGAN. *Michigan Jewish Hist. 1977 17(1): 3-10.* Chronicles the presence of Jews and the growth of their community in Pontiac, Michigan, 1915-77.

381. Lapomarda, Vincent A., S. J. MAURICE JOSEPH TOBIN AND THE BOSTON JEWISH COMMUNITY: THE MOVEMENT FOR THE STATE OF ISRAEL, 1926-1948. *Am. Benedictine Rev. 1973 24(1): 59-73.* Maurice Joseph Tobin, the sixth Secretary of Labor (1948-53), supported the establishment of a Jewish state in Palestine. Reviews Tobin's firm support of Zionist objectives in relationship to his career as Boston's Mayor, Massachusetts' Governor, and President Truman's Secretary of Labor. Based on primary and secondary sources; 57 notes. J. H. Pragman

382. Laqueur, Walter. JEWISH DENIAL AND THE HOLOCAUST. *Commentary 1979 68(6): 44-55.* Describes the dissemination of information about Hitler's Final Solution during the 1940's and Jews' reluctance to believe the extent of Nazi genocide.

383. Lavender, Abraham D. DISADVANTAGES OF MINORITY GROUP MEMBERSHIP: THE PERSPECTIVE OF A "NONDEPRIVED" MINORITY GROUP. *Ethnicity 1975 2(1): 99-119.* Though perceived by outside society to be nondeprived, minorities such as Jews actually feel cultural or social

disadvantages because of stereotyping, anti-Semitism, discrimination, exclusion, prejudice, separatism, and marginality.

384. Lavender, Abraham D. JEWISH COLLEGE WOMEN: FUTURE LEADERS OF THE JEWISH COMMUNITY? *J. of Ethnic Studies 1977 5(2): 81-90.* The American Jewish community deprives itself of needed talents by not encouraging participation of Jewish women in its leadership. Based on a questionnaire study of 488 Jewish undergraduate students at the University of Maryland during 1971, Jewish females are similar to Jewish males in their plans to obtain graduate degrees. They plan to combine their traditional mother-housewife role with that of a separate career. They have a higher degree of religious identity than their corresponding males, are more likely to date only Jews and oppose intermarriage, and have more concern than men on the vital issues of Israel and the treatment of Soviet Jews. Jewish women in America today have more opportunity than non-Jewish women for equality, though the situation is not as good as a few decades ago. Their religious position, although improving in non-Orthodox congregations, still remains far from one of equality. Primary and secondary sources; 7 tables, 11 notes. G. J. Bobango

385. Lavender, Abraham D. THE SEPHARDIC REVIVAL IN THE UNITED STATES: A CASE OF ETHNIC REVIVAL IN A MINORITY-WITHIN-A-MINORITY. *J. of Ethnic Studies 1975 3(3): 21-31.* The Sephardim number about 180,000 and comprise some 3% of the total US Jewish community, most of them in New York. Until now they have been neglected by laymen and social scientists as well, perhaps because they are non-Yiddish speakers and have "non-Jewish" names. Gives a brief background of the group and shows recent events of a scholarly and educational revival, such as the work of The American Society of Sephardic Studies, new journals, and programs at Yeshiva University. The Sephardi Federation raises funds for youth programs in Israel, now about 60% Sephardic itself. Sociological reasons for this more intense ethnicity might be the increased numbers migrating here since the 1950's, and the current Middle East situation which now has a "a power of arousal" to overcome previous apathy, as well as the increased ethnic consciousness of America in general. We must adopt a multidimensional view of Jews as is used in Spain and Islamic lands, rather than the one-dimensional portrait confined to Europe's Ashkenazim areas; few countries provide such a "living laboratory" of ethnic group relations as does Israel. Secondary materials; 46 notes. G. J. Bobango

386. Lavender, Abraham D. STUDIES OF JEWISH COLLEGE STUDENTS: A REVIEW AND A REPLICATION. *Jewish Social Studies 1977 39(1-2): 37-52.* A comparison of Jewish college students at the University of Maryland in 1971 with those surveyed at the same school by Irving Greenberg in 1949 indicates Jewish college students rank below their parents in overall observance of the Jewish religion, and in the preservation of their Jewish identity. However, the difference is not as great in 1971 as it had been in 1949. Specific findings show that the families of the 1971 freshmen students were economically better off than those of 1949; that synagogue attendance of the parents in both surveys was similar; that by 1971 observance of *kashruth* had declined; that Conservative Judaism had gained in strength at the expense of Orthodoxy; and that Reform Judaism made only minor percentile gains. Based on survey-questionnaires. N. Lederer

387. Lawson, Michael L. FLORA LANGERMANN SPIEGELBERG: GRAND LADY OF SANTA FE. *Western States Jewish Hist. Q. 1976 8(4): 291-308.* In 1875 Flora Langermann Spiegelberg (1857-1943) and her husband Willi (1844-1929) moved to Santa Fe. Willi and his five brothers operated a wholesale business that, along with new family enterprises, dominated the economy of the Southwest for several years. In 1893, the now wealthy Spiegelberg family moved to New York City. "Garbage Can Flora" became involved in the movement to clean up the city and she campaigned for investigations of war profits in the munitions industry during World War I. In 1914, she helped organize the Metropolitan Protective Association to work for improved wages for the city street cleaners. After Willi died she donated many family items to the Museum of New Mexico. Based primarily on Flora's manuscripts; 3 photos, 33 notes.   R. A. Garfinkle

388. Lazerwitz, Bernard. RELIGIOUS IDENTIFICATION AND ITS ETHNIC CORRELATES: A MULTIVARIATE MODEL. *Social Forces 1973 52(2): 204-220.* Studies the religious and ethnic identifications of white Protestants and Jews in Chicago, using eight identification dimensions. There is a mainstream of identification that runs from childhood home religious background to religious education to religious behavior to activity in ethnic organizations and to concern over one's children's religious education. Lenski's findings that ethnic community life and religious institutions were somewhat separated is supported for Protestants, but not for Jews. The findings for high-moderate status Jews show weak or negative relations between identification measures and liberalness. Low-status Jews show positive relations between five dimensions and liberalness. Protestants display weak relations between their identity dimensions and liberalness with no evidence of an interaction with social status.   J

389. Lease, Richard J. EUGENE J. STERN: MERCHANT, FARMER AND PHILANTHROPIST OF LAS CRUCES, NEW MEXICO. *Western States Jewish Hist. Q. 1977 9(2): 161-166.* Eugene J. Stern emigrated from Hungary in 1903. For several years he worked in the western states of Texas and Colorado before homesteading in New Mexico in 1914. In 1917 he moved to Las Cruces and opened a general store while continuing farming in the area of the Rio Grande Valley. Stern's philanthropies included contributing to the student loan fund at New Mexico State University and the building fund of every church in Las Cruces. He also helped establish a Salvation Army unit and a chapter of the Boys' Club of America. On the 50th anniversary of his affiliation with Masonry he gave a half million dollars for the construction of a new Scottish Rite Temple in Las Cruces. Based on interviews with the subject and his family; 2 photos, note.   B. S. Porter

390. Ledeen, Michael. LIBERALS, NOT THE JEWS, HAVE CHANGED. *Society 1979 16(4): 5, 19.* Examines sociopolitical attitudes of US Jews, 1969-79, and observes that the Jewish community has actually remained quite faithful to its liberalism while many former liberal spokespersons have shifted to conservatism in foreign policy.

391. Leibo, Steven A. OUT THE ROAD: THE SAN BRUNO AVENUE JEWISH COMMUNITY OF SAN FRANCISCO, 1901-1968. *Western States Jewish Hist. Q. 1979 11(2): 99-110.* The first synagogue, Ahabat Achim, was

formed in 1901, but the major growth of the San Bruno Avenue Jewish community took place after the 1906 earthquake. In its prime, the area comprised about 1200 Jewish residents, most of them poor, Eastern European immigrants. The Esther Hellman Settlement House, usually referred to as the "Clubhouse," was financed by wealthy "downtown" Jews, and provided for educational and social needs of the community. San Bruno Avenue, the main thoroughfare, had numerous stores and businesses operated by the local Jewish residents. Beginning in the 1930's, as they became more affluent, the younger generations moved out of the old neighborhood. Based on interviews and published sources; 3 photos, 47 notes.

B. S. Porter

392.   Lerner, Samuel and Kaplan, Rose.   A BRIEF HISTORY OF THE DE-TROIT JEWISH FAMILY AND CHILDREN'S SERVICE: AN OVERVIEW. *Michigan Jewish Hist. 1976 16(2): 22-26.* The Jewish Family and Children's Service is a community organization interested in the education and Americanization of Detroit's Jewish community, 1876-1976.

393.   Lerski, George J.   JEWISH-POLISH AMITY IN LINCOLN'S AMER-ICA.   *Polish Rev. 1973 18(4): 34-51.* Describes the participation of Polish Americans and Polish Jews in the Civil War, their social organizations, and cooperation in reacting to the 1863 Polish insurrection.   S

394.   Leventman, Paula Goldman and Leventman, Seymour.   CONGRESS-MAN DRINAN S. J., AND HIS JEWISH CONSTITUENTS.   *Am. Jewish Hist. Q. 1976 65(2): 215-248.* Robert Drinan in 1970 became the political representative of one of the largest areas of Jewish concentration outside of New York City. The importance of the "Jewish vote" for victory in this district encouraged a series of Jewish candidates to run against Father Drinan in subsequent elections. Nevertheless Drinan retained the active support of religious, communal, and political leaders and at least 50 percent of the Jewish voters, as is shown by analyses of the 1972 and 1974 returns. 28 notes.   F. Rosenthal

395.   Levin, Arthur.   A SOVIET JEWISH FAMILY COMES TO CAL-GARY.   *Can. Ethnic Studies [Canada] 1974 6(1-2): 53-66.* Describes the experience of the first Soviet Jewish family to come to Calgary, Alberta, during the post-1971 wave of Jewish emigration from the USSR, as reported in interviews held in September and October 1974.

396.   Levin, N. Gordon, Jr.   ZIONISM IN AMERICA.   *Rev. in Am. Hist. 1975 3(4): 511-515.* Melvin I. Urofsky's *American Zionism from Herzl to the Holocaust* (Garden City, New York: Anchor Pr., 1975) considers primarily the years 1880-1930, the efforts to adapt European Zionism to liberal American society, and the "major domestic and diplomatic events impinging on Jews in America and in Palestine."

397.   Levinson, Robert E.   AMERICAN JEWS IN THE WEST.   *Western Hist. Q. 1974 5(3): 285-294.* Barred for centuries from farming and the professions, most Jews who participated in the settlement of the West used the occupational skills developed by their ancestors in merchandising. Some sold food, clothing, and hardware in the mining areas. Others concentrated on the farming regions where they frequently acted as agents for the shipping of farm produce. Many settled in urban communities as wholesale merchants. Much more research

needs to be done to raise western Jewish history above the genealogical "begats" and the who's who of organization founders. 34 notes.   D. L. Smith

398.   Levinson, Robert E.   KETUBOT FROM EARLY CALIFORNIA. *Michael: On the Hist. of the Jews in the Diaspora [Israel] 1975 3: 34-41.* During the first eight years of Californian statehood, no standardized state marriage certificate existed. County recorders usually simply copied statements from clergymen or judges who officiated at weddings. Two such certificates, dated 1855 and 1861, closely resemble the traditional Jewish marriage contract, the *ketubah.* They are printed here, as is an advertisement from the San Francisco *Weekly Gleaner* (6 Nov. 1857) for "kethuboth" in English and Hebrew at $3.00 per dozen. Primary sources; 16 notes.   T. Sassoon

399.   Levitt, Abraham H.   IMPRESSIONS OF THE SAN FRANCISCO EARTHQUAKE-FIRE OF 1906.   *Western States Jewish Hist. Q. 1973 5(3): 191-197.* Recounts the confusion and destruction of this natural disaster, and the effect of the attitudes and edifices of the city's Jews.

400.   Levy, Abraham R.   CENTRAL NORTH DAKOTA'S JEWISH FARMERS IN 1903.   *Western States Jewish Hist. Q. 1978 11(1): 3-17.* The author was a founder of the Jewish Agriculturists' Aid Society of America (JAASA) which sponsored a "back to the soil" movement for Eastern European immigrants. In North Dakota, Jewish families had established homesteads on 160-acre plots where they raised flax, corn, oats, potatoes, and garden vegetables. Most of the settlers were from Russia, Rumania, and Galicia. They had worked in factories or small businesses in eastern American cities before obtaining loans from the JAASA and taking up homesteads on free government land. Reprinted from Charles S. Bernheimer, ed., *The Russian Jew in the United States* (Philadelphia, 1905). Photo, 22 notes.   B. S. Porter

401.   Levy, Eugene.   "IS THE JEW A WHITE MAN?": PRESS REACTION TO THE LEO FRANK CASE, 1913-1915.   *Phylon 1974 35(2): 212-222.* An analysis of white, black, and Jewish press reactions to the trial, conviction, and appeal of Leo Frank, a Jew, for the murder of a young Gentile girl in Atlanta, Georgia, in 1913. Frank's conviction depended on the testimony of James Conley, a black. The big city, white newspapers questioned the character of Conley, an ex-convict. The Jewish press perceived a shift in prejudices from Negroes to Jews. During the appeals processes, the black newspapers decried the attempt to substitute a black man for the Jew as perpetrator of the crime. 50 notes.
          V. L. Human

402.   Levy, J. Leonard.   A RABBI SAYS "NO."   *Western States Jewish Hist. Q. 1973 5(4): 270-272.* J. Leonard Levy (1865-1917), the rabbi in Sacramento 1889-93, rejected an 1892 offer from San Franciscans to head their congregation.

403.   Levy, William.   A JEW VIEWS BLACK EDUCATION: TEXAS 1890. *Western States Jewish Hist. Q. 1976 8(4): 351-360.* Reprints a speech given 6 August 1890 by William Levy at the cornerstone laying of the Northwest Texas Colored Citizens College in Sherman, Texas. Levy, the Mayor of Sherman, told his black audience that the way for Negroes to advance socially and economically was through the education of their children just like the Jews had done after their enslavement in Egypt. He told them that "Nothing upon earth elevates people

more than learning and good moral conduct, nothing can civilize nations more than knowledge, progress and refinement." 4 notes. R. A. Garfinkle

404. Lewis, Stuart A. THE JEWISH AUTHOR LOOKS AT THE BLACK. *Colorado Q. 1973 21(3): 317-330.* Until recently Jewish-black antagonism was negligible. While Jewish authors saw blacks as members of another minority, there was still a feeling of uneasiness and lack of acceptance of the Jewish minority by the black minority. In recent years blacks have often singled out Jews as major antagonists. However, there exists a dream of love between the races which expresses itself symbolically in many Jewish authors' works.

B. A. Storey

405. Lewis, Theodore. THE PLIGHT OF ISAAC TOURO. *Rhode Island Jewish Hist. Notes 1977 7(3): 442-443.* Reprints a 1782 document in which Rabbi Isaac Touro of Rhode Island petitions the British Commander-in-Chief for funds to take his family to Jamaica due to persecution by the British during their invasion of Rhode Island.

406. Lewis, Theodore. TOURO SYNAGOGUE, NEWPORT, R. I. *Newport Hist. 1975 48(3): 281-320.* Offers a history of the presence of Jews in Newport, Rhode Island, 1658-1963, and the synagogue built by them, eventuating in the construction of the Touro Synagogue, 1759. 3 reproductions, 19 photos, appendix.

407. Lichten, Joseph L. POLISH AMERICANS AND AMERICAN JEWS: SOME ISSUES WHICH UNITE AND DIVIDE. *Polish Rev. 1973 18(4): 52-62.* Read at a conference (in Chicago, 1970) on Polish American-Jewish community relations. S

408. Lieberman, Samuel S. and Weinfeld, Morton. DEMOGRAPHIC TRENDS AND JEWISH SURVIVAL. *Midstream 1978 24(9): 9-19.* Discusses reasons for the decrease in the American Jewish population and speculates on the future of the Jewish community.

409. Liebman, Arthur. THE TIES THAT BIND: THE JEWISH SUPPORT FOR THE LEFT IN THE UNITED STATES. *Am. Jewish Hist. Q. 1976 65(2): 285-321.* From the 1880's through the early 1920's a massive immigrant Yiddish-speaking working class led by indigenous radicals and attuned to Marxist-socialist values emerged in the United States. Post-World War II developments have eroded this basis of the Jewish left; nevertheless, in the 1950's and beyond, the middle-class college student, comfortably American and Jewish, became the cutting edge of social action and political activism. The story of the American Communist Party and its Jewish members illustrates these changing patterns. 45 notes. F. Rosenthal

410. Liebman, Charles S. ORTHODOX JUDAISM TODAY. *Midstream 1979 25(7): 19-26.* Discusses Orthodoxy in comparison to Conservative and Reform in terms of Jewish commitment, strength, and status in the Jewish community, distinguishing between the positions of strict and modern Orthodoxy.

411. Lifshitz, Yehezkel. SHNEI MIKHTAVIM AMERIKANIIM 'AL ZEKHUYOT-HAMI'UTIM SHEL HAYEHUDIM BEMIZRAH-EIROPA [Two American letters on Jewish minority rights in Eastern Europe]. *Gal-Ed: On the Hist. of the Jews in Poland [Israel] 1975 (2): 340-352.* A 1927 exchange of letters between Morton W. Royse, a young sociologist, and Isaiah Bowman, director of the American Geographical Society, illuminated American attitudes toward the League of Nations' responsibilities regarding Jewish minority rights in Eastern Europe.

412. Likhten, Iosyf L. ARNOL'D MARGOLIN: IOHO ZHYTTIA I PRATSIA [Arnold Margolin: his life and work]. *Sučasnist [West Germany] 1977 (5): 68-73.* Traces the life of Ukrainian American Jew Arnold Margolin, his participation in the Ukrainian struggle for independence, 1917-20, and his work on Ukrainian-Jewish relations.

413. Lima, Robert. SEPHARDIC LEGACY. *Américas (Organization of Am. States) 1978 30(9): 2-8.* Discusses the Portuguese Sephardic Jews in the United States, beginning with their arrival in 1654 at the Dutch colony of New Amsterdam to escape persecution in Portugal.

414. Lindberg-Seyersted, Brita. A READING OF BERNARD MALAMUD'S *THE TENANTS*. *J. of Am. Studies [Great Britain] 1975 9(1): 85-102.* Reviews Malamud's *The Tenants* (New York: Farrar, Straus and Giroux, 1971) in which Malamud emphasizes that minorities merit patience and understanding as they try to overcome social and cultural inequality. 11 notes.

H. T. Lovin

415. Littell, Franklin H. UPROOTING ANTISEMITISM: A CALL TO CHRISTIANS. *J. of Church and State 1975 17(1): 15-24.* Christian anti-Semitism, rooted in the theological teaching that Jews are guilty of the crucifixion of Christ, has had social and political implications, exhibited notably in the Holocaust of World War II, as well as in the theology and historiography of such anti-Semitic liberals as Arnold Toynbee.

416. Lobenthal, Richard H. FINDINGS OF THE COMMITTEE OF THE MICHIGAN DEPARTMENT OF EDUCATION ON REVIEWING HISTORY TEXTBOOKS. *Michigan Jewish Hist. 1973 13(2): 19-21.* Examines the report of the Michigan Department of Education on the portrayal of Jews in elementary and secondary social studies textbooks. S

417. Loewenberg, Robert. THE THEFT OF LIBERALISM—A JEWISH PROBLEM. *Midstream 1977 23(5): 19-33.* The contradictions of modern Jewish liberalism put Jews at odds with reality and force them to choose between particularism and universalism or, more specifically, between Judaism and liberalism.

418. Losben, Andrea Finkelstein. NEWPORT'S JEWS AND THE AMERICAN REVOLUTION. *Rhode Island Jewish Hist. Notes 1976 7(2): 258-276.* Discusses activities of the Jews in Newport, Rhode Island, during the American Revolution, including political and economic support, as well as those who enlisted and fought, 1763-76.

419. Lubin, David. A LETTER ON ZIONISM. *Western States Jewish Hist. Q. 1973 5(2): 100-109.* David Lubin (1849-1920), a Sacramento Jewish merchant, in a 1918 letter, advocated the establishment of an industrial state for Jews in Palestine.

420. Luttwak, Edward N. THE DEFENSE BUDGET AND ISRAEL. *Commentary 1975 59(2): 27-35.* Discusses the dilemma of Jewish liberals and liberal Senators who support the existence of Israel but oppose defense spending in the United States.

421. Lynch, Joseph D. THE BANKER OF THE SOUTHLAND IN 1885. *Western States Jewish Hist. Q. 1977 9(3): 226-228.* The Farmers' and Merchants' Bank of Los Angeles was founded in 1868 with $200,000 in paid up capital. Under Mr. Isaias W. Hellman, the president and major stockholder, it grew to be the sixth largest in the state in volume of business. By avoiding speculation and investing only where growth and natural development were certain, the bank gained the confidence and esteem of the business community. Reprint of article in the *Los Angeles Herald* "Annual" issue of January 1885; photo.

B. S. Porter

422. Magnes, Judah L. and Frenkel, Lee K. CONDITION OF SAN FRAN-CISCO JEWRY FOLLOWING THE 1906 EARTHQUAKE-FIRE. *Western States Jewish Hist. Q. 1979 11(3): 239-242.* The authors were sent to San Francisco by the National Conference of Jewish Charities to ascertain the needs of the Jewish community after the 1906 earthquake. They investigated refugee camps and found that about 1,000 Jews were housed in tents and shacks with the rest of the populace, and were adequately fed in the camps. Another 200 families were taken care of in Oakland. On the advice of the Jewish Relief Committee, they reported to their agency headquarters that no immediate appeal for funds in behalf of San Francisco's Jewish community was necessary. Reprinted from the Fourth Biennial Session of the National Conference of Jewish Charities (New York, 1907), pp. 262-265.

B. S. Porter

423. Maibaum, Matthew. THE ENERGY CRISIS IN THE U.S.A.: FUEL TO PREJUDICE. *Patterns of Prejudice [Great Britain] 1974 8(1): 1-4.* Discusses the possible role the oil shortage may play in changing public opinion toward Jews in the United States in the 1970's, emphasizing the dangers of anti-Semitism.

424. Maller, Allen S. CLASS FACTORS IN THE JEWISH VOTE. *Jewish Social Studies 1977 39(1-2): 159-162.* A study of the mayoral campaign in Los Angeles, California, in 1969 between liberal black candidate Tom Bradley and conservative Sam Yorty indicates the extent to which class factors amid the Jewish voting population are beginning to divide Jews into ascertainable subgroups. Reform rabbis and spokesmen supported Bradley in public meetings as part of their liberal commitment while Orthodox rabbis threw their allegiance to the far more conservative Yorty. Although a majority of Los Angeles Jewish voters supported Bradley, the percentage of Bradley supporters in the most highly affluent Jewish neighborhoods was significantly higher than that in less prosperous Jewish areas. The influence of changing neighborhoods and the school desegregation issue suggests that although Jewish voting patterns are still unique,

various issues affecting the well-being and personal status of Jews are having their effect on voting behavior.   N. Lederer

425. Mann, Peggy. THE DENTIST AND THE BISHOP: "I KNEW THE MAN WAS A SATAN . .." *Present Tense 1974 1(4): 29-35.* Charles H. Kremer has tried to expose Rumanian (now US-based) Bishop Valerian Trifa's role in the murder of Jews during World War II.

426. Marcus, Jacob Rader. JEWS AND THE AMERICAN REVOLUTION: A BICENTENNIAL DOCUMENTARY. *Am. Jewish Arch. 1975 27(2): 103-276.* When the civil war which we call the American Revolution entered its military phase in 1775, it proved impossible for British North America's tiny Jewish community of perhaps 2,500 souls to remain aloof from the conflict. Most of them, for political or socio-economic reasons or a combination of the two, abandoned their loyalty to the British crown and attached themselves to the Revolutionary cause. When the United States won its independence in 1783, it seemed to the Jews that the world had begun again.   J

427. Mark, Yudel. MENDEL ELKIN (ZU ZEIN ZENTEN YAHRZEIT) [Mendel Elkin (on the occasion of his 10th anniversary)]. *Yivo Bleter 1973 44: 292-295.* Presents, on the anniversary of his death, highlights of the life of one of the founders of the Yivo Library—his manifold activities, assistance and advice to writers, immigrants, and poor, and his love for the theater. Based on personal recollection.   B. Klein

428. Marshutz, Siegfried G. HISTORY OF THE MOVEMENT TO ESTABLISH A JEWISH ORPHANS' HOME IN LOS ANGELES. *Western States Jewish Hist. Q. 1977 9(2): 155-160.* Los Angeles Lodge No. 487, Independent Order of B'nai B'rith, determined in 1907 to organize and maintain a home for orphaned and half-orphaned Jewish children, and for the temporary maintenance of destitute and abandoned Jewish children. The Stern home on Mission Road was leased for this purpose. Jewish merchants and citizens subscribed to the home's annual support. The Jewish Orphans' Home of Southern California was informally opened on 4 January 1909 with a capacity of 50 children. This institution today (1977) is known as the Vista Del Mar Child Care Service. Reprints article published in the *B'nai B'rith Messenge*, Los Angeles, 29 January 1909; 5 notes.   B. S. Porter

429. Mashberg, Michael. AMERICAN DIPLOMACY AND THE JEWISH REFUGEE, 1938-1939. *Yivo Ann. of Jewish Social Sci. 1974 (15): 339-365.* Discusses the American planning and participation in the Évian Conference dealing with the resettlement of German-Jewish refugees. The conference made it clear that the "Jew was a universal minority having no national representation or protection. Once a state revoked the protection of a hyphenated Jew, be he a German-Jew or an Austrian-Jew, he was isolated from the nation state system. . . . The Jewish refugee became a legal freak in the diplomacy of the nation-state." 52 notes.   R. J. Wechman

430. Mashberg, Michael. DOCUMENTS CONCERNING THE AMERICAN STATE DEPARTMENT AND THE STATELESS EUROPEAN JEWS, 1942-1944. *Jewish Social Studies 1977 39(1-2): 163-182.* A collection of documents from the papers of Franklin D. Roosevelt's wartime Secretary of the

Treasury, Henry M. Morgenthau, Jr., indicates the efforts of the Treasury Department to investigate and bring to the attention of the President the role of State Department officials in preventing any tangible efforts to rescue European Jewry from extermination at the hands of the Nazis. Treasury Department investigators, especially general counsel Randolph E. Paul, believed that the State Department prevented Jewish rescue through procrastination and failure to act, that it refused to work with private rescue agencies, that it prevented public disclosure of news about the exterminations, and that it covered up its role in regard to the Jewish situation. The actions of Morgenthau and his staff finally resulted in the creation of the War Refugee Board and efforts to retrieve refugees from the hands of the Nazis. Based on documents in the Franklin D. Roosevelt Library.

N. Lederer

431. Mashberg, Michael. PREJUDICE THAT MEANT DEATH: THE WEST AND THE HOLOCAUST. *Patterns of Prejudice [Great Britain] 1978 12(3): 19-32.* Examines social and scientific attitudes toward Jews, 1880's-1900's, and their effects on US immigration quotas in the 20th century and later, during World War II, on the lethargy displayed by the US government and other Allied governments as well as other Allied nations in organizing the rescue of European Jews.

432. Masilamoni, E. H. Leelavathi. THE FICTION OF JEWISH AMERICANS: AN INTERVIEW WITH LESLIE FIEDLER. *Southwest Rev. 1979 64(1): 44-59.* Literary critic and novelist Leslie Fiedler discusses forces in American society—anti-Semitism, ethnic identification, and religious differences—as they affect Jews, especially Jewish writers, 1970's.

433. Maslow, Will. JEWISH POLITICAL POWER: AN ASSESSMENT. *Am. Jewish Hist. Q. 1976 65(2): 349-362.* The proper assessment of Jewish political power or influence in the United States, aside from the voting pattern in areas of Jewish concentration, should include the following: a network of Jewish organizations, skilled professionals and dedicated laymen, an educated, affluent and committed membership, many political and governmental contracts, and concentration on three major issues (security of Israel, Arab boycott, and Soviet Jewry). 30 notes.

F. Rosenthal

434. Maslow, Will. THE STRUGGLE AGAINST THE ARAB BOYCOTT: A CASE HISTORY. *Midstream 1977 23(7): 11-26.* The American Jewish Committee, the American Jewish Congress, and the Anti-Defamation League of B'nai B'rith have tried during 1975-77 to effect legislation against the Arab boycott of Israel.

435. Maurer, Marvin. QUAKERS IN POLITICS: ISRAEL, P.L.O. AND SOCIAL REVOLUTION. *Midstream 1977 23(9): 36-44.* The American Friends Service Committee sponsored a conference in Chevy Chase, Maryland, in February 1977 on "New Imperatives for Israeli-Palestinian Peace" at which the Religious Society of Friends showed a definite bias toward the Palestinians, comparing today's Palestinians to holocaust victims and criticizing Israel for alleged behavior of a kind which the Society has apparently ignored among groups and nations whom it considers its "clients."

436. Maydell, Bodo von. JUEDISCH-KABBALISTISCHE ELEMENTE IN DER RELIGIOESEN GESELLSCHAFT DER FREUNDE (QUAEKER) [Jewish-cabalistic elements in the religious Society of Friends (Quakers)]. *Judaica [Switzerland] 1973 29(3): 97-98.* Cabalistic Jews and Quakers share some basic beliefs, including the concept of the "inner light," the spark of the divine in every human being, and a distrust of hard and fast dogmas.

437. Mayer, Egon. GAPS BETWEEN GENERATIONS OF ORTHODOX JEWS IN BORO PARK, BROOKLYN, N.Y. *Jewish Social Studies 1977 39(1-2): 93-104.* The generation gap between Jewish parents and children takes on a unique form in the Orthodox Jewish neighborhood of Boro Park. The generations in Boro Park exhibit definite continuities in economic and cultural success from parents to children. However, while the children of Orthodox parents have continued the successful patterns of their parents and have been dependent in their success on that of their elders, tensions generated by status conflict have evolved. Children claim to be more Orthodox than their parents by asserting more sophisticated and deeper understanding of Orthodox ritual and practice. The economic successes of the parents are countered by their children's claims to academic and professional gains. Although both parents and children surround themselves with material evidences of success, the generations display different tastes in the acquisition of such objects. Largely based on survey research.   N. Lederer

438. Mayo, Louise Abbie. HERMAN MELVILLE, THE JEW AND JUDAISM. *Am. Jewish Arch. 1976 28(2): 172-179.* Melville is the only major American writer in the nineteenth century to include a serious consideration of Jews and Judaism in one of his works—*Clarel.*   J

439. McKillop, Lucille. THE TOURO INFLUENCE—WASHINGTON'S SPIRIT PREVAILS. *Rhode Island Jewish Hist. Notes 1974 6(4): 614-628.* An address on religious liberty made at the Touro Synagogue, Newport, Rhode Island to commemorate an exchange of letters in 1790 between Moses Seixas, President of the Newport Congregation, and George Washington.   S

440. McQuaid, Kim. AN AMERICAN OWENITE: EDWARD A. FILENE AND THE PARAMETERS OF INDUSTRIAL REFORM, 1890-1937. *Am. J. of Econ. and Sociol. 1976 35(1): 77-94.* Edward A. Filene introduced industrial democracy in his Boston department store in 1891. He was deposed from the presidency of the store in 1928. His experiment ceased and thereafter he was denied any effective authority. He also directed his liberal energies to local, state, and national affairs such as his ambitious plan of urban reform, "Boston 1915." Such efforts were equally unsuccessful. He was a spokesman for the New Capitalism and a supporter of the New Deal, but in both movements his integrity isolated him from his peers. His enduring contributions were the cooperative and credit union movements.   P. Travis

441. Medovy, Harry. THE EARLY JEWISH PHYSICIANS IN MANITOBA. *Tr. of the Hist. and Sci. Soc. of Manitoba 1972/73 Series 3(29): 23-39.* Discusses the development of medical practice among Jewish doctors in Manitoba. Thirteen doctors are described in biographical sketches which include anecdotal material. These were men who "helped the community come of age."   J. A. Casada

442. Mendelsohn, Ezra. THE RUSSIAN ROOTS OF THE AMERICAN JEWISH LABOR MOVEMENT. *Yivo Ann. of Jewish Social Sci. 1976 (16): 150-177.* The large emigration of Russian Jews to the United States following the pogroms of 1881-82 was mainly a movement of poor artisans and traders who came looking for an opportunity to work, grow prosperous, and live without fear. In addition, there were Russian Jewish intellectuals who felt themselves mentally superior to the masses. From the Russian Jewish intellectuals grew the Jewish US labor movement. 74 notes.   R. J. Wechman

443. Mergen, Bernard. "ANOTHER GREAT PRIZE": THE JEWISH LABOR MOVEMENT IN THE CONTEXT OF AMERICAN LABOR HISTORY. *Yivo Ann. of Jewish Social Sci. 1976 (16): 394-423.* Emphasizes the uniqueness of the American Jewish labor movement within the context of American labor history. Shows the various relationships between the Jewish labor movement and the American labor movement, demonstrating similarities, differences, and influences.   R. J. Wechman

444. Merowitz, Morton J. MAX LILIENTHAL (1814-1882)—JEWISH EDUCATOR IN NINETEENTH CENTURY AMERICA. *Yivo Ann. of Jewish Social Sci. 1974 (15): 46-65.* Discusses Rabbi Max Lilienthal's educational endeavors, including his establishment of a boarding school, his directorship of the Noyoth Institute, and his work with the Mound St. Temple Sabbath School. Also stressed was Dr. Lilienthal's founding of the first Jewish children's magazine in America, *The Hebrew Sabbath School Visitor*, and his starting of the confirmation of boys and girls in America. 107 notes.   R. J. Wechman

445. Meshcheryakov, V. AT THE SERVICE OF US REACTION. *Internat. Affairs [USSR] 1975 (2): 90-95.* Zionism is an integral aspect of American reactional foreign policy. Zionists have a broad network of influential organizations in the United States with strong ties to government and the news media. These organizations actively spread Zionist propaganda. 24 notes.
                                                      D. K. McQuilkin

446. Mesmer, Joseph. SOME OF MY LOS ANGELES JEWISH NEIGHBORS. *Western States Jewish Hist. Q. 1975 7(3): 191-199.* Personal accounts by the author (1855-1947), written in the 1930's about several of his close friends in Los Angeles. He wrote about his relationships with Maurice Kremer (1824-1907) and his wife Matilda, the daughter of Rabbi Joseph Newmark; Eugene Meyer (1842-1925) and his wife Harriet, youngest daughter of Rabbi Newmark; Ephraim Greenbaum; and Isaiah M. Hellman. In the 1870's, Rabbi and Mrs. Newmark lived next door to the author. 18 notes.   R. A. Garfinkle

447. Meyer, Eugene and Stern, Norton B. MY EARLY YEARS. *Western States Jewish Hist. Q. 1973 5(2): 87-99.* Meyer (1842-1925), a leading Jew of Los Angeles, provides a personal account of his boyhood in France, and his stay in San Francisco in 1859-60.

448. Meyer, Michael A. THE HEBREW UNION COLLEGE—ITS FIRST YEARS. *Cincinnati Hist. Soc. Bull. 1975 33(1): 7-25.* Discusses the activities of Rabbi Isaac Mayer Wise as founder of the Hebrew Union College, America's first rabbinical seminary, in Cincinnati, Ohio, 1817-90's, including students' curricula in Jewish history.

449.   Meyer, Michael A.   LETTERS OF ISAAC MAYER WISE TO JOSEPH
STOLZ.   *Michael: On the Hist. of the Jews in the Diaspora [Israel] 1975 3:
48-58.* Publishes 10 letters written during 1882-1900 by Rabbi Isaac Mayer Wise
to Joseph Stolz, one of the early graduates of the rabbinical seminary Wise
founded, Hebrew Union College. The letters reveal aspects of a poorly documented area of Wise's activities: the placement and advancement of HUC graduates in American congregations. The letters reflect Wise's fatherly concern for
Stolz, as well as his hard-headed approach to rabbinical salaries and prerogatives,
and relations with better-established rabbis. Primary and secondary sources; 28
notes.   T. Sassoon

450.   Michel, Sonya.   CHILDREN, INSTITUTIONS, AND COMMUNITY:
THE JEWISH ORPHANAGE OF RHODE ISLAND, 1909-1942.   *Rhode
Island Jewish Hist. Notes 1977 7(3): 385-400.* Although the community favored
foster parents and one-to-one relations, Jews in Rhode Island founded an orphanage in 1909 which functioned well until 1942, when federal funds were made
available to dependent children.

451.   Michel, Sonya.   FAMILY AND COMMUNITY NETWORKS
AMONG RHODE ISLAND JEWS: A STUDY BASED ON ORAL HISTO-
RIES.   *Rhode Island Jewish Hist. Notes 1978 7(4): 513-533.* These individual
accounts of the lives of American Jews date as far back as 1882; based on
interviews of residents of the Jewish Home for the Aged of Rhode Island, in
Providence, in 1978.

452.   Michelman, Irving S.   A BANKER IN THE NEW DEAL: JAMES P.
WARBURG.   *Rev. Int. d'Hist. de la Banque [Italy] 1974 8: 35-59.* James P.
Warburg, scion of one of the great German Jewish banking houses in the United
States, was one of the few Wall Streeters to become part of the FDR administration. Drawn into the frantic preparations to reopen the banks in March 1933,
Warburg became a delegate to the World Economic Conference in London, only
to resign shortly after his appointment. Roosevelt made it clear that domestic
monetary policy could not be compromised by international agreements. Roose-
velt's decision to take the United States off the gold standard and to accept
legislation which gave him far-reaching power to increase the money supply led
Warburg to break with the administration. A successful polemicist and writer,
Warburg became associated with the anti-New Deal faction and the Liberty
League. Secondary sources; 24 notes.   D. McGinnis

453.   Miller, Sally M.   FROM SWEATSHOP WORKER TO LABOR LEA-
DER: THERESA MALKIEL, A CASE STUDY.   *Am. Jewish Hist. 1978 68(2):
189-205.* Theresa Serber Malkiel (1874-1949) is an example of a female Jewish
leader in the labor movement and in a minor political party (Socialist Labor
Party, and later the Socialist Party of America). On the Women's National
Committee of the Socialist Party in the decade before 1914 she gave her greatest
attention to women and the party, unionization of women workers, foreign-born
women, woman suffrage, and the party commitment to sexual equality. Her most
lasting accomplishment was the establishment of the Brooklyn Adult Students
Association. 20 notes.   F. Rosenthal

454. Mintz, Jacqueline A. THE MYTH OF THE JEWISH MOTHER IN THREE JEWISH, AMERICAN, FEMALE WRITERS. *Centennial Rev. 1978 22(3): 346-353.* Despite the prevalence of the "Molly Goldberg" caricature, the most damaging stereotype of the Jewish mother has been that of the source of ideal mother love. Tillie Olsen, Anzia Yezierska, and Susan Fromberg Schaeffer have dealt with this myth and the terrible burdens it placed on women who were expected to live up to its demands of total involvement with family and endless, selfless giving and nurturing. In showing the pernicious side of the myth, these writers contribute to its death, to the benefit of all caught up in it.

T. L. Powers

455. Moltmann, Günter. DIE AMBIVALENZ DES AMERIKANISCH-SCHWEIZERISCHEN VERTRAGES VON 1850/1855 [The ambivalence of the American-Swiss treaty of 1850-55]. *Schweizerische Zeitschrift für Geschichte [Switzerland] 1976 26(1-2): 100-133.* In 1850 the United States and Switzerland signed a "Convention of Friendship, Commerce and Extradition." It was not ratified until 1855. The treaty came under attack because it contained a clause that made the treatment of citizens subject to existing laws. Because some Swiss cantons still discriminated against non-Christians, US Jews were hostile to the treaty and remained so even after its ratification. The motives of the originator of the treaty, A. Dudley Mann, nonetheless had been truly liberal. Inspired by the French General Louis Cavaignac, Special Agent Mann prevailed upon Washington to make a treaty with the Helvetic sister republic to demonstrate to the reactionary powers of Europe that America supported republican ideals. Sheds new light on the Cavaignac-Mann role. 62 notes.

H. K. Meier

456. Mongerman, Freda. PIONEERS IN SOCIAL SERVICE: THE JEWISH COMMITTEE FOR PERSONAL SERVICE IN STATE INSTITUTIONS IN THE 1920'S. *Western States Jewish Hist. Q. 1974 6(2): 83-99.* Studies the Jewish Committee for Personal Service in State Institutions founded in 1920 by Rabbi Martin A. Meyer. The purpose of this group was to help Jews who were in, or had been in, California mental hospitals and prisons. Elsie Shirpser, Executive Secretary of the JCPSSI for 24 years, pioneered the use of psychiatric social histories of the inmates. Primary and secondary sources; 32 notes.

R. A. Garfinkle

457. Moonman, Jane; Buckley, Berenice; and Lacks, Roslyn. "GUESS WHO'S COMING TO DINNER?" *Present Tense 1974 1(2): 11-15.* Describes Jewish intermarriage in Great Britain, Australia and the United States. S

458. Moore, Deborah Dash. FROM KEHILLAH TO FEDERATION: THE COMMUNAL FUNCTIONS OF FEDERATED PHILANTHROPY IN NEW YORK CITY, 1917-1933. *Am. Jewish Hist. 1978 68(2): 131-146.* The Federation for the Support of Jewish Philanthropic Societies as an alternative communal structure to that of the Kehillah with its relgious and almost obligatory nuances began in New York City in 1917. A fund raising apparatus that recognized class differences but stressed mass participation and emphasized nonsectarianism remained the framework for a minimal community into the 1930's. Samson Benderly and other Federation leaders recognized early that potentially it could be transformed into a viable, broad, and truly Jewish community. 24 notes.

F. Rosenthal

459. Morgan, David T. JUDAISM IN EIGHTEENTH-CENTURY GEORGIA. *Georgia Hist. Q. 1974 58(1): 41-54.* Traces the development of Judaism in Georgia until it achieved a permanent institutional form. The first group of Jewish immigrants met official opposition, but they freely observed their religion and remained until the War of Jenkins' Ear brought their departure. A second group arrived in 1762; they were forced out during the American Revolution. They returned after the peace. The state incorporated a Jewish congregation in 1790, evidence that religious freedom had become a reality. 34 notes.

D. L. Smith

460. Morgan, David T. THE SHEFTALLS OF SAVANNAH. *Am. Jewish Hist. Q. 1973 62(4): 348-361.* Benjamin Sheftall arrived in Savannah, Georgia, in 1733. The Sheftall Papers indicate that the family acquired real estate throughout the state before the Revolution. Mordecei and Levi Sheftall suffered imprisonment, banishment, and loss of livelihood for espousing the American cause when the British captured Savannah in 1778. Although the government did not reimburse the Sheftalls for losses suffered, they prospered again after 1790 and remained active in the affairs of Savannah's Jewish community. The Sheftall Papers, Keith Reid Collection, University of Georgia; 39 notes.

F. Rosenthal

461. Morris, Jeffrey B. THE AMERICAN JEWISH JUDGE: AN APPRAISAL ON THE OCCASION OF THE BICENTENNIAL. *Jewish Social Studies 1976 38(3-4): 195-223.* Jews have played an interesting and important role as members of the judiciary in American history. As judges they have displayed significant differences in their behavior and legal attitudes but have also revealed certain similarities. Among the characteristics common to many Jewish members of the judiciary are a realization of the need for the law to conform to contemporary society, an awareness of the need to break away from mechanical jurisprudence, and a sensitivity to civil liberties and social justice. The marked Jewish affinity for the law as well as the concern for social justice may have its roots in Jewish practice and belief.

N. Lederer

462. Mosbacker, George. PRESIDENT'S REPORT, FEDERATION OF JEWISH CHARITIES, LOS ANGELES, 1917. *Western States Jewish Hist. Q. 1978 11(1): 91-94.* Dora Berres, a social worker, was hired to coordinate the activities of charitable organizations of the Federation of Jewish Charities (FJC). Many families were made self-supporting by business concerns that hired applicants for employment. The Kaspare Cohn Hospital, the several orphans' homes, and the benevolent societies helped many in the community. The FJC began the year 1916 with a large funding deficit which was reduced; however, there was a continuing need for increased subscriptions. Reprinted from *B'nai B'rith Messenger,* Los Angeles, 16 February 1917.

B. S. Porter

463. Moshe, Meir. THE YOM KIPPUR WAR IN MIDDLE AMERICA. *Midstream 1974 20(6): 74-79.* Comments on public opinion about the 1973 Arab-Israeli War in a Middle American university town, where the majority of Jews are assimilated.

S

464. Mosk, Stanley. A MAJORITY OF THE CALIFORNIA SUPREME COURT. *Western States Jewish Hist. Q. 1976 8(3): 224-231.* For three months in 1852, the three-member California Supreme Court had two Jews on the bench. Henry A. Lyons (1809-72) was Chief Justice and Solomon Heydenfeldt (1816-90) was elected to the bench that year. Lyons was a poor justice who spent little time on court matters and wrote few opinions. Heydenfeldt was a brilliant legal scholar who wrote 45 opinions during his five years on the bench. Both men were from the South and were strong southern sympathizers during the Civil War. They both left large estates. 2 photos.   R. A. Garfinkle

465. Myers, Carmel. FILM INDUSTRY RECOLLECTIONS. *Western States Jewish Hist. Q. 1976 8(2): 126-135.* An early movie star tells how she got started in films. Her father was Rabbi Isidore Myers (1856-1922). Rabbi Myers was asked by film director David Wark Griffith to be a consultant for his film *Intolerance*. As payment for his services, Rabbi Myers' daughter was allowed to try out for a movie part in Griffith's next film. She got a part and that started her career in which she played leading roles opposite such male stars as Rudolph Valentino, Douglas Fairbanks, Jr., John Gilbert, Lew Cody, and William Haines. She was also very active in Jewish community affairs in Los Angeles. Based on personal recollection; 4 photos, 12 notes.   R. A. Garfinkle

466. Narell, Irena Penzil. BERNHARD MARKS: RETAILER, MINER, EDUCATOR, AND LAND DEVELOPER. *Western States Jewish Hist. Q. 1975 8(1): 26-38.* In 1852, Bernhard Marks (1832-1913) arrived in California from Providence, Rhode Island. He worked at various jobs and the got into gold mining. He became a partner in several mines, but met with little success. In 1859, he married Cornelia D. Barlow, a schoolteacher. In 1860, they opened a private school in Columbia. During 1862-72, he was principal of Lincoln Grammar School, San Francisco. In 1874, he established a raisin-growing colony in Fresno County. He failed at ranching, farming, and real estate development. 37 notes.   R. A. Garfinkle

467. Naske, Claus-M. JEWISH IMMIGRATION AND ALASKAN ECONOMIC DEVELOPMENT: A STUDY IN FUTILITY. *Western States Jewish Hist. Q. 1976 8(2): 139-157.* During the 1930's when Nazi Germany was persecuting Jews, the United States provided little aid to help the Jews to emigrate. No area in the United States wanted a large group of Jewish immigrants. It was proposed that they be settled in Alaska, but the leaders in Alaska fought all efforts to enact special federal legislation to allow the refugees to settle there, stating that Alaska could not support a mass immigration at that time. The 1940 King-Havenner bill proposed that public purpose corporations be set up to establish colonies in Alaska for the refugees if Congress passed the necessary laws, but the bill never passed and by then it was too late to save the Jews. Based on primary sources; 46 notes.   R. A. Garfinkle

468. Neu, Irene D. THE JEWISH BUSINESSWOMAN IN AMERICA. *Am. Jewish Hist. Q. 1976 66(1): 137-154.* Provides thumbnail sketches of Jewish businesswomen in America from colonial days to the present. The scarcity of such individuals in the past is a reflection of the social mores of the 19th century which saw women as homemakers and at their best in communal and philanthropic activities. These patterns are now changing. 53 notes.   F. Rosenthal

469. Neusner, Jacob. DEPARTMENTS OF RELIGIOUS STUDIES AND CONTEMPORARY JEWISH STUDIES. *Am. Jewish Hist. Q. 1974 63(4): 356-360.* Although much material of contemporary Jewish studies is not religious in nature, it is often placed in religious studies departments. One of nine related articles in this issue.   S

470. Neusner, Jacob. THE STUDY OF RELIGION AS THE STUDY OF TRADITION: JUDAISM. *Hist. of Religions 1975 14(3): 191-206.* Defines tradition as "something handed on from the past which is made contemporary and transmitted because of its intense contemporaneity." Stresses the importance of literary and legal sources for proper understanding of Jewish tradition. Draws distinctions between the aims and methods of historians of religion and regular historians. Contribution to a Symposium on Methodology and World Religions at the University of Iowa; 8 notes.   T. L. Auffenberg

471. Newman, Phyllis. A SAN BERNARDINO CENTENNIAL. *Western States Jewish Hist. Q. 1975 7(4): 303-307.* On 2 May 1875, Paradise Lodge No. 237 of the Independent Order of B'nai B'rith was established in San Bernardino, California, and was granted its charter by Isidor N. Choynski, president of the Grand Lodge of B'nai B'rith, District No. 4. The Paradise Lodge was the first B'nai B'rith lodge in southern California. In 1883, it acquired a Jewish cemetery. The lodge is still active. 2 photos, 8 notes.   R. A. Garfinkle

472. Newman, William M. and Halvorson, Peter L. AMERICAN JEWS: PATTERNS OF GEOGRAPHIC DISTRIBUTION AND CHANGE, 1952-1971. *J. for the Sci. Study of Religion 1979 18(2): 183-193.* Also discusses the effects of geographic change on patterns of American religious pluralism.

473. Newmark, Abraham. A ST. LOUIS VISITOR VIEWS SOUTHERN CALIFORNIA IN 1883. *Western States Jewish Hist. Q. 1978 10(3): 212-215.* Abraham Newmark visited Los Angeles on the occasion of the marriage of a close relative. Newmark wrote several letters to his wife and daughters about the beauty of the city, the mildness of the climate, and the lushness and variety of the agricultural products. Reprints two letters written in 1883; photo, 17 notes.   B. S. Porter

474. Newmark, Helen. A NINETEENTH CENTURY MEMOIR. *Western States Jewish Hist. Q. 1974 6(3): 204-218.* Autobiography of Helen Newmark (1840-1911), written in 1900. Immigrating in 1855 from Posen, Poland, Newmark gives a good account of life in San Francisco in the latter half of the 19th century. 3 photos, 15 notes.   R. A. Garfinkle

475. Newmark, Rosa. A LETTER FROM MOTHER TO DAUGHTER— LOS ANGELES TO NEW YORK, 1867. *Western States Jewish Hist. Q. 1973 5(4): 274-284.* Mrs. Joseph Newmark, née Rosa Levy, describes the Jewish marriage celebration, and attendant social customs, of her daughter, Harriet, to Eugene Meyer in Los Angeles.

476. Nieto, Jacob. A 1906 SAN FRANCISCO PROTEST AND APPEAL. *Western States Jewish Hist. Q. 1977 9(3): 246-250.* Rabbi Jacob Nieto criticized the way relief money was distributed to casualties of the San Francisco earthquake of 18 April 1906. After the immediate needs for food, clothing, and shelter

had been cared for, financial aid should have been given with a view to reestablishing commercial activities and religious institutions. Many who suffered great losses were too proud to seek aid, and these cases should have been sought out and ministered to in a way that would maintain their privacy and dignity. Reprint of article in *The Jewish Times and Observer,* San Francisco, 9 November 1906, pp. 8-9.   B. S. Porter

477. Osipova, N. V. PROIZRAIL'SKAIA KOALITSIIA V AMERIKAN-SKOM KONGRESSE, [The pro-Israeli lobby in the American Congress]. *Voprosy Istorii [USSR] 1974 (6): 78-86.* Taking the activity of US Congress as an example, the author examines the influence exerted by American Zionists on the Administration's Middle East policy. The article describes in detail the forms and methods employed by the Zionists to exert pressure on congressmen. Analyzing the composition of this coalition, the author makes a point of stressing that it consists in the main of the representatives of military-industrial circles which are resolutely opposed to any relaxation of international tension.   J

478. Oxman, Daniel K. CALIFORNIA REACTIONS TO THE LEO FRANK CASE. *Western States Jewish Hist. Q. 1978 10(3): 216-224.* In August 1913, Leo Frank, a Jewish factory superintendent in Atlanta, Georgia, was tried and convicted of murdering a 14-year-old girl. Despite some indication of improper legal procedures, the verdict was upheld after several appeals. The case received nationwide publicity, resulting in thousands of letters and petitions to Georgia's governor. In June 1915, the governor commuted the death sentence to life imprisonment, but on 17 August 1915, a vigilante group removed Frank from prison and lynched him. Throughout the trial and period of appeals, and after the lynching, California newspapers accused Georgia officials and common citizens of moral injustice. Contemporary newspapers and secondary works; 34 notes.   B. S. Porter

479. Panitz, Esther. LOUIS DEMBITZ BRANDEIS AND THE CLEVELAND CONFERENCE. *Am. Jewish Hist. Q. 1975 65(2): 140-162.* The culmination of a prolonged controversy between European and American Zionist leaders occurred at the 1921 Cleveland Conference of the Zionist Organization of America. This contest of wills and personalities over attitudes and techniques to adopt in the achievement of a common goal ultimately pitted Louis Brandeis against Chaim Weizmann. Since the final vote went against him, Brandeis and Judge Julian Mack of Chicago resigned from their Zionist offices but continued to work for the economic development of Palestine's Jewish colonists.
                                                        T. Rosenthal

480. Papanek, Miriam Lewin. PSYCHOLOGICAL ASPECTS OF MINORITY GROUP MEMBERSHIP: THE CONCEPTS OF KURT LEWIN. *Jewish Social Studies 1974 36(1): 72-79.* Lewin's conceptions about Jews as a minority group can be applied to other minority groups for social psychological study. Based on primary and secondary sources in English; 28 notes.
                                                        P. E. Schoenberg

481. Papermaster, Isadore. A HISTORY OF NORTH DAKOTA JEWRY AND THEIR PIONEER RABBI. *Western States Jewish Hist. Q. 1977 10(1): 74-89; 1978 10(2): 170-184, (3): 266-283.* Part I. Rabbi Benjamin Papermaster

was born in Lithuania in 1860. He agreed to come to America in 1890 to serve a party of immigrants as its religious leader and teacher. He settled in Grand Forks, North Dakota, amid a growing congregation of Jews from the Ukraine, Rumania, Poland, and Germany. Most of the Jews at that time were peddlers who mortgaged their houses and wagons to build the first synagogue. Rabbi Papermaster was enthusiastic about America; his letters to his family in Lithuania brought many relatives to join him. Grand Forks was considered a boom town because of the building of the Great Northern Railway. The influx of eastern capital helped the development of Jewish merchants. Based on personal experience and family records; 2 photos, 6 notes. Part II. Until the turn of the century, Rabbi Papermaster of Grand Forks was the only rabbi serving Jews in all of North Dakota and western Minnesota. Jewish families who started as peddlers became prosperous enough to move out to towns and villages where they opened small shops and stores. Other families followed the Great Northern Railway along its branch lines toward the Canadian border. In Grand Forks, the Jewish community established a modern Hebrew school, a Ladies' Aid Society, and a burial society. 2 photos, 11 notes. Part III. The city of Grand Forks, at the urging of Rabbi Papermaster, acquired a sanitary meat slaughtering facility with a special department for kosher beef. Rabbi Papermaster maintained an active interest in local politics, generally favoring the Republican Party but supporting Democrats when he knew them to be good men. Although a member of a Zionist organization, he worried about the antireligious character of the modern movement. During World War I he urged Jewish youths to their patriotic duty of joining the American armed forces. Rabbi Papermaster died on 24 September 1934. 3 photos, 14 notes.   B. S. Porter

482. Parzen, Herbert.   THE ENLARGEMENT OF THE JEWISH AGENCY FOR PALESTINE: 1923-1929 A HOPE—HAMSTRUNG. *Jewish Social Studies 1977 39(1-2): 129-158.* The confirmation of the World Zionist Organization as the Jewish Agency for Palestine created serious dissension in Jewish ranks, especially with regard to the positions of European Zionists led by Chaim Weizmann and the governing board of the Zionist Organization of America headed by Louis D. Brandeis. Distrust between these two groups was exacerbated by the distrust of Zionists in general exhibited by the non-Zionist American Jews, perhaps best represented by the position of Louis Marshall, president of the American Jewish Committee, who felt that the Zionists desired complete control over Palestine developments through the use of monetary contributions by non-Zionists. The terrific infighting of these various groups colored the deliberations of various international convocations held during the 1920's to discuss approaches to the Palestine situation. The creation in 1929 of an enlarged Jewish Agency including non-Zionists did not fulfill expectations for any group.
                                                                      N. Lederer

483. Parzen, Herbert.   LOUIS MARSHALL, THE ZIONIST ORGANIZATION IN AMERICA, AND THE FOUNDING OF THE JEWISH AGENCY. *Michael: On the Hist. of the Jews in the Diaspora [Israel] 1975 3: 226-253.* In 1920 the Zionist movement split over the launching of the Keren Hayesod fund for the development of Jewish Palestine. Louis D. Brandeis and his supporters withdrew from Zionist leadership, while Louis Lipsky (1876-1963) led the US Zionists who backed Chaim Weizmann's alliance with prominent non-Zionist

American Jews such as Louis Marshall (1856-1929). In 1924 a strengthened Jewish agency for Palestine assumed control of the fund, and had to deal with "Palestine Securities", a rival investment scheme, and the Crimea colonization program, then being advocated for Russian Jews. A memorandum prepared by Meyer W. Weisgal in 1925 concerning the "Understanding between Mr. Marshall and the Zionist Organization" is reproduced. 22 notes, appendix.

T. Sassoon/S

484. Parzen, Herbert. THE PURGE OF THE DISSIDENTS, HEBREW UNION COLLEGE AND ZIONISM, 1903-1907. *Jewish Social Studies 1975 37(3-4): 291-322.* The assumption of the presidency of this Reform Judaism college in Cincinnati by Dr. Kaufmann Kohler in the fall of 1903 led to the expulsion of its Zionist faculty. Kaufmann, a vehement assimilationist and anti-Zionist, paid only lip service to academic freedom as he moved to curb pro-Zionist utterances and writings by Caspar Levias, Max L. Margolis, and Max Schloessinger. His success in purging the faculty of these individuals met with the general approval of the Reform Judaism constituency. Includes a letter from Max L. Margolis explaining his position to Rabbi Clarke S. Levi. Primary and secondary sources.

N. Lederer

485. Passow, Isidore David. SHMUEL NIGER'S IDEAS ON BUILDING A JEWISH COMMUNITY IN THE UNITED STATES, 1920-1933. *Yivo Ann. of Jewish Social Sci. 1974 (15): 188-203.* Shmuel Niger was appalled by the East European Jewish immigrant's cultural stultification, urging Jews to retain their culture. The Jew in America should become more conscious of the heritage of East European Jewry.

R. J. Wechman

486. Petrusak, Frank and Steinert, Steven. THE JEWS OF CHARLESTON: SOME OLD WINE IN NEW BOTTLES. *Jewish Social Studies 1976 38(3-4): 337-346.* An analysis of survey data indicates that Jewry in Charleston, South Carolina, constitutes a well-defined, highly structured, nonassimilated ethnic group. The Jewish community retains its distinctiveness as a separate entity from the majority population despite great pressures to assimilate. The community has considerable self-identification, and the synagogue and the state of Israel play important roles as ethnic referents. Politically the Charleston Jews are strongly Democratic and have a social welfare and liberal orientation. Primary sources.

N. Lederer

487. Petuchowski, Jakob J. ABRAHAM GEIGER AND SAMUEL HOLDHEIM: THEIR DIFFERENCES IN GERMANY AND REPERCUSSIONS IN AMERICA. *Leo Baeck Inst. Year Book [Great Britain] 1977 22: 139-160.* In the emergence of a 19th-century German Reform Jewish ideology Abraham Geiger (1810-74) and Samuel Holdheim (1806-60) were dialectic opposites, with Geiger representing the right, traditionalist and Holdheim the left, modernist wing of the movement: evolutionary change versus a revolutionary break with the past. When translated to the United States by German-Jewish immigrants, this dichotomy was represented by Isaac Mayer Wise (1819-1900) and David Einhorn (1809-97). To this day the basic question remains: whether Reform Judaism is predicted on organic growth, i.e. on evolution, or whether it stands for revolution, a break with tradition. 79 notes.

F. Rosenthal

488.   Pierce, Lorraine E.   THE JEWISH SETTLEMENT ON ST. PAUL'S
LOWER WEST SIDE.   *Am. Jewish Arch. 1976 28(2): 143-161.* Much of what
is known about life on the Lower West Side of St. Paul, Minn., between the late
1800's and 1920—when the neighborhood was for the most part, peopled by
Jewish immigrants from Eastern Europe—"suggest[s] parallels with New York's
Lower East Side."   J

489.   Pinsker, Sanford.   PIETY AS COMMUNITY: THE HASIDIC VIEW.
Social Res. 1975 42(2): 230-246. Discusses the life, philosophy, and attitudes of
Hasidic Jews in the United States, speculating on whether the traditional Jewish
community is currently disintegrating.

490.   Pinsker, Sanford.   SAUL BELLOW'S CRANKY HISTORIANS.
Hist. Reflections [Canada] 1976 3(2): 35-47. Saul Bellow's most recent fiction is
dominated by the protagonist-as-historian, rather than by the traditional concerns of "historical novels." History reflects individual sensibilities and mirrors
that which must be synthesized for the culture's good, while, simultaneously, it
transcends the heart's deepest needs. The embattled "historians" of *Herzog*
(1964), *Mr. Sammler's Planet* (1970), and *Humboldt's Gift* (1975), suggest something of what a vision of history might mean to a contemporary novelist.
                                                                                    P. Travis

491.   Pinsky, Mark.   ASSIMILATED IN MILLTOWN.   *Present Tense 1978
5(3): 35-39.* Studies the socioeconomic patterns of several Jewish families in
"Milltown" (not the real name), an average-sized city in the American South,
from the 1890's to the present, as representative of the individual goals and
attitudes of southern Jews.

492.   Pitterman, Marvin and Schiavo, Bartholomew.   HAKHAM RAPHAEL
HAIM ISAAC CARIGAL: SHALIAH OF HEBRON AND RABBI OF NEW-
PORT, 5533 (1773).   *Rhode Island Jewish Hist. Notes 1974 6(4): 587-603.*
Biographical sketch of Hakham Raphael Haim Isaac Carigal's career as rabbi of
Newport, Rhode Island (1773), and his contribution to the community's culture
and history.   S

493.   Podet, Allen H.   ANTI-ZIONISM IN A KEY U.S. DIPLOMAT: LOY
HENDERSON AT THE END OF WORLD WAR II.   *Am. Jewish Arch. 1978
30(2): 155-187.* Describes Loy Henderson as the "single diplomat most centrally
involved in questions of Zionism, of Palestine, and of the world Jewish movement
that centered on these issues," at the end of World War II. The case of Loy
Henderson must be seen as central to any understanding and evaluation of State
Department policy during this important and controversial period leading to the
creation of Israel.   J

494.   Poliakov, Léon.   RÉFLEXIONS SUR "HOLOCAUSTE"   [Reflections
on "Holocaust"].   *Études [France] 1979 350(6): 759-765.* Analyzes the factors in
present day Western society which contributed to the overwhelming emotional
effect of the television film "Holocaust" on its viewers.

495.   Polishook, Sheila Stern.   THE AMERICAN FEDERATION OF LA-
BOR, ZIONISM, AND THE FIRST WORLD WAR.   *Am. Jewish Hist. Q.
1976 65(3): 228-244.* The period of World War I brought with it recognition of

organized labor as an essential element in the nation's development, whose support the Wilson administration sought and needed. Thus, even though the AFL leadership readily accepted the principle of national self-determination, its endorsement of a Jewish national state in Palestine came as a surprise which Samuel Gompers was able to push through against vociferous opposition by the pacifist and socialist spokesmen of the ILGWU. Labor's commitment to a Jewish homeland has strengthened over the years. 39 notes.   F. Rosenthal

496. Polos, Nicholas C. BLACK ANTI-SEMITISM IN TWENTIETH-CENTURY AMERICA: HISTORICAL MYTH OR REALITY? *Am. Jewish Arch. 1975 27(1): 8-31.*

497. Popkin, Richard H. MOSES MENDELSSOHN AND FRANCISCO DE MIRANDA. *Jewish Social Studies 1978 40(1): 41-48.* Latin American revolutionary Francisco de Miranda visited Moses Mendelssohn and other prominent Jewish intellectuals in Berlin in 1785. *Journey to Prussia* records the events of this visit. Miranda wrote the Spanish passages in the book and Colonel William Stephens Smith, an aide-de-camp to John Adams, then American envoy to London, almost certainly penned the English section. Unfortunately, the passage relating the conversation with Mendelssohn does not reveal the substance of the subjects discussed. Mendelssohn, a champion of the separation of church and state, would have been unhappy with Miranda's later espousal of Catholicism as the official religion for his Latin American constitution. The other Jewish intellectuals visited by the team expressed support for and interest in the United States, a republic founded on Enlightenment principles.   N. Lederer

498. Porter, Jack Nusan. THE JEWISH INTELLECTUAL. *Midstream 1979 25(1): 18-25.* Discusses Jews within the American intellectual elite, 1945-78, assessing their divisions and intergroup conflicts as well as their role in modern American social circles.

499. Porter, Jack Nusan. JEWISH SINGLES. *Midstream 1975 21(10): 35-43.* Proposes various Jewish community responses to the problems faced by adult singles in the 1970's.

500. Porter, Jack Nusan; Rockovsky, Boris; and Agrillo, Anita Bach. THE JEWISH STUDENT: A COMPARATIVE ANALYSIS OF RELIGIOUS AND SECULAR ATTITUDES. *Yivo Ann. of Jewish Social Sci. 1974 (15): 297-338.* Gives the results of a study during April 1968-May 1969 of Jewish students at Yale and Northwestern Universities. The study surveyed attitudes of students on observance, attitudes toward Judaism and "Jewishness," Israel, intermarriage, assimilation, sex, God, and the Bible. 7 tables.   R. J. Wechman

501. Porter, Jack Nusan. A NAZI RUNS FOR MAYOR: DANGEROUS BROWNSHIRTS OR MEDIA FREAKS? *Present Tense 1977 4(4): 27-31.* Discusses the resurgence of Matt Koehl's National Socialist White People's Party. Traces the Party's activities during 1974-76 in Milwaukee, Wisconsin. Examines the political repercussions and the split in the Jewish community. Analyzes Jewish reactions: the activist-confrontationists vs. the minimalists. Primary and secondary sources; 4 photos.   R. B. Mendel

502. Porter, Jack Nusan. ROSA SONNENSCHEIN AND *THE AMERI-CAN JEWESS:* FIRST INDEPENDENT ENGLISH LANGUAGE JEWISH WOMEN'S JOURNAL IN THE UNITED STATES. *Am. Jewish Hist. 1978 68(1): 57-63.* Rosa Sonnenschein (1847-1932) published and edited the periodical *The American Jewess* during its short life, 1895-99. This "first English-language journal independently edited by women" addressed itself to upper-middle to upper class German and Sephardic Jewish women. Its articles reflected the tumultuous events of the period (Russian pogroms, Dreyfus affair, early Zionism, etc.) and reflected the women's suffrage movement and the noblesse oblige of the upper class to the poor. The magazine died in 1899, partly because of the strong assimilationist attitudes of so many Jews.   F. Rosenthal

503. Pratt, Norma Fain. TRANSITIONS IN JUDAISM: THE JEWISH AMERICAN WOMAN THROUGH THE 1930S. *Am. Q. 1978 30(5): 681-702.* A study of the slow, but steady growth in the status of women in American Judaism, particularly during the 1920's-30's. Rapidity of status growth has depended partly on whether the country of origin was Eastern or Western Europe, but economic factors in the adopted country also had some influence. One can see very clear differences between Reform, Conservative, Orthodox, and secular Jews in their reaction to liberalizing tendencies and demands. A number of Jewish women's organizations have developed significant programs where women have found opportunity for making unique contributions. However, the fear of assimilation into Gentile culture patterns has been a strong inhibiting force among the women themselves. 60 notes.   R. V. Ritter

504. Quinn, Carin C. THE JEANING OF AMERICA—AND THE WORLD. *Am. Heritage 1978 29(3): 14-21.* A German immigrant, Levi Strauss (1829-1902), came to New York in 1848 and went to San Francisco in 1850, intent on selling canvas for tents. Finding a need for a sturdy material for men's pants, Strauss made a pair from some of his canvas. From then on, he was in business. Spreading to the eastern United States during the 1930's, today the market for jeans is worldwide. 16 illus.   J. F. Paul

505. Raab, Earl. BLACKS AND JEWS ASUNDER? *Midstream 1979 25(9): 3-9.* Discusses the political and social development of blacks and Jews in the United States since the 1930's, and views with alarm the disintegration of the traditional black-Jewish political coalition.

506. Raab, Earl. IS ISRAEL LOSING POPULAR SUPPORT? THE EVIDENCE OF THE POLLS. *Commentary 1974 57(1): 26-29.* Discusses public opinion in the United States about US foreign policy toward Israel.   S

507. Rabkin, Yakov M. SOVIET JEWS: THE BITTER AFTERMATH OF EMIGRATION. *Bull. of the Atomic Scientists 1975 31(6): 35-38.* Focuses on the legal, social, and psychological adjustment and the resettlement of Jewish emigrant scientists in the United States and Israel. Contrasts the situation of Soviet immigrants with the more favorable situation of German Jewish scientists in the United States in the 1930's. Primary and secondary sources; 14 notes.   D. J. Trickey

508. Rachleff, Owen. JEWISH COMICS. *Midstream 1976 22(4): 51-56.*
Discusses humor themes and stereotypes of Jewish comedians in the United
States in the 1960's and 70's, including Woody Allen, David Steinberg and Don
Rickles.

509. Rafael, Ruth. ERNEST BLOCH AT THE SAN FRANCISCO CON-
SERVATORY OF MUSIC. *Western States Jewish Hist. Q. 1977 9(3): 195-215.*
Ada Clement and Lillian Hodghead, founders of the San Francisco Conservatory
of Music, persuaded Ernest Bloch (1880-1959) to leave the Cleveland Institute
of Music to become the director of their organization in 1925. Bloch contributed
his prestige and administrative talents to acquire instruments and other equipment to aid in the school's expansion. He hired artists, established an orchestra
and choir, and created a theory department after a survey of San Francisco's
musical needs. On 6 June 1928, Bloch won first prize in a symphony contest for
the score, "America, I Build for You." Bloch resigned as director of the Conservatory on 11 February 1930 due to financial considerations and his desire to have
more time for composing. Primary and secondary sources; 2 photos, 74 notes.
B. S. Porter

510. Rakeffet-Rothkoff, Aaron. THE ATTEMPT TO MERGE THE JEW-
ISH THEOLOGICAL SEMINARY AND YESHIVA COLLEGE, 1926-1927.
Michael: On the Hist. of the Jews in the Diaspora [Israel] 1975 3: 254-280. The
merger attempt of the two leading American traditional rabbinical seminaries was
prompted by the fund-raising campaigns launched by both institutions for new
campuses in New York City. Some American Jewish lay leaders could not discern
the differences between Jewish Theological Seminary and Yeshiva College, for
many in the JTS administration and faculty were Orthodox in their theology and
practice. Presents 26 documents relating to the attempted merger and serving as
the basis for the description in the author's book, *Bernard Revel: Builder of
American Jewish Orthodoxy* (Philadelphia, 1972), pp. 94-114. Primary and secondary sources; 40 notes.

511. Raphael, Marc Lee. EUROPEAN JEWISH AND NON-JEWISH
MARITAL PATTERNS IN LOS ANGELES, 1910-1913: A COMPARATIVE
APPROACH. *Western States Jewish Hist. Q. 1974 6(2): 100-106.* Examines
more than 25,000 marriage licenses for the years 1910-1913, and concludes that
European national animosities persisted when immigrants moved to Los Angeles.
There were few intermarriages between people of different nationalities. Jews
tended to marry Jews from the same geographic homeland areas—for instance,
East Europeans married East Europeans but did not marry Jews from other parts
of Europe. 7 tables.   R. A. Garfinkle

512. Raphael, Marc Lee. FEDERATED PHILANTHROPY IN AN
AMERICAN JEWISH COMMUNITY: 1904-1948. *Am. Jewish Hist. 1978
68(2): 147-162.* The story and development of the Federation movement in one
American Jewish community, that of Columbus, Ohio, illustrates the paths taken
during those decades throughout the country. The shift from local to national and
overseas allocations and the increase in contributors and contributions, especially
after 1937-38, were accompanied by gradual democratization of the board, even
though the bulk of the money continued to be contributed by a tiny minority. Yet
the Federation, because of its control of philanthropy, brought secular and reli-

gious, traditional and non-traditional, Zionist and non-Zionist Jews together, the only true forum in the community. 28 notes.   F. Rosenthal

513. Raphael, Marc Lee. THE GENESIS OF A COMMUNAL HISTORY: THE COLUMBUS JEWISH HISTORY PROJECT. *Am. Jewish Arch. 1977 29(1): 53-69.* Writes of the Columbus (Ohio) Jewish History Project as a joint undertaking of the Columbus Jewish Federation, the Ohio Historical Society, and the Ohio State University. Believes that "the writing of serious American Jewish communal history is still in its infancy," though "such studies are valuable for the insights they offer into particular historical processes, . . . the information they offer indirectly about a society, and . . . the questions they raise about similar cases."   J

514. Raphael, Marc Lee. THE INDUSTRIAL REMOVAL OFFICE IN COLUMBUS: A LOCAL CASE STUDY. *Ohio Hist. 1976 85(2): 100-108.* Studies an organization responsible for relocating (in Columbus, Ohio) Jewish immigrants from the East Coast (1901-16). Based on archival sources; illus., 26 notes.   T. H. Hartig

515. Raphael, Marc Lee. THE JEWISH COMMUNITY AND ELLIS IS-LAND, 1909. *Michael: On the Hist. of the Jews in the Diaspora [Israel] 1975 3: 172-187.* The Baron de Hirsch Fund, established in 1891, paid for an agent of the United Hebrew Charities of New York to meet Jewish immigrants at Ellis Island. Publishes condensed and edited document highlighting the activities of this agent, I. Irving Lipsitch (1884-1935) in 1909. Interviewed by David M. Bressler (1879-1942), general manager of the Industrial Removal Office, Lipsitch's testimony illuminates the plight of the immigrants and the complexity, frustration, and conflicts accompanying the self-help efforts of the American Jewish community in the early 20th century.   T. Sassoon

516. Raphael, Marc Lee. ORAL HISTORY IN AN ETHNIC COMMU-NITY: THE PROBLEMS AND THE PROMISE. *Ohio Hist. 1977 86(4): 248-257.* Discusses techniques in oral history interviews. Using brief excerpts from the tapes of the Jewish History Project of Columbus, Ohio, since 1920, the author touches on the strengths and weaknesses of recording and transcribing oral history. Secondary sources; 23 notes.   N. Summers

517. Raphael, Marc Lee. RABBI JACOB VOORSANGER OF SAN FRAN-CISCO ON JEWS AND JUDAISM: THE IMPLICATIONS OF THE PITTS-BURGH PLATFORM. *Am. Jewish Hist. Q. 1973 63(2): 185-203.* Rabbi Voorsanger (1852-1908) utilized 19th-century Biblical criticism and current philosophies to support his interpretation of the Pittsburgh Platform, the 1885 statement of principles of American Reform Judaism. Strongly influenced by Darwin's studies, he rejected any notions of supernatural revelation and adjusted Jewish theology to the accepted scientific theories of the day. 41 notes.
                                                                                      F. Rosenthal

518. Raphael, Marc Lee. THE UTILIZATION OF PUBLIC LOCAL AND FEDERAL SOURCES FOR RECONSTRUCTING AMERICAN JEWISH LOCAL HISTORY: THE JEWS OF COLUMBUS, OHIO. *Am. Jewish Hist. Q. 1975 65(1): 10-35.* Using 19th-century and early 20th-century statistics from various sources, discusses the history of the majority of Jews in Columbus, Ohio,

whose activities were not recorded by the local Jewish newspaper. Examines the validity of quantitative methods in history. 10 tables, 43 notes.

F. Rosenthal

519. Rapp, Michael G. SAMUEL N. DEINARD AND THE UNIFICA-TION OF JEWS IN MINNEAPOLIS. *Minnesota Hist. 1973 43(6): 213-221.* Rabbi Samuel N. Deinard (1873-1921), founder and editor of *The American Jewish World,* was the prime mover in bringing German and East European Jews together as a community in Minneapolis. His weekly newspaper is the principal source for this analysis. 5 illus., 28 notes. D. L. Smith

520. Rausch, David. AMERICAN EVANGELICALS AND THE JEWS. *Midstream 1977 23(2): 38-41.* Discusses American Jews' fears of anti-Semitism by Protestant Fundamentalists and Evangelicals; considers trends in Fundamentalists' Messianic beliefs, 1970's.

521. Rausch, David A. ARNO C. GAEBELEIN (1861-1945): FUNDA-MENTALIST PROTESTANT ZIONIST. *Am. Jewish Hist. 1978 68(1): 43-56.* Arno C. Gaebelein (1861-1945), originally of the Methodist Episcopal Church, was a central figure in the formulation of Fundamentalism in America. He became a student of Hebrew and Yiddish and a missionary to Jews of New York. In 1893 he began publishing, in Yiddish, *Tiqweth Israel,* or *The Hope of Israel Monthly,* on the pages of which he actively encouraged Jewish settlement of Palestine. This strong Zionist concern was to characterize his work as an evangelist and a teacher at the Dallas Theological Seminary. 28 notes.

F. Rosenthal

522. Rausch, David A. OUR HOPE: PROTOFUNDAMENTALISM'S AT-TITUDE TOWARD ZIONISM, 1894-1897. *Jewish Social Studies 1978 40(3-4): 239-250.* Our Hope, founded by Arno C. Gaebelein and edited for its first three years by Dr. Ernst F. Stroeter, was an English-language Christian publication designed to further Fundamentalism in the United States and emphasizing the importance of the Jews and their place in biblical prophecy. Original articles and those taken from Jewish publications were pro-Zionist and stressed the everlasting quality of the nation of Israel. Other pieces discussed Christian missions to the Jews and the Jewish colonization of Palestine. In 1897 the periodical changed from its original purpose to a popular Bible study publication. Attitudes similar to those in the early years of *Our Hope* regarding the restoration of the Jews to Palestine were expressed in the international prophetic conference movement and the Christian missions to the Jews in the 19th century.

N. Lederer

523. Resnik, Bezalel Nathan. MEMOIR OF MY LIFE. *Rhode Island Jewish Hist. Notes 1978 7(4): 471-500.* The author (b. 1891) left his native Lithuania in 1933 for the United States, and became a businessman in Providence, Rhode Island.

524. Reutlinger, Andrew S. REFLECTIONS ON THE ANGLO-AMERI-CAN JEWISH EXPERIENCE: IMMIGRANTS, WORKERS AND ENTRE-PRENEURS IN NEW YORK AND LONDON, 1870-1914. *Am. Jewish Hist. Q. 1977 66(4): 473-484.* Many of the factors responsible for the divergent pattern of communal development among the East European Jewish immigrants in Lon-

don and New York City lay in the process of migration itself and in the differences between British and American values and institutions. For example, financial difficulties or religious predilections of an orthodox nature might be determining factors in remaining in Great Britain. Even a temporary sojourn in London made possible changes in the factory method of garment manufacture and in the men working in it to humanize the consequences of this system. Also, the Jewish labor movement benefited from the experience of many of its leaders in London's sweat shops. English models made for communal paternalism exercised by the "Cousinhood" (Rothschilds, Montefiores, etc.), but American conditions precluded national institutions or the same degree of deference to the Jewish elite.

F. Rosenthal

525. Rezneck, Samuel. THE MARITIME ADVENTURES OF A JEWISH SEA CAPTAIN, JONAS P. LEVY, IN NINETEENTH-CENTURY AMERICA. *Am. Neptune 1977 37(4): 239-252.* Jonas Phillips Levy (1807-83) went to sea in 1823 as a cabin boy and eventually owned and commanded several sailing ships. Focuses on Levy's services as a sea captain in the Peruvian Revolution and the Mexican War. Based on Levy's unpublished memoirs; illus., 31 notes.

G. H. Curtis

526. Rezneck, Samuel. A NOTE ON THE GENEALOGY OF AN EIGHTEENTH-CENTURY FAMILY OF JEWISH ORIGIN: THE NUNEZ FAMILY OF LEWES, DELAWARE. *Am. Jewish Arch. 1978 30(1): 20-23.* In colonial America, Jews occasionally left the security of the Jewish community to migrate into the hinterland. Often, deprived of essential contacts, they ceased to be Jewish. Reconstruction of three generations of one such family.   J

527. Rezneck, Samuel. THE STRANGE ROLE OF A JEWISH SEA CAPTAIN IN THE CONFEDERATE SOUTH. *Am. Jewish Hist. 1978 68(1): 64-73.* Jonas Phillips Levy (1807-83), the younger brother of Commodore Uriah Levy, rose to the rank of captain in the American merchant marine. He was a participant in a Peruvian revolution in the 1830's and was made the harbor master of Vera Cruz during the Mexican War (1846-48). During the Civil War he conducted business activities for the Confederate government and frequently offered his advice and his services from Wilmington, North Carolina. His children became respected members of the Jewish and general community of New York. 22 notes.

F. Rosenthal

528. Rice, Dan. REINHOLD NIEBUHR AND JUDAISM. *J. of the Am. Acad. of Religion 1977 45(1): 72.* Identifies and investigates the main themes in the Jewish-Christian dialogue as Reinhold Niebuhr conceived them. Some attention is given to the history of this dialogue. Four major themes are discussed: Zionism and the state of Israel; anti-Semitism; theological issues dividing the two faiths; and the problem of missions.

E. R. Lester

529. Richtik, James M. and Hutch, Danny. WHEN JEWISH SETTLERS FARMED IN MANITOBA'S INTERLAKE AREA. *Can. Geographical J. [Canada] 1977 95(1): 32-35.* In an effort to escape persecution in tsarist Russia, Jews migrated to Canada in 1884, settling primarily in the interlake districts of Manitoba; in the 1920's they set up agricultural communities in Saskatchewan and Alberta.

530. Ripinsky, Sol. AN ALASKAN REPORT: 1909. *Western States Jewish Hist. Q. 1978 11(1): 56-59.* The author (1850-1927) came to Alaska in the early 1880's. He reported that there were about 300 Jews in Alaska in 1909. They were active in commercial, financial, educational, and political development. Rothschilds and Guggenheims had vast holdings of mineral claims of gold, copper, coal, and iron. The author operated a general store at Chilkat Peninsula—later known as Haines, Alaska. Reprinted from the *Jewish Tribune,* Portland, Oregon, 17 December 1909. 2 photos, 6 notes. B. S. Porter

531. Rivlin, Helen Anne B. THE HOLY LAND: THE AMERICAN EXPE-RIENCE: AMERICAN JEWS AND THE STATE OF ISRAEL. *Middle East J. 1976 30(3): 369-389.* The authenticity of the American commitment to Israel derives from the nature of American society, "while the American Jewish consensus regarding Israel has arisen out of the exceptional circumstances of the Jewish experience in this country." No group benefited more from the American Revolution than the Jews. Assistance to the Jews of Palestine began as early as the 18th century. Covers American-Jewish relations up to the present. 58 notes. E. P. Stickney

532. Rockaway, Robert A. ANTISEMITISM IN AN AMERICAN CITY: DETROIT, 1850-1914. *Am. Jewish Hist. Q. 1974 64(1): 42-54.* Detroit, headquarters of the anti-Semitic activities of Henry Ford and Charles E. Coughlin in the 1920's and 1930's, was the site of many earlier instances produced by party politics in the 1850's and the emotionalism of the Civil War. After the great migration of Jews from eastern Europe to the city anti-Semitism became increasingly apparent and led to the formation of the Jewish Peddlers Protective Association in 1892. This decade also witnessed the first explicit act of social discrimination involving the Detroit Athletic Club. Overt anti-Semitism in the city created anxiety and apprehension among Detroit's Jewish citizens and led some of them to reevaluate their position as Americans and as Jews. 36 notes. F. Rosenthal

533. Rockaway, Robert A. "CAUSE FOR RICHUS"; MAGNUS BUTZEL OF DETROIT TO MEYER SAMUEL ISAACS OF NEW YORK: AN EXAMPLE OF NINETEENTH CENTURY AMERICAN JEWISH INSECURITY. *Michigan Jewish Hist. 1974 14(2): 3-5.* Discusses Jewish reluctance in the 19th century to join Jewish organizations which were "international in scope," fearing that it would lead to a questioning of "Jewish loyalty," and possibly be used as a pretext for anti-Semitism. S

534. Rockaway, Robert A. THE EASTERN EUROPEAN JEWISH COM-MUNITY OF DETROIT, 1881-1914. *Yivo Ann. of Jewish Social Sci. 1974 (15): 82-105.* Most East European Jews coming to Detroit in this period lived in the crowded downtown sections of the city. Author discusses the religious, economic, social and cultural life of the community, its religious identification, reaction to cultural change, and relations with non-Jews. "Although the Eastern European Jews made great strides in coming to terms with their American environment by 1914, they were still viewed with hostility and suspicion by native-born and foreign-born Detroiters." 83 notes. R. J. Wechman

535. Rockaway, Robert A. LOUIS BRANDEIS ON DETROIT. *Michigan Jewish Hist. 1977 17(1): 17-19.* Reprints a letter from Louis Brandeis to his brother Alfred about anti-Semitism in Detroit, 1914.

536. Rockaway, Robert A. THE PROGRESS OF REFORM JUDAISM IN LATE 19TH AND EARLY 20TH CENTURY DETROIT. *Michigan Jewish Hist. 1974 14(1): 8-17.*

537. Rockaway, Robert A. THE ROOSEVELT ADMINISTRATION, THE HOLOCAUST, AND THE JEWISH REFUGEES. *Rev. in Am. Hist. 1975 3(1): 113-118.* Review article prompted by Saul S. Friedman's *No Haven for the Oppressed: United States Policy toward Jewish Refugees, 1938-1945* (Detroit, Mich.: Wayne State U. Pr., 1973).

538. Rockaway, Robert A. "WORTHY SIR . . . ": A COLLECTION OF IMMIGRANT LETTERS FROM THE INDUSTRIAL REMOVAL OFFICE. *Michael: On the Hist. of the Jews in the Diaspora [Israel] 1975 3: 152-171.* A hitherto untapped source of Jewish immigrant life in the United States in the early 20th century are the letters to the Industrial Removal Office (IRO). This correspondence is housed in the American Jewish Historical Society. The IRO's function was to disperse Jewish immigrants throughout the United States, persuading and assisting Jewish workers to leave the large cities on the East Coast for smaller cities where Jewish communities existed and jobs were available. Some 75,000 Jews were thus relocated in 1900-17. Publishes 11 immigrant letters from Detroit, most addressed to and answered by David Bressler (1879-1942) and Philip Seman (1881-1957). T. Sassoon

539. Roditi, Edouard. NEO-KABBALISM IN THE AMERICAN JEWISH COUNTER-CULTURE. *Midstream 1979 25(8): 8-13.* In response to middle-class Jewish traditionalism and rationalism, young dissident Jews have turned to the mysticism of the Cabala for inspiration, 1940's-70's.

540. Rodrigues, Eusebio L. SAUL BELLOW'S HENDERSON AS AMERICA. *Centennial R. 1976 20(2): 189-195.* Saul Bellow's novel *Henderson The Rain King* (1965) is a "daring parable about America and the American dream." Henderson, a man of gigantic size, symbolizes the size and potential of America; he combines technological achievement with the power of the human spirit. His voice is the voice of hope, which has always been present in the new world. Henderson restores to 20th-century America the ideals of brotherhood, love, and service, and represents Bellow's rejection of an America doomed to enslavement to the processes of technology. 7 notes. A. R. Stoesen

541. Rogers, Barbara. TO BE OR NOT TO BE A JEWISH HOSPITAL. *Western States Jewish Hist. Q. 1978 10(3): 195-201.* On 3 November 1887, a group of San Francisco citizens agreed to establish a charitable hospital for deserving and needy Israelites and others. Rabbi M. Friedlander of Oakland openly opposed the hospital's policy and urged that it accept only Jewish patients. San Francisco's prominent rabbis, Jacob Voorsanger, Jacob Nieto, and Myer S. Levy agreed with the hospital's board of directors that it should be nonsectarian in its admissions policy. Critics today claim the hospital is no longer Jewish because many patients and doctors are not Jewish; but supporters say that a high proportion of Bay area Jews are served by Mount Zion Hospital and it will

continue to grow and develop with the San Francisco Bay area. Based on Board of Directors' minutes, secondary sources; 13 notes.   B. S. Porter

542. Rogoff, Abraham S. HARRY T. MADISON, PAST NATIONAL COMMANDER OF THE JEWISH WAR VETERANS OF U.S.A. *Michigan Jewish Hist. 1974 14(2): 6-8.* Madison joined the Detroit, Michigan, chapter of this organization in 1938, and in 1953 was elected National Commander.   S

543. Rolle, Andrew. UPROOTED OR UPRAISED? IMMIGRANTS IN AMERICA. *Rev. in Am. Hist. 1978 6(1): 95-98.* Review article prompted by Thomas Kessner's *The Golden Door: Italian and Jewish Immigrant Mobility in New York City, 1880-1915* (New York: Oxford U. Pr., 1977).

544. Romanofsky, Peter. "AN ATMOSPHERE OF SUCCESS": THE KEREN HAYESOD IN MISSOURI, 1921-1922. *Jewish Social Studies 1978 40(1): 73-84.* The World Zionist Organization (WZO) founded the Keren Hayesod organization in the United States in 1921 to provide an umbrella organization for the receipt of all funds, donations, and investments designed to implement the creation of a Jewish national homeland in Palestine. Opposed by the American group led by cultural Zionists Louis D. Brandeis and Julian W. Mack, the Keren Hayesod and the Brandeis group competed for the allegiance and funds of American Jews. The Missouri situation, especially in Kansas City and St. Louis, revealed that the Keren Hayesod gained the full support of the majority of American-born leaders as well as European-born, American-educated Jews. These persons not only supported but led the campaign to provide backing for the instrument of the WZO. The overwhelming majority of Missouri Zionists supported Keren Hayesod owing to its "atmosphere of success," based on efficient and speedy organization and the skillful employment of attention gaining publicity.   N. Lederer

545. Romanofsky, Peter. "... TO RID OURSELVES OF THE BURDEN..." NEW YORK JEWISH CHARITIES AND THE ORIGINS OF THE INDUSTRIAL REMOVAL OFFICE, 1890-1901. *Am. Jewish Hist. Q. 1975 64(4): 331-343.* Various motives combined to induce the primarily German-Jewish leadership of New York Jewish charities to actively support removal of new immigrants to other parts of the country. Overcrowding, the possibility of political radicalism, and the fear of renewed antisemitism led to various programs for job training, agricultural settlements, and resettlement outside New York. Both the Industrial Removal Office of 1901 and the Galveston Plan of 1907 were created to prevent limitation of Jewish immigration to the United States. By 1914 some 70,000 men and their families had been placed outside New York City, allowing Jewish charities to expand and develop their services to the children, widows, and the sick of the Jewish community. 31 notes.   F. Rosenthal

546. Romanofsky, Peter. "TO SAVE... THEIR SOULS": THE CARE OF DEPENDENT CHILDREN IN NEW YORK CITY, 1900-1905. *Jewish Social Studies 1974 36(3/4): 253-261.* During 1903-05 a small number of dependent children were placed in foster homes of working class families rather than families of middle class background. The program was initiated by the United Hebrew Charities of New York City in order to cope with the increasing number of orphans and other children that needed help as Jewish immigration from Eastern

Europe increased. Ideological opposition and lack of financial support terminated the program but its pioneering prepared the way for a change in the general American approach. Primary and secondary sources; 27 notes.

P. E. Schoenberg

547.　Roseman, Kenneth D.　JONAS LEVI, A JEW.　*Am. Jewish Arch. 1975 27(1): 67-69.* Presents a 1780 deposition of Jonas Levy, an American Jew, on the difficulties encountered in France.

548.　Rosen, Benton H.　KING DAVID'S LODGE, A.F. & A.M., NO. 1 OF NEWPORT, RHODE ISLAND.　*Rhode Island Jewish Hist. Notes 1974 6(4): 578-586.* A history of the King David's Masonic Lodge of Newport, Rhode Island (1780-90); includes copies of a letter from George Washington, ledger entries, and voting records.　　　　　　　　　　　　　　　　　　　　　　　S

549.　Rosen, Benton H.　SAMUEL STARR, M.D., 1884-1950.　*Rhode Island Jewish Hist. Notes 1976 7(2): 294-296.* Provides a short history of Samuel Starr, including his schooling and medical practice in Providence, Rhode Island, 1910-50.

550.　Rosen, Norma.　THE HOLOCAUST AND THE AMERICAN-JEW-ISH NOVELIST.　*Midstream 1974 20(8): 54-62.*

551.　Rosenberg, Bernard and Howe, Irving.　ARE AMERICAN JEWS TURNING TO THE RIGHT?　*Dissent 1974 21(1): 30-45.* If there is a new Jewish conservatism, it is possibly the result of affluence, assimilation, decline in the Jewish labor movement, fear of Negroes, or reaction to Communist anti-Semitism.　　　　　　　　　　　　　　　　　　　　　　　　　　　　　S

552.　Rosenblum, Herbert.　IDEOLOGY AND COMPROMISE: THE EVO-LUTION OF THE UNITED SYNAGOGUE CONSTITUTIONAL PREAM-BLE.　*Jewish Social Studies 1973 35(1): 18-31.* Traces the ideological and institutional development of the Conservative branch of American Judaism, 1910-13. The preambles of the articles of incorporation of the United Synagogue of America, the association for Conservative rabbis, indicate the ideological compromises among diverse groups to achieve unity. Based on primary and secondary sources, particularly letters and documents in the archives of the Jewish Theological Seminary of America; 45 notes.　　　P. E. Schoenberg

553.　Rosenfeld, Alvin H.　INVENTING THE JEW: NOTES ON JEWISH AUTOBIOGRAPHY.　*Midstream 1974 20(4): 54-66.*

554.　Rosenfeld, Stephen S.　THE POLITICS OF THE JACKSON AMEND-MENT: "A PIECE OF POLITICAL BAGGAGE WITH MANY DIFFER-ENT HANDLES."　*Present Tense 1974 1(4): 17-23.* Details the efforts of Senator Henry M. Jackson, supported by American Jews, to attach a free emigra-tion condition to the Nixon administration's bill granting the USSR "most fa-vored nation" status in international trade.　　　　　　　　　　　　　　S

555.　Rosenshine, Jay.　HISTORY OF THE SHOLOM ALEICHEM INSTI-TUTE OF DETROIT, 1926-1971.　*Michigan Jewish Hist. 1974 14(2): 9-20.*

556. Rosenthal, Marcus. THE JEWISH IMMIGRATION "PROBLEM." *Western States Jewish Hist. Q. 1974 6(4): 278-289.* On 27 January 1905, Rabbi Jacob Voorsanger, the editor of *Emanu-El*, published his feelings against the immigration of large numbers of East European Jews. The author's rebuttal attacks Rabbi Voorsanger's ideas, stating that if American Jews turn against the new arrivals the Christian community will use that as a sign to start a new round of anti-Semitism. Reprinted letter-to-the-editor from *Emanu-El*, San Francisco, 24 February 1905. R. A. Garfinkle

557. Rosenwaike, Ira. ESTIMATING JEWISH POPULATION DISTRIBUTION IN U.S. METROPOLITAN AREAS IN 1970. *Jewish Social Studies 1974 36(2): 106-117.* Uses the Yiddish mother tongue data of the 1970 US census to determine the Jewish population and pattern of settlement in major metropolitan centers, concentrating on four Standard Metropolitan Statistical Areas: Baltimore, Cleveland, St. Louis, and Washington, D. C. The data implies that a high degree of geographical concentration still exists among Jews in most metropolitan areas, despite the transition to predominantly suburban residence. Yiddish mother tongue data of the 1970 US census is highly reliable and useful for similar studies of other cities. Primary and secondary sources are in English; 25 notes. P. E. Schoenberg

558. Rosenwaike, Ira. THE FIRST JEWISH SETTLERS IN LOUISVILLE. *Filson Club Hist. Q. 1979 53(1): 37-44.* By 1832 the Jewish population of Louisville was large enough to support the establishment of the Israelite Benevolent Society. Most of the community was highly mobile at this time; few of the early Jewish settlers remained in the city for more than a decade. Based on local government records and the federal census. 38 notes. G. B. McKinney

559. Rosenwaike, Ira. THE FOUNDING OF BALTIMORE'S FIRST JEWISH CONGREGATION: FACT VS. FICTION. *Am. Jewish Arch. 1976 28(2): 119-125.* Disputes the claim that Isaac Leeser's uncle Zalma Rehine was a founder of the Baltimore Hebrew Congregation. Writers of local history, he urges, "would do well not to rely on some of the hearsay evidence of their predecessors, who often lacked scholarly training." J

560. Rosenwaike, Ira. THE JEWS OF BALTIMORE: 1810 TO 1820. *Am. Jewish Hist. Q. 1977 67(2): 101-124.* The Jewish population of Baltimore during this period, although subject to considerable flux, remained small (less than 25 families). These individuals, nevertheless, seem to have been broadly representative of American Jewry; because of their mobility, they were also the Jews of Philadelphia and New York. Short biographical sketches are provided for both foreign-born and native-born heads of families. 2 tabulations, 74 notes. F. Rosenthal

561. Rosenwaike, Ira. THE JEWS OF BALTIMORE TO 1810. *Am. Jewish Hist. Q. 1975 64(4): 291-320.* The systematic examination of the Jewish population of Baltimore from 1770 to 1810 reveals that by 1810 a rough outline of the communal trends in the next stage of development had been shaped: differentiation had taken place between the relatively well-off older "American" Jews and the recent immigrant arrivals. Another two decades passed, however, before the first congregation was set up. Over 40 individuals and their families provide material for this study. 85 notes. F. Rosenthal and S

562. Rosenwaike, Ira. THE JEWS OF BALTIMORE: 1820 TO 1830. *Am. Jewish Hist. Q. 1978 67(3): 246-259.* Provides biographical surveys of most of the 30 individuals whose families constituted the Jewish community of Baltimore, Maryland. One-fourth were native-born by 1830. Dutch Jews predominated among European newcomers. All but two of these heads of household practiced middle class occupations, and 10 of the 24 families contained one or more blacks. This small group of men founded the first congregations, led them for many years, and thus founded an enduring organizational structure. 26 notes.
F. Rosenthal

563. Rosenwaike, Ira. LEON DYER: BALTIMORE AND SAN FRANCISCO JEWISH LEADER. *Western States Jewish Hist. Q. 1977 9(2): 135-143.* Earlier accounts of the life of Leon Dyer (1807-83) have too often relied on legend instead of valid documentary sources. In fact, Dyer was a Baltimore butcher and real estate dealer who developed a business interest in California when his younger brother, Abraham, joined a group of immigrants to that state. Leon Dyer went to San Francisco in 1850 for business reasons and in the few months he spent there, he was chosen the religious leader of a temporary congregation of Jewish settlers. After his return to Baltimore he made several trips to Europe before settling in Louisville, Kentucky, in 1875. Based on documents in the National Archives, Baltimore Land Records, other primary, and secondary sources; 31 notes.
B. S. Porter

564. Rosenwaike, Ira. LEVY L. LAURENS: AN EARLY TEXAN JOURNALIST. *Am. Jewish Arch. 1975 27(1): 61-66.* Discusses the death by duelling of Levy L. Laurens in 1837.
S

565. Rosenwaike, Ira. THE PARENTAGE AND EARLY YEARS OF M. H. DE YOUNG, LEGEND AND FACT. *Western States Jewish Hist. Q. 1975 7(3): 210-217.* A San Francisco publisher and civil leader in the late 1800's, Michael H. De Young dictated some autobiographical material which became the basis for a description of himself and his family in the *Encyclopedia of American Biography*. The author has disproved much of the information about his background that De Young passed on as fact. Primary and secondary sources; 25 notes.
R. A. Garfinkle

566. Roth, Henry and Friedman, John S. ON BEING BLOCKED AND OTHER LITERARY MATTERS. *Commentary 1977 64(2): 27-38.* Discusses Roth's childhood in New York City, his student days at City College of New York, his authorship of *Call It Sleep,* his membership in the Communist Party, his growing sympathy for Israel, and his eventual reunion with Judaism.
D. W. Johnson

567. Rothchild, Sylvia. BRANDEIS UNIVERSITY: THE MAKING OF A FIRST CLASS INSTITUTION. *Present Tense 1979 7(1): 31-36.* Briefly discusses the history of Brandeis University from its founding in Waltham, Massachusetts, in 1948, to the present focusing on the diverse cultural backgrounds of the students and faculty.

568. Rothchild, Sylvia. A GREAT HAPPENING IN BOSTON: REVOLT OF THE YOUNG. *Present Tense 1976 3(3): 21-26.* Traces the development of the Jewish Student Movement, a renaissance born in 1960 radicalism, from

Jewish Boston establishment antipathy to uneasy acceptance by urban and suburban Jewish and Gentile Boston. Describes the establishment and the impact of the student quarterlies *Response* and *Genesis 2*, the Jewish Student Projects, the communal Havurat Shalom, and the *Jewish Catalogue* on the educational and administrative policies of such religious and educational institutions as the Hillel Foundation(s), Boston University, Harvard-Radcliffe, and suburban synagogues. Quotes such movement notables as Alan Mintz, first editor of *Response*; writers Elie Wiesel and Bill Novak; activists Hillel Levine and Rav Kuk; rabbis Arthur Green, Zalman Schachter, Joseph Polak, Ben-Zion Gold, and Lawrence Kushner; professors Bernard Reisman and Leonard Fein. 4 photos.

R. B. Mendel

569. Rothchild, Sylvia. RETURN TO "NORTHRUP," MASS. *Present Tense 1975 2(4): 36-41.* Author's comments on the community she once lived in, describing the social changes in the Jewish suburb. S

570. Rothchild, Sylvia. TRAVELING THROUGH MIDDLE AMERICA. *Present Tense 1975 2(2): 37-40.* Discusses patterns of assimilation in three generations of Jewish families in the United States, 1925-75, and how each generation has responded to the social and religious attitudes of its parents.

571. Rothman, Sheila. THE LIMITS OF SISTERHOOD. *Rev. in Am. Hist. 1979 7(1): 92-97.* Review article prompted by *The Maimie Papers,* edited by Ruth Rosen and Sue Davidson (Old Westbury, N.Y.: The Feminist Pr., 1977), a record of the correspondence between Fanny Quincy Howe, the wife of a wealthy Boston writer, and Maimie Pinzer, a poor Jewish immigrant, during 1910-22, which represents the intimate friendships that transcend class boundaries.

572. Rothman, Stanley. GROUP-FANTASIES AND JEWISH RADICALISM: A PSYCHODYNAMIC INTERPRETATION. *J. of Psychohistory 1978 6(2): 211-239.* In the last century, Jews have made up a significant proportion of members of radical movements in Western culture. The source of Jewish radicalism is both sociological and psychodynamic, stemming from the Jews' historical social marginality and childrearing patterns which produce paranoid masochistic personalities. The combination pushes many Jews toward radical action. Secondary historical and psychiatric sources and original research with student radicals in the United States; 105 notes. R. E. Butchart

573. Rothschild, Janice. PRE-1867 ATLANTA JEWRY. *Am. Jewish Hist. Q. 1973 62(3): 242-249.* The first Jewish family—Jacob and Jeanetta Hirsch Haas with their four children—came to Atlanta in 1845, soon followed by Henry Levi, Herman Haas, David Mayer, and others, mostly from southern Germany. Sketches family, business, and social activities. Mayer was instrumental in organizing the Hebrew Benevolent Society and a Jewish cemetery, and led the small community during the Civil War. Based on contemporary newspaper data and family recollections; 26 notes. F. Rosenthal

574. Rozen, Frieda Shoenberg. THE PERMANENT FIRST-FLOOR TENANT: WOMEN AND *GEMEINSCHAFT. Mennonite Q. Rev. 1977 51(4): 319-328.* Discusses the role of women in Amish and Hutterite communities, based on written materials, and includes a comparison with the Jewish Chassidim

of Brooklyn and the kibbutzim of Israel. In all such societies the women are subordinate to the men. Structures have been built to maintain this position even in the face of avowed equality. This much is known, but otherwise a number of questions remain unanswered. Studies are needed to determine whether women are in inferior positions or merely subordinate ones, and to determine how satisfied and happy they are in comparison with their liberated sisters of the larger society. 6 notes.   V. L. Human

575.   Rozenstain, Yael.   MEMOIRS OF AN ALASKAN MERCHANT. *Western States Jewish Hist. Q. 1977 9(3): 253-261.* The author left Russia as a boy of 12 in 1900. He worked as a cabin boy on an English ship, and as a peddler in Australia until 1906 when he came to the United States. Joining the gold rush to Alaska, he became an apprentice in a general store in Fairbanks, later opening his own business and following the placer miners from one mining camp to another. After World War I, he bought a lot and built a store in the mining town of Hyder in southern Alaska. The decline of the mining industry forced him to move to the big fishing camp at Dillingham in 1938. The fishing business proved too risky for Rozenstain. He sold his outfit in 1944 and retired to southern California. 5 photos, 7 notes.   B. S. Porter

576.   Rubenstein, Richard L.   STUDYING AT HEBREW UNION COLLEGE: 1942-45. *Midstream 1974 20(6): 68-73.* From the author's *Power Struggle* (New York: Scribner's, 1974).   S

577.   Rubin, Lois.   DISAPPOINTED EXPECTATIONS: AN IMMIGRANT ARRIVES IN WESTERN PENNSYLVANIA.   *Western Pennsylvania Hist. Mag. 1976 59(4): 445-462.* Reprints excerpts from the unpublished memoir of a Jewish immigrant to western Pennsylvania, 1913-45, Harry Jackson.

578.   Rubin, Steven J.   CONTEMPORARY AMERICAN ETHNIC LITERATURE IN FRANCE.   *J. of Ethnic Studies 1975 3(1): 95-98.* The French regard Jewish and Negro writings as representations of unique American experiences and not as important commentaries on universal themes. Argues that these ethnic writings lose much of their flavor and meaning when translated into French. 6 notes.   T. W. Smith and S

579.   Rubinoff, Michael W.   C. E. H. KAUVAR: A SKETCH OF A COLORADO RABBI'S LIFE.   *Western States Jewish Hist. Q. 1978 10(4): 291-305.* Charles Eliezer Hillel Kauvar (1879-1971) was elected rabbi of Denver's Beth Ha Medrosh Hagodol Synagogue in 1902. Kauvar's devotion to Zionism caused friction between him and Rabbi William S. Friedman of Denver's Temple Emmanuel. The schism between the two rabbis affected the community at large when, in 1903, Rabbi Kauvar helped found the Jewish Consumptives' Relief Society (later the American Medical Center), open to Jews and non-Jews alike. In 1899 Temple Emmanuel had helped start the Jewish Hospital for Consumptives, an institution with a restricted admission policy. In 1920 Rabbi Kauvar was invited to the chair of rabbinic literature at the Methodist-sponsored University of Denver; he held this post for 45 years. Rabbi Kauvar became rabbi emeritus of his synagogue in 1952. In his later years he received many civic and religious awards and honors. Based on archival and published sources; 2 photos, 39 notes.   B. S. Porter

580. Rubinoff, Michael W. RABBI IN A PROGRESSIVE ERA: C.E.H. KAUVAR OF DENVER. *Colorado Mag. 1977 54(3): 220-239.* Russian-born (1879) and New York-educated, Rabbi Charles Eliezer Hillel Kauvar served Denver's orthodox Beth Ha Medrosh Hagodol synagogue during 1902-71. A leading progressive reformer, Kauvar founded the Jewish Consumptives' Relief Society and an orphanage, worked closely with Judge Banjamin Barr Lindsey in attacking juvenile delinquency, and was a long-time leader of Denver's Community Chest. He was a Zionist, urged ecumenism, and vigorously opposed the Ku Klux Klan in the 1920's. Primary and secondary sources; 10 illus., 51 notes.

O. H. Zabel

581. Rubinoff, Michael W. THE REACTION TO HITLER BY THE INTERMOUNTAIN JEWISH NEWS OF DENVER. *Western States Jewish Hist. Q. 1977 9(4): 301-314.* Between 1932 and 1935 the *Intermountain Jewish News* (IJN) of Denver, under editor Carl Mandel, encouraged its readers to respond to Nazi anti-Semitism by raising funds for refugees, boycotting German products, and protesting US participation in the 1936 Olympics in Germany. Early in this period the IJN was optimistic about the overthrow of Hitler and the future of German Jews. After 1935 the IJN muted its call for positive action to aid German Jews and overthrow Hitler. The apparent reasons for this were: 1) fear of latent anti-Semitism in the U.S. and 2) financial hardship caused by the Depression. Despite the failure of many Jews to take militant action against Nazi Germany, they were by no means "disinterested bystanders" to Hitler's persecution of the Jews. Based on the *Intermountain Jewish News* and other primary and secondary sources; 51 notes.

B. S. Porter

582. Rubinstein, Aryeh. ISAAC MAYER WISE: A NEW APPRAISAL. *Jewish Social Studies 1977 39(1-2): 53-74.* Traditional interpretations of the role of Isaac Mayer Wise as a leader of 19th-century American Judaism depict him as a proponent of moderate reform in Judaism and as a champion of religious unity in the Jewish community. In fact, he was a radical Reformist whose advocacy of reform led to religious disunity and the generation of enemies in the Jewish community. Wise was an opportunistic advocate of reform who craved popularity and a position at the head of American Jewry, and often tailored his pronouncements to suit the audience he was addressing at the moment. Basically, however, his conservative statements were a cover for his almost Deistic views, stressing the role of rationalist thought in Reform Judaism. Primary sources.

N. Lederer

583. Rubinstein, W. D. THE LEFT, THE RIGHT, AND THE JEWS. *Midstream 1979 25(8): 3-7.* Jews in the Western world are disproportionately represented among the elite, thanks to the inegalitarianism and plurality of power centers under capitalism; 20th century.

584. Ruchames, Louis. MORDECAI MANUEL NOAH AND EARLY AMERICAN ZIONISM. *Am. Jewish Hist. Q. 1975 64(3): 196-223.* Discusses the intellectual history of Mordecai Manuel Noah (1785-1847), for many years America's most prominent Jew, a man devoted to alleviating the sufferings of his people by advocating a return to Palestine. Noah's adherence to Zionism grew from his family background and the strong influence exerted upon him by Gershom Mendes Seixas (1743-1816). 51 notes.

F. Rosenthal

585. Rudavsky, David. LOUIS D. BRANDEIS AT THE LONDON IN-
TERNATIONAL ZIONIST CONFERENCE OF 1920. *Yivo Ann. of Jewish
Social Sci. 1974 (15): 145-165.* Delves into Louis D. Brandeis's conflicts with
Chaim Weizmann at the London Conference on the questions of including the
National Jewish Councils, and over Dubnow's doctrine of diaspora nationalism
which Brandeis was against. Brandeis complained that the Zionist confederations
in English-speaking countries were carrying too much of the financial burden,
and wanted the World Zionist Executive to be moved to Jerusalem. 76 notes.
R. J. Wechman

586. Rudd, Hynda. AUERBACH'S: ONE OF THE WEST'S OLDEST DE-
PARTMENT STORES. *Western States Jewish Hist. Q. 1979 11(3): 234-238.*
Auerbach's Department Store was founded in Salt Lake City, Utah, in 1864. The
Auerbach brothers had earlier stores in the mining camps of California. In the
1860's the Auerbachs operated tent stores along the route of the transcontinental
railroad while it was under construction. The main store in Salt Lake City
remained in the family from 1864 to 1977, although it had many changes of
location. Published and archival sources; 7 photos, 3 notes.   B. S. Porter

587. Rudd, Hynda.   CONGREGATION KOL AMI: RELIGIOUS
MERGER IN SALT LAKE CITY. *Western States Jewish Hist. Q. 1978 10(4):
311-326.* Congregation Kol Ami was formed in 1972 by the merger of Congregations B'nai Israel (begun in 1873) and Montefiore (begun ca. 1880). Different
opinions about ritual originally had divided Salt Lake City's Jewish community.
Eventually grievances dissipated and new religious, social, and economic problems brought the people together. A consolidation committee was formed to
discuss the issue, and members of both congregations voted in favor of the merger.
The old synagogues were sold and a new synagogue was constructed in 1976.
Based on archival, other primary, and secondary sources; 3 photos, 67 notes.
B. S. Porter

588. Rudd, Hynda.   SAMUEL NEWHOUSE: UTAH MINING MAG-
NATE AND LAND DEVELOPER. *Western States Jewish Hist. Q. 1979
11(4): 291-307.* Samuel Newhouse (18554-1930) had a freighting business to
mining camps in Colorado, 1879-86, when he made several successful mining
investments. He moved to Utah in 1896 as a millionaire investor and developer
of mining properties. Newhouse, and his partner Thomas Weir, developed rich
copper mines in Bingham Canyon, near Salt Lake City. British investors backed
Newhouse and Weir in the 1898 establishment of the Boston Consolidated Copper and Gold Mining Company, Ltd. Fluctuations in the copper market
prompted the merger of Boston Consolidated with the Utah Copper Company
in 1910. At the same time, Newhouse financed the construction of many large
commercial buildings, including a luxury hotel, in Salt Lake City. These investments overextended Newhouse financially, leading to bankruptcy in 1915. Newhouse moved to France to live with his sister in 1920. He died in 1930. Interviews
and published sources; 5 photos, 58 notes.   B. S. Porter

589. Rudd, Hynda. SHAREY TZEDICK: SALT LAKE'S THIRD JEWISH
CONGREGATION. *Western States Jewish Hist. Q. 1976 8(3): 203-208.* Some-
time during 1916-19, Congregation Sharey Tzedick of Salt Lake City was formed.
The founding members had belonged to the Montefiore synagogue but had

become discouraged with the gradual movement away from Orthodox traditions. Sharey Tzedick was set up as an Orthodox temple and the congregation erected a synagogue. For reasons still unclear the congregation folded during the 1930's, and in 1948 its property was sold to the Veterans of Foreign Wars. Photo, 22 notes.   R. A. Garfinkle

590.   Rudd, Hynda.   THE UNSINKABLE ANNA MARKS.   *Western States Jewish Hist. Q. 1978 10(3): 234-237.* Anna Marks (1847-1912) and her husband Wolff Marks (1842-1918) operated a store in Eureka City, Utah during the 1880's and 90's. They made a fortune in real estate and mining investments. Anna earned a reputation as a feisty character, especially concerning disputed property boundaries. She was handy with a gun and had a full vocabulary of cuss words. Secondary sources; 3 photos, 5 notes.   B. S. Porter

591.   Rudin, Marcia R. and Rudin, A. James.   BLACK JEWS IN AMERICA. *Present Tense 1979 7(1): 37-41.* Interviews black Rabbi Moshe Paris from New York City about the problems of black Jews attempting integration into the white Jewish community in America.

592.   Rustin, Bayard.   JEWS AND BLACKS: A RELATIONSHIP RE-EXAMINED.   *Midstream 1974 20(1): 3-12.*

593.   Ruxin, Robert H.   THE JEWISH FARMER AND THE SMALL-TOWN JEWISH COMMUNITY: SCHOHARIE COUNTY, NEW YORK. *Am. Jewish Arch. 1977 29(1): 3-21.* A small percentage of American Jews maintain their existence in a rural environment. Examines the effort of one such group to remain a part of "country" life without sacrificing its Jewish identity.
                                                                                                J

594.   Ryan, Frances B.   SIG STEINER: FATHER OF ESCONDIDO'S GRAPE DAY.   *Western States Jewish Hist. Q. 1976 8(4): 361-369.* In 1886 Sigmund Steiner arrived in Escondido, California and in 1886 opened the town's first store with P. A. Graham. The store served the rural community until 1912 when Steiner retired to Los Angeles. He was very active in Escondido's community affairs and served as mayor for twelve years (1894-1906). In 1908, he organized the first Grape Day which became an annual event there. 3 photos, 42 notes.
                                                                                    R. A. Garfinkle

595.   Salomon, H. P.   JOSEPH JESURUN PINTO (1729-1782): A DUTCH HAZAN IN COLONIAL NEW YORK.   *Studia Rosenthaliana [Netherlands] 1979 13(1): 18-29.* Recounts the scholarly, professional, and personal activities of a Sephardic cantor who traveled from Amsterdam to London and New York, where he lived, 1759-66, while serving at the Congregation Shearith Israel, whence he returned to London and to Amsterdam, where he died in 1782.

596.   Sandler, Bernard I.   HOACHOOZO—ZIONISM IN AMERICA AND THE COLONIZATION OF PALESTINE.   *Am. Jewish Hist. Q. 1974 64(2): 137-148.* At the beginning of the 20th century, many of the East European Jewish immigrants to America had succeeded in improving their economic position. Some, however, still aspired to live in a totally Jewish environment in Palestine and were imbued with the spirit of Jewish nationalism. An ingenious program for land acquisition in Palestine eventually led to the establishment of colonies.

Simon Goldman of St. Louis and Dr. Arthur Ruppin were leading members of these early undertakings. Herzlia, Afule, Raanana, and Gan Yavne were among the colonies founded by these Achoosa-Zionists between 1908 and 1934, settlements which continue to thrive and develop in modern Israel. 21 notes.

F. Rosenthal

597.   Sarna, Jonathan D.   A GERMAN-JEWISH IMMIGRANT'S PERCEPTION OF AMERICA, 1853-54: SOME FURTHER NOTES ON MORDECAI M. NOAH, A JEWEL ROBBERY, AND ISAAC M. WISE. *Am. Jewish Hist. 1978 68(2): 206-212.* Prompted by Gershon Greenberg's translation of *Deutsch-Amerikanische Skizzen . . . .* Greenburg and the 1854 author of *D.A.S.* erred regarding Mordecai Manuel Noah's Ararat colony, Noah's role in the Polari jewel theft case, and the lack of comment on *D.A.S.* (as disproved by Isaac Mayer Wise's denunciation of it). Reprints Noah's "The Crown Jewels" in his *Sunday Times and Noah's Weekly Messenger* of 27 January 1850. 18 notes.

598.   Schappes, Morris U.   EXCERPTS FROM ROBERT MORRIS' "DIARIES IN THE OFFICE OF FINANCE, 1781-1784," REFERRING TO HAYM SALOMON AND OTHER JEWS. *Am. Jewish Hist. Q. 1977 67(1): 9-49; (2): 140-161.* Part I. In his "Diaries" Robert Morris (1734-1806), then Superintendant of Finance, refers 162 times to seven Jewish businessmen and financial agents, of which 114 mentioned Haym Solomon. This relatively large number reflects great credit on the small Jewish communities of America. The allusions to Haym Solomon help to dispel some of the exaggerated myths that surround his career as well as reveal his contributions to the cause of the Republic. 71 notes. Part II. Concludes the reproduction and analysis of the diary entries. 114 notes.

F. Rosenthal

599.   Schappes, Morris U.   HOW AMERICAN WRITERS SAW THE JEWS: REVIEW ESSAY. *J. of Ethnic Studies 1978 6(2): 75-92.* Surveys and comments on Louis Harap, *The Image of the Jew in American Literature: From Early Republic to Mass Immigration* (1974), "a seminal work opening and defining new areas of perception and evaluation in American life and letters," and "exemplary in conception and execution." Harap examines not only belles lettres, but also popular forms from folklore to journalism and from the dime novel to mass-circulation popular fiction, and concludes that "the history of the Jewish character in American literature is also a chapter in the history of anti-Semitism." Schappes finds Harap even too mild in his criticisms in places, but calls his section on Emma Lazarus "the best single essay in print," and that on Abraham Cahan excellent. Still Harap is inadequate in his understanding of the Jewish transformation to a primarily ethnic rather than a religious entity.   G. J. Bobango

600.   Schappes, Morris U.   THE POLITICAL ORIGINS OF THE UNITED HEBREW TRADES, 1888. *J. of Ethnic Studies 1977 5(1): 13-44.* Details the origins, planning, and organizational meetings which produced the United Hebrew Trades (UHT) organization in New York City, a product of Branch 8 and Branch 17 of the Socialist Labor Party. The leaders were Yiddish-speaking workingmen such as Jacob Magidow, Lev Bandes, and Bernard Weinstein, who were products of the Jewish working class rather than the older middle-class composition of American Jewry. Demonstrates the close contacts and clearly imitative nature of the UHT and the older *Vereinigte Deutsche Gewerkschaften* (German

Central Labor Union). The UHT faced opposition by Jewish middle class organs such as *The Jewish Messenger* and the *American Hebrew,* who called the Farein anarchistic. The opposition of Samuel Gompers, who objected to the socialist nature of the group's program and its religious basis, also took several years to overcome. Gompers' writings later falsely claimed him as one of the organizers of the UHT. For 25 years this union was a vital factor in organizing Jewish workers and bringing them into the American labor movement. Primary and secondary sources, 88 notes.   G. J. Bobango

601. Schatt, Stanley. THE GHETTO IN RECENT AMERICAN LITERA-TURE. *J. of Ethnic Studies 1973 1(1): 44-54.* Concludes from an extensive examination of recent black and Jewish literature, that an understanding of Jewish and black ghetto culture is necessary in order to understand ethnic litera-ture. This literature can in turn provide deep insights into the nature of Jewish and black culture. Based on contemporary literature and related scholarship; 37 notes.   T. W. Smith

602. Schless, Nancy Halverson. PETER HARRISON, THE TOURO SYNA-GOGUE, AND THE WREN CITY CHURCH. *Winterthur Portfolio 1973 (8): 187-200.* The Touro Synagogue, Newport, Rhode Island, 1759-63, demonstrates the reliance of Peter Harrison (1716-75) on English architectural books. In spite of brief mention by other authors, the existence of a specific architectural model for the Newport synagogue has been overlooked. The prototype was the Bevis Marks Synagogue in London. The London building was derived from two sources. First, the design recalls the first London synagogue of the Resettlement, the Creechurch Lane synagogue. Secondly, Bevis Marks is related to the most common type of Wren city church of the late 17th century. The Bevis Marks Synagogue marks a halfway point and a catalyst in the "amalgamation of aisled, galleried basilica into religious architecture on both sides of the Atlantic." Based on primary and secondary sources; 19 illus., 16 notes.   N. A. Kuntz

603. Schmidt, Sarah. HORACE M. KALLEN AND THE "PROGRES-SIVE" REFORM OF AMERICAN ZIONISM. *Midstream 1976 22(10): 14-23.* Examines the efforts of Horace M. Kallen to bring about progressive reform within American Zionism during the early 20th century.

604. Schmidt, Sarah. HORACE M. KALLEN AND THE "AMERICAN-IZATION" OF ZIONISM—IN MEMORIAM. *Am. Jewish Arch. 1976 28(1): 59-73.* Discusses the life of Horace M. Kallen (1882-1974), especially detailing Kallen's beliefs about Zionism and American Jews.

605. Schmidt, Sarah. THE *PARUSHIM*: A SECRET EPISODE IN AMERICAN ZIONIST HISTORY. *Am. Jewish Hist. Q. 1975 65(2): 121-139.* Horace M. Kallen, best known in American intellectual history for his theory of cultural pluralism, became a Zionist in 1903 as a means to retain Jewish identity. Ten years later he founded a secret Zionist society which he called *Parushim* (separate ones) to realize his ideas on Zionism and to bring about statehood in Palestine. Even though the *Parushim* failed in these endeavors, their activities stirred and directed an unwieldy organizational structure, bedevilled by clashes of strong personalities, such as Rabbi Wise, Justice Brandeis, and Henrietta Szold. Contains excerpts of letters written in 1914.   F. Rosenthal

606.   Schmidt, Sarah.   THE ZIONIST CONVERSION OF LOUIS D. BRAN-
DEIS.   *Jewish Social Studies 1975 37(1): 18-34.* Brandeis's change in attitude
from a long-held, deeply felt belief in Jewish assimilation to that of an espousal
of a Zionist state was based to a considerable extent on his contacts with and the
influence of Horace Kallen, ca. 1912-15. Kallen's papers reveal that before Brandeis's agreement to take over leadership of the American Zionism movement, he
and Kallen met on various occasions for the exchange of ideas on the subject.
Brandeis's Zionist speeches are quite similar to Kallen's recorded thought. Based
on primary and secondary sources, and the author's interviews with Kallen.
N. Lederer

607.   Schmier, Louis.   THE FIRST JEWS OF VALDOSTA.   *Georgia Hist.*
Q. 1978 62(1): 32-49. Valdosta's first Jews, Abraham Ehrlich and Bernard Kaul,
arrived in 1866, closely followed by some of Ehrlich's relatives. Although the
number of Jews in Valdosta, Georgia, during this period was never greater than
17, they were very involved with business and town affairs. Business ventures as
well as acceptance by and involvement in the gentile community, particularly by
the Ehrlichs and the Engels, are detailed. Based on primary sources, mainly
newspapers, legal records, and interviews; 63 notes.   G. R. Schroeder

608.   Schneider, William; Berman, Michael D.; and Schilut, Mark.   BLOC
VOTING RECONSIDERED: "IS THERE A JEWISH VOTE?"   *Ethnicity*
1974 1(4): 345-392. Analysis of voting behavior among Jews, 1952-72, indicates
similar patterns to other "bloc voters" with tendencies toward liberalism, adherence to the Democratic Party, and the influence of "bloc forces."

609.   Schoenbaum, David.   THE UNITED STATES AND THE BIRTH OF
ISRAEL.   *Wiener Lib. Bull. [Great Britain] 1978 31(45-46): 87-100.* In 1946-47,
three possibilities existed for US policy toward Palestine: support partition, oppose it, or adopt neutrality. The first one raised the possibility of military responsibility for the protection of the Jews; neutrality would open the area to the
Russians. What remained was a cantonized federal Palestine under some kind of
trusteeship. However, Jewish successes led US foreign policy to recognize a de
facto partition. Shows variety of pressures on Harry S. Truman, from domestic
political concerns to the exigencies of the Cold War, and concludes that his policy
was "neither an opportunistic nor an incompetent one." It helped create Israel
while maintaining the Anglo-American alliance, keeping up the ties with the
Arab states, and avoiding being pulled into a major war. Summarizes contemporary opinions, for example, Secretary Forrestal's note in his diary in 1948 that
unless the United States had access to Middle Eastern oil, American motorcar
companies would have to design a four-cylinder motorcar. 77 notes.
R. V. Layton

610.   Schoenberg, Philip Ernest.   THE AMERICAN REACTION TO THE
KISHINEV POGROM OF 1903.   *Am. Jewish Hist. Q. 1974 63(3): 262-283.*
American reaction to the Kishinev pogrom (in which 47 Jews were killed, more
than 400 injured, and 10,000 made homeless and dependent on relief) led first to
the organization of financial help for the victims and then to plans for their
orderly immigration. Perhaps most surprising was the strong protest which the
Roosevelt administration tried to lodge in St. Petersburg. The events were, after
all, an internal affair within Russia, persecution of minority groups was taking

place in other parts of the world as well, and America's treatment of its own ethnic minorities left much to be desired. The formation of the American Jewish Committee was to permanently affect Jewish communal and organizational structure. 57 notes. F. Rosenthal

611. Schwartz, Henry. THE FIRST TEMPLE BETH ISRAEL: SAN DIEGO. *Western States Jewish Hist. Q. 1979 11(2): 153-161.* A surge in population growth following rail connection with the east in 1885 helped the growth of San Diego's Jewish congregation and led to the construction of Temple Beth Israel in 1889. The facilities were expanded for another population increase after World War I, but continued growth demanded a new synagogue, built in 1926. The old building was sold at that time but was repurchased by congregation Beth Israel in 1978. The community now intends to restore the historic building and move it to Heritage Park in Old Town. Primary and secondary sources; photo, 45 notes. B. S. Porter

612. Schwartz, Henry. THE LEVI SAGA: TEMECULA, JULIAN, SAN DIEGO. *Western States Jewish Hist. Q. 1974 6(3): 161-176.* A biography of Simon Levi (1850-1918) and his brother Adolph Levi (1858-1943), who came to San Diego from Bohemia, set up stores in several locations, and became successful businessmen. Examines their many years of public service. Primary and secondary sources; 5 photos, 53 notes. R. A. Garfinkle

613. Schwartz, Henry. THE UNEASY ALLIANCE: JEWISH-ANGLO RELATIONS IN SAN DIEGO, 1850-1860. *J. of San Diego Hist. 1975 20(3): 53-60.* Describes the generally harmonious relations between Jewish and other settlers in San Diego during the 1850's. S

614. Schwartz, Lita Linzer and Isser, Natalie. FORGOTTEN MINORITIES, SELF-CONCEPT, AND THE SCHOOLS. *Social Studies 1978 69(5): 187-190.* Textbooks written about Chinese, Japanese, and Jewish children are biased because they show unrealistic views of their cultures and life-styles. Covers the periods 1880-1920 and 1945-65. Bias against minorities may lead to damage of their self-image. 15 notes. L. R. Raife

615. Scult, Melvin. MORDECAI M. KAPLAN: CHALLENGES AND CONFLICTS IN THE TWENTIES. *Am. Jewish Hist. Q. 1977 66(3): 401-416.* Mordecai M. Kaplan was an immigrant who grew up on the lower East Side of New York City and who tried to reconcile his Orthodox Jewish upbringing with the new American culture. The struggle assumed both intellectual and spiritual aspects and was the basis for Kaplan's ambivalence toward the Jewish Theological Seminary where he served as head of its Teacher's Institute and as professor of Homiletics. Analyzes the gradual development of reconstructionist thoughts, clashes with Orthodoxy and seminary colleagues, relations with administrators and the lengthy negotiations with Stephen Wise and the Jewish Institute of Religion. 39 notes. F. Rosenthal

616. Segal, Beryl. THE EDUCATION OF AN IMMIGRANT. *Rhode Island Jewish Hist. Notes 1976 7(2): 277-293.* Reminiscences of Russia before World War I and of the immigration of a Jewish family to Canada and the United States, 1900-70's.

617. Segal, Beryl and Goldowsky, Seebert J. JAMES JACOBS, EARLY JEWISH MERCHANT OF PROVIDENCE, RHODE ISLAND. *Rhode Island Jewish Hist. Notes 1978 7(4): 461-470.* James Jacobs, possibly the first Jew to settle in Providence, was successful and prominent there, 1820's-30's and 1850's.

618. Segal, Beryl. JEWISH SCHOOLS AND TEACHERS IN METROPOLITAN PROVIDENCE: THE FIRST CENTURY. *Rhode Island Jewish Hist. Notes 1977 7(3): 410-419.* Covers 1854-1946.

619. Segal, Sheila F. FEMINISTS FOR JUDAISM. *Midstream 1975 21(7): 59-65.* Discusses the compatibility of Judaism and feminism (1970's).　　　S

620. Selavan, Ida Cohen. THE EDUCATION OF JEWISH IMMIGRANTS IN PITTSBURGH, 1862-1932. *Yivo Ann. of Jewish Social Sci. 1974 (15): 126-144.* Looks at the education of the Jewish immigrants in public school, night school, and adult education. Jews flocked to the public education system and did well. Hebrew, religious, and Yiddish education are also briefly covered. 85 notes.
R. J. Wechman

621. Selavan, Ida Cohen. THE FOUNDING OF COLUMBIAN COUNCIL. *Am. Jewish Arch. 1978 30(1): 24-42.* The Columbian Council of Pittsburgh was founded as a local section of the National Council of Jewish Women. Dr. Selavan examines the early years of the Council and highlights its most important contributions to the life of Pittsburgh Jewry.
J

622. Selavan, Ida Cohen. JEWISH WAGE EARNERS IN PITTSBURGH, 1890-1930. *Am. Jewish Hist. Q. 1976 65(3): 272-285.* The formation of a Jewish proletariat in Pittsburgh began after the influx of a large number of Jews from Eastern Europe. During the 40 years under discussion Jewish wage earners were found in large numbers among stogy makers, the needle trades, and the bakery trade, which was unionized in 1906. These three industries, each different in conditions, wages, and work force, are described on the basis of oral interviews, contemporary journals, newspapers, etc. Attempts to unionize tailors and seamstresses were successful only in the larger shops before 1914. 39 notes.
F. Rosenthal.

623. Seretan, L. Glen. DANIEL DE LEON, "WANDERING JEW" OF AMERICAN SOCIALISM: AN INTERPRETIVE ANALYSIS. *Am. Jewish Hist. Q. 1976 65(3): 245-256.* A psychohistorical analysis of the life of Daniel DeLeon (1850-1914), socialist leader and theoretician, and American labor radical and organizer, is provided in this essay, using Eugene Sue's literary concept of the Wandering Jew as a frame of reference. 19 notes.　　　F. Rosenthal

624. Sergeyev, S. NEKOTORYE OSOBENNOSTI RAZVITIIA SIONIZM V SSHA [Certain peculiarities attending the development of Zionism in the United States]. *Voprosy Istorii [USSR] 1973 11: 66-80.* Analysis of the development of American Zionism as the ideology and practice of the Jewish bourgeoisie, focussing on the close connection between the objectives of Zionism and the interests of America's ruling class as a whole, which is one of the principal factors determining the specific features of the development of Zionism in the United States. The article highlights the multi-various forms and methods of Zionism's

activity on the US political scene and gives a careful appraisal of the Zionist potential to exert influence on America's home and foreign policies. The author also examines the question concerning the role of America's Zionist movement in the over-all system of international Zionism.   J/S

625. Shack, Sybil. THE IMMIGRANT CHILD IN THE MANITOBA SCHOOLS IN THE EARLY TWENTIETH CENTURY. *Tr. of the Hist. and Sci. Soc. of Manitoba [Canada] 1973-74 (30): 17-32.* Discusses the history of the public schools in Winnipeg during 1900-20, concentrating on the educational difficulties of Jewish Central European immigrant children. Examines the school attendance records. The lack of incentive was due in part to the academic program reflecting a strong Protestant British tradition taught by English-speaking teachers who paid little attention to the children's heritage, and to the clash with the impoverished home situation. Primary and secondary works; 14 notes.
S. R. Quéripel

626. Shaffir, William. THE ORGANIZATION OF SECULAR EDUCATION IN A CHASSIDIC JEWISH COMMUNITY. *Can. Ethnic Studies [Canada] 1976 8(1): 38-51.* Examines how the religious community of Lubavitcher chassidim in Montreal, Quebec, attempts to minimize their children's exposure to contradictive materials during their secular learning; covers late 1969 to 1971.

627. Shafir, Shlomo. TAYLOR AND MCDONALD: TWO DIVERGING VIEWS ON ZIONISM AND THE EMERGING JEWISH STATE. *Jewish Social Studies 1977 39(4): 323-346.* Myron Taylor and James G. McDonald were public-spirited citizens involved in President Roosevelt's pre-World War II effort to ameliorate the condition of European Jews persecuted by Nazism. Taylor, head of the intergovernmental committee on refugees and later presidential emissary to the Vatican, was anti-Zionist; he felt that Jews should be absorbed by various countries rather than be allowed to migrate in large numbers to a newly created Israel. McDonald, one of the few Americans early aware during the 1930's of the Nazi threat to European Jews, became deeply involved in refugee activities and eventually, under President Truman, became the first US ambassador to Israel. McDonald understood the central position of Palestine as a place of refuge and rehabilitation for Jewish survivors of the Holocaust and consequently strongly supported unrestricted Jewish immigration to Palestine and the creation of Israel.
N. Lederer

628. Shain, Samson Aaron. ODE TO THE UNITED STATES ON ITS BICENTENNIAL AND TO THE REDEDICATION OF ITS PEOPLE TO THE PRINCIPLES OF THE DECLARATION OF INDEPENDENCE. *J. of the Lancaster County Hist. Soc. 1976 80(2): 109-112.* The late author (1906-76), a contributor to this journal, was Rabbi to Congregation Shaarai Shomayim in Lancaster 1956-76; presents Hebrew and English versions of his Bicentennial poem.

629. Shankman, Arnold. ATLANTA JEWRY—1900-1930. *Am. Jewish Arch. 1973 25(2): 131-155.* Though little research has been devoted to the subject, few ethnic groups have made as important a contribution to Atlanta history as have her Jewish citizens.   J

630.   Shankman, Arnold.   HAPPYVILLE, THE FORGOTTEN COLONY. *Am. Jewish Arch. 1978 30(1): 3-19.* The name Happyville, South Carolina, has become a forgotten chapter in the history of the American Jewish agricultural colonies. Yet Happyville needs to be remembered, more for the idealism and devotion of its colonists than for the failures which marked its short-lived existence. [Covers 1900-08].   J

631.   Shankman, Arnold.   THE PECULIAR PEOPLE AND THE JEWS. *Am. Jewish Hist. Q. 1975 64(3): 224-235.* During the last decades of the 19th century, when thousands of European Jews fled to the United States to escape religious persecution, Christian evangelical groups intensified their missionary efforts to convert Jews to Christianity. Among the religious periodicals founded to show the Jew "his need of repentance and of a saviour" was *The Peculiar People*, founded in New York City by the Reverend Herman Friedlaender as a weekly newspaper in 1888. On his sudden death four months later the magazine was taken over by the Reverend William C. Daland, backed by a group of Seventh Day Baptists. Daland served as editor until the paper's demise in 1898. Since Daland's efforts were primarily directed toward conversion of Jews, his interests in Palestinian colonization and his arguments against anti-Semitism were not effective in a wider sense.   F. Rosenthal

632.   Shapiro, Edward S.   AMERICAN JEWRY AND THE STATE OF ISRAEL.   *J. of Ecumenical Studies 1977 14(1): 1-16.* Changing attitudes of American Jews toward Israel, especially the increasing pro-Israel sentiment created by the wars of 1967 and 1973, helped to develop a uniquely American Zionism that makes criticism or indifference toward Israel within the United States seem anti-Semitic.

633.   Shapiro, Edward S.   GERMAN AND RUSSIAN JEWS IN AMERICA. *Midstream 1979 25(4): 42-51.* Discusses the reactions of established German Jews in America to the mass immigration of Jews from Russia between 1880 and 1920, and their assimilation into American culture.

634.   Shapiro, Howard M.   PERCEIVED FAMILY STRUCTURE AS AN EXPLANATION OF JEWISH INTELLECTUALITY.   *Sociol. Q. 1977 18(4): 448-463.* Focuses on the perceived structure of parent-adolescent relations for its effect on intellectuality in young adulthood. In addition, position in the wider societal structure and integration into a supposed intellectually oriented subculture are considered for their effects on this personality characteristic. The data reported are based on a questionnaire survey of 181 Jewish men age 22-29 residing in metropolitan St. Paul. There is a clear association between the perception structure of parent-child relations and later intellectuality. On the other hand, integration into the Jewish subculture neither leads directly to intellectuality nor is associated with the relationship between perceived family structure, and intellectuality. Position in the wider social structure, however, is important in the development of intellectuality both directly and in terms of its effect on perceived family structure.   J

635.   Shechner, Mark.   ISAAC ROSENFELD'S WORLD.   *Partisan Rev. 1976 43(4): 524-543.* Isaac Rosenfeld was a literary journalist who wrote book reviews, critical essays and occasional fiction. He wrote during and after World

War II for such publications as *New Republic*, *Nation*, *Commentary* and *Partisan Review*. As a Jewish intellectual, Rosenfeld's theme was alienation. He often used the ideas of Whilhelm Reich in his cultural analysis. While a minor figure in his own life-time, Rosenfeld's work demonstrated the continuing and significant contribution of Jewish intellectuals to America's moral and cultural life. Undocumented. D. K. Pickens

636. Shook, Robert W. ABRAHAM LEVI: FATHER OF VICTORIA JEWRY. *Western States Jewish Hist. Q. 1977 9(2): 144-154.* Victoria, Texas, was a trade and cattle center serving Texas and northern Mexico since before the Civil War. Abraham Levi (1822-1902) was among the earliest Jewish settlers in Victoria, arriving in 1848 or 1849. By the 1870's the Jewish community included 15 families and had organized a reform congregation. Levi operated a retail store, and engaged in land transactions and private banking. The Levi Bank and Trust Company (now the Victoria Bank and Trust) was franchised in 1910. Levi's activities in the community included serving as president of the Jewish congregation and as a city alderman. Primary and secondary sources; 3 photos, 26 notes. B. S. Porter

637. Showalter, Dennis E. A RIVER OF BLOOD AND TIME: IMAGES OF JEWISH-GENTILE RELATIONS IN CONTEMPORARY PULP CULTURE. *South Atlantic Q. 1977 76(1): 12-31.* Traditional literary images of Jewish-Gentile relations define the Jew by the acts of his Christian oppressors. Until recently, the Jew was either physically brutalized or spiritually assimilated by the Christian world, whether he resisted or not. Post-World War II portrayals make the Jew into freedom fighters of a classically heroic mode, or into members of a matured, independent Israel. This shift has left the American Jew all the more self-conscious of his non-Israeli, nonoppressed, highly ambivalent cultural position. 25 notes. W. L. Olbrich

638. Shumsky, Neil Larry. ZANGWILL'S *THE MELTING POT:* ETHNIC TENSIONS ON STAGE. *Am. Q. 1975 27(1): 29-41.* The widely held interpretation of Israel Zangwill's play as a hymn to ethnic assimilation in America oversimplifies its contradictions and inconsistencies. Zangwill expresses ambivalence over the immigrant acceptance of Americanization at the expense of ethnic tradition. The hero, David Quixano, consciously tries to reject his Judaic heritage while other characters praise it. The play is a depiction of the tormented immigrant mind, including the dilemma of generational conflict. N. Lederer

639. Sichel, Carolyn Meyberg. LOS ANGELES MEMORIES. *Western States Jewish Hist. Q. 1974 7(1): 49-58.* The author relates her experiences growing up in Los Angeles at the turn of the century. Relatives and close family friends included civic, business, and religious leaders in Los Angeles. As a second generation Jewish family, their goal was Americanization. Yiddish was not spoken in her home, but the family was very religious. 2 photos, 6 notes. R. A. Garfinkle

640. Silberschlag, Eisig. THE THRUST OF HEBREW LETTERS IN AMERICA: A PANORAMIC VIEW. *Jewish Social Studies 1976 38(3-4): 277-288.* Hebrew literature in America has been a literature of immigrants and displays a concern with affairs of the homeland and a spiritual yearning for the

shtetl as well as for the Holy Land. The literature, predominantly poetic in form, has been highly romantic and draws on Victorian and American models for some of its themes. Among the themes have been those concerned with blacks and the American Indian. Despite its foreign focus, Hebrew literature has been most cognizant of American ideals. Primary sources.   N. Lederer

641. Silverberg, David. "HEAVENLY DECEPTION": REV. MOON'S HARD SELL. *Present Tense 1976 4(1): 49-56.* Describes the growth and decline of Reverend Sun Myung Moon's Unification Church. Discusses the Moonie experience, deprogramming, the Divine Principle, anti-Semitism, Jewish involvement and reaction. Primary and secondary sources; 5 photos.
R. B. Mendel

642. Silverberg, David. HILLEL ON THE CAMPUS. *Present Tense 1978 5(2): 53-59.* The Hillel Foundation is a Jewish association active in colleges and universities since 1923.

643. Silverberg, David. JEWISH STUDIES ON THE AMERICAN CAMPUS. *Present Tense 1978 5(4): 52-56.* Both academic and community interest are reflected in the growth of Jewish studies programs in US colleges and universities, 1967-77; the movement resulted from growing ethnic consciousness and the Israeli victory in the 1967 Six-Day War.

644. Silverberg, David. THE "OLD" POOR—AND THE "NEW": WHAT'S HAPPENING TO THEM? *Present Tense 1977 4(3): 59-64.* Examines the plight of American urban Jewish poor. Presents case studies, and quotes Ann G. Wolfe, Misha Avramoff, Yisroel Rosenfeld, Yaakov Tzimman, Rose Fefelman, Leonard Haber, Eugene Weiss, Jack Simcha Cohen, Max Friedson, Alfred P. Miller, and Steven Robbins. Cites official government, local community, and Hassidic sources. Primary and secondary sources; 4 photos.
R. B. Mendel

645. Simms, Adam. A BATTLE IN THE AIR: DETROIT'S JEWS ANSWER FATHER COUGHLIN. *Michigan Jewish Hist. 1978 18(2): 7-13.* A memorandum written in 1939 by executive director William I. Boxerman outlines the initial stages of the Jewish Community Council's radio campaign against Charles Edward Coughlin's anti-Semitism.

646. Simons, Leonard N. MY YEARS OF COMMUNAL ACTIVITIES IN THE DETROIT JEWISH COMMUNITY: SOME PERSONAL MEMOIRS. *Michigan Jewish Hist. 1975 15(2): 9-33.* Short autobiographical sketch of the author (1901-75) and his community involvement, including work with the Detroit Jewish Welfare Federation, the Jewish Home for the Aged, and the Sinai Hospital in Detroit, Michigan.   S

647. Sinclair, Clive. A CONVERSATION WITH ISAAC BASHEVIS SINGER. *Encounter [Great Britain] 1979 52(2): 20-28.* Records a recent interview with Isaac Bashevis Singer, winner of the 1978 Nobel Prize for literature, in which he discusses his life in Poland and the United States, Jews, his writings, and the work of his brother, Israel Joshua Singer, author of *The Brothers Ashkenazi, Yoshe Kalb, East of Eden* and others.

648. Singer, David. LIVING WITH INTERMARRIAGE. *Commentary 1979 68(1): 48-53.* Discusses the issue of marriage between Jews and Christians in the United States, which was discussed at a national symposium on intermarriage in 1963, and provides data on intermarriage from studies since 1962.

649. Singer, David. THE PRELUDE TO NAZISM: THE GERMAN-AMERICAN PRESS AND THE JEWS 1919-1933. *Am. Jewish Hist. Q. 1977 66(3): 417-431.* Analyzes editorial and news materials which appeared in the German-American presses, particularly those of the Midwest during 1919-33. Shows that attitudes toward Jews changed from support to strong unfriendliness. Newspapers, such as the Illinois *Staats-Zeitung,* the Milwaukee *Herald,* and the St. Louis *Weltiche Post,* reflected the rise of anti-Semitism, racism and xenophobia in America and Western Europe. 35 notes.   F. Rosenthal

650. Singer, David. A PROFILE OF THE JEWISH ACADEMIC: SOME RECENT STUDIES. *Midstream 1973 19(6): 57-64.*

651. Singer, David. VOICES OF ORTHODOXY. *Commentary 1974 58(1): 54-60.* In view of the "Orthodox renaissance," describes ideological differences between modernist and sectarian branches of Orthodox Judaism.   S

652. Singer, Isaac Bashevis and Howe, Irving. YIDDISH TRADITION VS. JEWISH TRADITION: A DIALOGUE. *Midstream 1973 19(6): 33-38.*

653. Singerman, Robert. AMERICAN-JEWISH REACTIONS TO THE SPANISH CIVIL WAR. *J. of Church and State 1977 19(2): 261-278.* Considers the background of Jews in Spain and examines the America Jewish press's reaction to the treatment of Jews during the Spanish Civil War, 1936-39. 58 notes.
E. E. Eminhizer

654. Singerman, Robert and Grumet, Elinor, eds. WAYWARD ETCHINGS: I. N. CHOYNSKI VISITS SOUTHERN CALIFORNIA, 1881. *Western States Jewish Hist. Q. 1979 11(2): 119-135.* Isidor Nathan Choynski (1834-99) was the West's foremost Jewish journalist of the 19th century. Choynski set out from his home in San Francisco in 1881 to visit several cities in southern, California. His reports on San Luis Obispo, Santa Barbara, Los Angeles, San Gabriel, San Bernardino, Riverside, and San Diego mention the numbers of Jews in these cities, praise their commercial success, and criticize their religious indifference. Based on articles published in *The American Isralite* on 8, 15, and 29 July 1881; 2 photos, 19 notes.   B. S. Porter

655. Siskin, Edgar E. CHAIM WEIZMANN AND JAMES H. BECKER: THE STORY OF A FRIENDSHIP. *Am. Jewish Arch. 1975 27(1): 32-50.* Chaim Weizmann sought the aid of successful businessman James H. Becker in furthering the cause of Zionism in the 1920's.   S

656. Sklare, Marshall. AMERICAN JEWRY—THE EVER-DYING PEOPLE. *Midstream 1976 22(6): 17-27.* Examines in the Bicentennial year the question of whether American Jewry will survive as a viable community in the United States in the next 100 years, and provides a brief history of the Jewish experience in America after 1880.

657. Sklare, Marshall. THE GREENING OF JUDAISM. *Commentary 1974 58(6): 51-57.* Reviews *The Jewish Catalog: A Do-It Yourself Kit,* Richard Siegel, Michael Strassfeld, and Sharon Strassfeld, eds. (Jewish Publication Society of America, 1974).   S

658. Sklare, Marshall. THE JEW IN AMERICAN SOCIOLOGICAL THOUGHT. *Ethnicity 1974 1(2): 151-173.* Jews in academia are more active professionally than non-Jews, but are quite often alienated from their own Jewish communities. Jewish sociologists involved in the study of Jews fall into three schools: assimilationists who see the Jewish community as a dying anachronism and advocate the right of assimilation, critical intellectuals who idealize the immigrant communities but are alienated from and critical of contemporary Jewry, and survivalists who see both continuity and assimilation, and are unsentimental about the old communities, but detect an ongoing liberalism. 28 notes.
E. Barkan

659. Sklare, Marshall. JEWISH RELIGION AND ETHNICITY AT THE BICENTENNIAL. *Midstream 1975 21(9): 19-28.* The survival of the Jewish religion in the United States has been deeply dependent upon the Jews' sense of ethnic unity.

660. Sklare, Marshall. PROBLEMS IN THE TEACHING OF CONTEMPORARY JEWISH STUDIES. *Am. Jewish Hist. Q. 1974 63(4): 361-368.* Contemporary Jewish studies is a newcomer in the academic world, and has several problems to resolve before it can become a fully developed discipline. One of nine related articles in this issue.   S

661. Smith, Judith E. OUR OWN KIND: FAMILY AND COMMUNITY NETWORKS. *Radical Hist. Rev. 1978 (17): 99-120.* Provides a study of immigrant family ties and traditions, particularly among southern Italian and eastern European Jewish immigrants as they experienced the urban industrial environment of Rhode Island during 1880-1940.

662. Sokolov, Raymond A. HARRY SALTZSTEIN, M.D. (1890-): A PERSONAL MEMOIR. *Michigan Jewish Hist. 1976 16(2): 5-9.* Reminisces about Harry Saltzstein, a fellow surgeon and leader in the Jewish community in Chicago, 1935-75.

663. Solomon, Joseph. AUTOBIOGRAPHY. *Am. Jewish Arch. 1976 28(1): 51-58.* Provides an autobiographical sketch of Joseph Solomon (b. 1905), from his birth until his admission to the bar in December 1928, including his education and his fascination with the law.

664. Spetter, Allan. THE UNITED STATES THE RUSSIAN JEWS AND THE RUSSIAN FAMINE OF 1891-1892. *Am. Jewish Hist. Q. 1975 64(3): 236-244.* The United States, aware of its world power status, became involved in the internal affairs of the Russian Empire in the early 1890's because of Russia's persecution of the Jews and the great famine. Diplomatic representations made by American foreign service personnel are surveyed along with the evasive answers of Russian officials. Even though the Benjamin Harrison administration was not able to ameliorate the lot of the Russian Jews, it provided a haven for those who left. Russian policy led ultimately to the cancellation of the 1832 commercial treaty.   F. Rosenthal

665. Sprenger, Bernice C. THE BURTON HISTORICAL COLLECTION AND ITS JEWISH ARCHIVES. *Michigan Jewish Hist. 1973 13(1): 5-7.* Covers items concerning Jews in Michigan from the Burton Historical Collection of the Detroit Public Library.   S

666. Starr, Jerold M. RELIGIOUS PREFERENCE, RELIGIOSITY, AND OPPOSITION TO WAR. *Sociol. Analysis 1975 36(4): 323-334.* Discusses the high percentage of Jewish youth involved in the anti-Vietnam War protest movements of the 1960's.

667. Steinberg, Jacob. THE MOSCOW BOOK FAIR—REVISITED. *Freedom at Issue 1978 (46): 27-30.* Discusses a vitriolic attack made on the Association of Jewish Book Publishers by a Soviet journal following a display of AJBP books at a Moscow book fair, 1977.

668. Steiner, Ruth Heller. "THE GIRLS" IN CHICAGO. *Am. Jewish Arch. 1974 26(1): 5-22.* Aunt Ernestine and Aunt Louise would have summed up their lives as "a combination of luck and nerve," but their niece, Mrs. Steiner, reflected that the word she would have chosen "would be character."   J

669. Stern, Malcolm H. GROWING UP IN PIONEER SAVANNAH: THE UNFINISHED MEMOIR OF LEVI SHEFTALL (1739-1809). *Michael: On the Hist. of the Jews in the Diaspora [Israel] 1975 3: 15-22.* Levi Sheftall was a son of Benjamin Sheftall (1692-1765), a native of Prussia and one of the first Jews to settle in Georgia; he was half-brother to Mordecai Sheftall. Reprints the oldest known memoir of an American Jew and possibly the earliest description of life in pioneer Savannah. Starting from scratch, Levi Sheftall accumulated a large fortune, including many slaves, but eventually lost most of it. Imprisoned as a rebel during the American Revolution, he denied entertaining such sentiments. He was active in Jewish community life. 10 notes.   T. Sassoon

670. Stern, Malcolm H. REFORMING OF REFORM JUDAISM—PAST, PRESENT, AND FUTURE. *Am. Jewish Hist. Q. 1973 63(2): 111-137.* Summarizes the history of Reform Judaism from its beginnings in France and Germany during the time of the French Revolution to its flowering in America during the past 100 years. Includes an extensive bibliography of its history, institutions, biographies, sociological studies, rituals, periodicals, and congregational histories by states.   F. Rosenthal

671. Stern, Norton B. and Kramer, William M. ANTI-SEMITISM AND THE JEWISH IMAGE IN THE EARLY WEST. *Western States Jewish Hist. Q. 1974 6(2): 129-140.* A study of California newspapers in the gold rush period; centers on anti-Semitic articles and stories, and Jewish responses to those articles. Primary sources; 21 notes.   R. A. Garfinkle

672. Stern, Norton B. and Kramer, William M. ARIZONA'S MINING WIZARD: BLACK JACK NEWMAN. *Western States Jewish Hist. Q. 1979 11(3): 255-264.* John B. (Black Jack) Newman (1862-1928) seemed to have an uncanny ability to locate rich copper ore deposits near Globe, Arizona, in the 1880's through 1910. With the money earned in the mining business, Newman invested real estate both in Arizona and in his new home in southern California (1910-28). His pet project in his later years was a cattle ranch and orchard in the

San Joaquin Valley. Beginning as a penniless, illiterate miner, he developed a fortune estimated at $12 million at the time of his death. Primary and secondary sources; 2 photos, 23 notes.   B. S. Porter

673. Stern, Norton B. AT THE SOUTHERN END OF THE MOTHER LODE. *Western States Jewish Hist. Q. 1976 8(2): 163-166.* Most of the Jews who lived in Mariposa County during the 1850's-60's resided in Mariposa and Hornitos, were foreign born, and were in business. By 1882 only two Jewish merchants were left in the county. The rest had left when the gold rush ended. No Jewish buildings, benevolent societies, or cemeteries were established in Mariposa County. 24 notes.   R. A. Garfinkle

674. Stern, Norton B. BAD DAY AT SAN BERNARDINO. *Western States Jewish Hist. Q. 1974 7(1): 61-66.* On 2 January 1862, Wolff Cohn was killed in his own store by Dick Cole, while Cole was wounded by Wolff's brother Isaac. In August 1861, 35 citizens of San Bernardino signed a petition requesting the army to come and protect the merchants from attacks by desperadoes. Isaac Cohn was arrested but the grand jury refused to indict him for shooting Cole. 18 notes.   R. A. Garfinkle

675. Stern, Norton B. THE BERNSTEINS OF BAJA CALIFORNIA. *Western States Jewish Hist. Q. 1975 7(2): 108-115.* Max Bernstein (1854-1914) went to Baja California during the gold rush of 1881. He became the resident agent of the International Company of Mexico, working to develop Ensenada for the company. He married Governor Teodoro Riveroll's daughter, Guadalupe, and had seven children. Includes information about their descendants living mainly in California. 9 photos, 5 notes.   R. A. Garfinkle

676. Stern, Norton B. CALIFORNIA'S JEWISH GOVERNOR. *Western States Jewish Hist. Q. 1973 5(4): 285-287.* Discusses Washington Bartlett (1824-87), journalist and politician in San Francisco and governor of the state in 1886.

677. Stern, Norton B. CHOLERA IN SAN FRANCISCO IN 1850. *Western States Jewish Hist. Q. 1973 5(3): 200-204.* Notes the charity efforts of Jews led by Samuel I. Neustadt to ameliorate conditions during the cholera epidemic.

678. Stern, Norton B. DENOUEMENT ON SAN DIEGO IN 1888. *Western States Jewish Hist. Q. 1978 11(1): 49-55.* David and Fannie Green, married in Ripin, Poland, in 1863, had a stormy marriage with a pattern of desertion and reconciliation until 1888 when Fannie decided to divorce her husband. By this time Fannie operated a boarding house in San Diego, California. David, who opposed the divorce, came to the house on the evening of 31 August 1888, and during an argument with his wife and her lawyer's clerk, wounded Fannie with a revolver and fatally shot himself. The Jewish press viewed the incident and the Green family as a disgrace to Judaism. Based on primary sources; 34 notes.   B. S. Porter

679. Stern, Norton B. and Kramer, William M. THE FIRST JEWISH ORGANIZATION, THE FIRST JEWISH CEMETERY AND THE FIRST KNOWN JEWISH BURIAL IN THE FAR WEST. *Western States Jewish Hist. Q. 1979 11(4): 318-324.* The first Jewish burial in the West took place in San Francisco in December 1849. The deceased was Henry D. Johnson, religious

rites were performed by Lewis A. Franklin, and burial was in the Yerba Buena public cemetery. Following this burial, the Jewish community organized the First Hebrew Benevolent Society and established a Jewish cemetery so that Jewish burials could take place in consecrated ground. The Benevolent Society was founded in January 1850, and the land for the cemetery was acquired in April 1950. Johnson's remains were moved to the new cemetery. The first funeral service in the Hart (Jewish) Cemetery was in the fall of 1850 when two victims of the Sacramento cholera epidemic were buried. Newspaper accounts and other published sources; photo, 22 notes. B. S. Porter

680. Stern, Norton B. THE FOUNDING OF THE JEWISH COMMUNITY IN UTAH. *Western States Jewish Hist. Q. 1975 8(1): 65-69.* Charges two authors, Leon L. Watters, *The Pioneer Jews of Utah* (New York: American Jewish Historical Society, 1952), and Juanita Brooks, *History of the Jews in Utah and Idaho* (Salt Lake City: Western Epics, 1973), with failing to research thoroughly for information about the founding of the Jewish community in Utah for their books on early Utah Jewish history. Cites a contemporary (1860's) report published in *The Hebrew* of San Francisco as the baisis for the facts. Watters and Brooks used other sources for their information. 16 notes. R. A. Garfinkle

681. Stern, Norton B. THE FRANKLIN BROTHERS OF SAN DIEGO. *J. of San Diego Hist. 1975 21(3): 32-42.* Describes the lives of Lewis Abraham Franklin (1820-79) and his brother Maurice Abraham Franklin (1817-74), pioneer merchants of San Diego during the 1850's. S

682. Stern, Norton B. HELENA, MONTANA JEWRY RESPONDS TO A FRENCH APPEAL IN 1868. *Western States Jewish Hist. Q. 1979 11(2): 170-172.* Jews in France established the Alliance Israelite Universelle in 1860 to improve the living conditions of Jews in North Africa, the Near East, and Eastern Europe. The Alliance's appeal for aid, published in *The American Israelite* of Cincinnati on 17 January 1868, was met with a generous reponse from the Jewish population of Helena, Montana. Sixty-seven individuals were listed as donors, giving evidence of a large Jewish population in the pioneer Western town. Based on an article in *The American Israelite,* 17 January 1868; 9 notes.
B. S. Porter

683. Stern, Norton B. and Kramer, William M. THE HISTORICAL RECOVERY OF THE PIONEER SEPHARDIC JEWS OF CALIFORNIA. *Western States Jewish Hist. Q. 1975 8(1): 3-25.* Virtually ignored by historians writing about Jews living in California in the 19th century, the Sephardic Jewish community has been rediscovered by historians. In 1853, the Sephardic Jews in San Francisco organized Congregation Shaar Hashamayim, but this group folded in less than a year. The members joined the two Ashkenazim congregations in the city. Because they were no longer an organized group, little was written about them. Discusses prominent California Sephardic Jews, including Abraham Cohen Labatt (and his sons), Joseph Rodriguez Brandon (1828-1916), Elcan Heydenfeldt, Solomon Heydenfeldt (1816-1890), Isaac Nunez Cardozo, California Governor Washington Bartlett (and his brothers Julian and Columbus), Joseph Simpson, Raphael Schoyer, Manuel Mordicai Noah, Elias De Sola, Seixas Solomons, Abraham H. L. Dias (1814-77), and Benjamin Franklin Davega. 3 photos, 78 notes. R. A. Garfinkle

684.   Stern, Norton B. and Kramer, William M.   AN ISAAC MAYER WISE 1890 PLACEMENT LETTER TO SAN FRANCISCO.   *Am. Jewish Hist. Q. 1973 63(2): 204-207.* A recently discovered letter of Rabbi Isaac Mayer Wise to Abraham J. Prager, president of Congregation Sherith Israel of San Francisco, 28 April 1890, shows the role of Wise in rabbinic placement. As the patriarch of American Jewry he felt it his responsibility and moral duty to provide objective information when men of his close acquaintance, whether students or colleagues, applied for rabbinic positions. Reproduces the letter. 9 notes.   F. Rosenthal

685.   Stern, Norton B.   JEWS IN THE 1870 CENSUS OF LOS ANGELES. *Western States Jewish Hist. Q. 1976 9(1): 71-86.* The federal census taken in 1870 showed there were 330 Jews (5.76% of the population) in the city of Los Angeles. This high proportion of Jews was probably duplicated in other cities of the early West. Demographic analysis shows the Jewish population to be predominantly young, Polish or Prussian-Polish, and employed in the merchandizing of wearing apparel. Based on the Federal Census of 1870, city and county directories, cemetery records, register of voters, secondary publications, and demographic and name listings; 11 notes.   B. S. Porter

686.   Stern, Norton B.   THE KING OF TEMECULA: LOUIS WOLF. *Southern California Q. 1976 58(1): 63-74.* Provides a profile of Louis Wolf (1833-87), merchant and rancher in the Temecula Valley, 60 miles north of San Diego. Born in France of Jewish parentage, Wolf arrived in San Francisco in 1852. By the late 1850's he had constructed a general store and hostelry in the Temecula Valley. For 30 years he dominated the economic life of the valley. His enterprises included livestock, hotel, retail sales, and real estate. Wolf and his wife, who was of Indian blood, met Helen Hunt Jackson in 1882. Jackson based characters on them in her novel *Ramona*, which she named after Wolf's wife. Known for his sympathy for the Indians in the region, he was called by them "King of Temecula." At his death in 1887 his estate was worth more than $100,000. Not an observant Jew, Wolf shared many characteristics of his coreligionists in his economic activities, participation in civic affairs, and friendship for Indians and Californios. Based on primary and secondary sources; 52 notes.
A. Hoffman

687.   Stern, Norton B. and Kramer, William M.   THE LILIENTHAL FAMILY PACT.   *Western States Jewish Hist. Q. 1975 7(3): 220-224.* The pact of seven families surnamed Lilienthal created on 20 August 1880 established a family corporation whereby the signers pooled their assets and their abilities to aid each other and "the furtherance of the common interest." "In this document the age-old Jewish ideal of family solidarity was formalized by a contractual agreement under the laws of the State of New York." Included are short biographies of the Lilienthals, the text of the pact, and the individual roles of the signers within the agreements of the pact. 5 notes.   R. A. Garfinkle

688.   Stern, Norton B.   LOS ANGELES JEWRY AND THE CHICAGO FIRE.   *Western States Jewish Hist. Q. 1974 6(4): 260-267.* Soon after the fire that destroyed most of Chicago in 1871, the Jews of Los Angeles collected $2,657 from several individuals and benevolent societies to send to the stricken city. 23 notes.   R. A. Garfinkle

689. Stern, Norton B. and Kramer, William M. THE MAJOR ROLE OF POLISH JEWS IN THE PIONEER WEST. *Western States Jewish Hist. Q. 1976 8(4): 326-344.* In the West many Polish Jews hid their Polishness as an effort to expedite their social movement. Polish Jews were considered inferior to German Jews. The myth therefore developed that few Polish Jews settled in the West. This is now being repudiated by scholars studying voter records, tombstones, and other sources. Census records show that Polish Jews outnumbered German Jews in early California. Many so-called German synagogues were really established by Polish Jews and followed the Minhag Polem (Polish custom). Contemporary accounts credited Germans with starting the congregations. 70 notes.

R. A. Garfinkle

690. Stern, Norton B. THE MASONIC CAREER OF BENJAMIN D. HYAM, CALIFORNIA'S THIRD GRAND MASTER. *Western States Jewish Hist. Q. 1975 7(3): 251-263.* Benjamin Daniel Hyam came to California in 1850. He organized the Benecia Lodge and held several offices within the Masonic order. In 1850 he attended a convention to form a Grand Lodge of California, and in 1852 was elected Grand Master. After trying to help a Jewish friend be reinstalled into the order, he was attacked by his fellow Masons and suffered their prejudice for many years. Hyam served as a quartermaster clerk during the Civil War and practiced law in Washington, D.C., until his death. Based on primary and secondary sources; photo, 46 notes.

R. A. Garfinkle

691. Stern, Norton B. MISSION TO SAN BERNARDINO IN 1879. *Western States Jewish Hist. Q. 1978 10(3): 227-233.* In the summer of 1879, Rabbi Aron J. Messing of San Francisco went to San Bernardino, California, for a "missionary visit." This unusual trip was undertaken to raise funds for construction of a synagogue for Messing's San Francisco Congregation Beth Israel. In San Bernardino Messing organized a Sabbath school and a Hebrew Association to promote the spiritual welfare of the community. Rabbi Messing undertook several fundraising journeys but was careful to avoid slander or suspicion by bringing along a trustee from his congregation to receive the collections. Primary and secondary sources; 25 notes.

B. S. Porter

692. Stern, Norton B. A "MURDER" TO BE FORGOTTEN. *Western States Jewish Hist. Q. 1977 9(2): 176-185.* On 20 May 1875 in the settlement of Rincon, California, in today's Riverside County, Simon Goldsmith fatally shot his business partner George Kallman. The dispute concerned Goldsmith's handling of a large sum of the firm's money. A popular and respected man in his community and in Los Angeles, Goldsmith was tried and found innocent. The general feeling in the community was that the universal practice of carrying concealed weapons was a large cause of the tragedy. Goldsmith continued to operate his store in Rincon until 1883 when he joined his brothers in a general merchandise business in Santa Ana, and later retired to San Francisco in 1902 or 1903. The reaction of the Jewish community was to repress the memory of the killing to the extent that none of the direct or collateral descendants has ever heard of it. Based on newspaper reports, court records, interviews and published sources; 2 photos, 40 notes.

B. S. Porter

693. Stern, Norton B. THE NAME OF LOS ANGELES' FIRST JEWISH NEWSPAPER. *Western States Jewish Hist. Q. 1975 7(2): 153-157.* Lionel L. Edwards, publisher, and Victor Harris, editor, established the first Los Angeles Jewish newspaper, the *Emanu-El*, on 10 March 1897. Rabbi Jacob Voorsanger, publisher of the well-established Jewish newspaper *Emanu-El* in San Francisco, criticized the fact that the southern paper had copied his paper's name. In 1898, the southern paper was changed to the *B'nai B'rith Messenger*, and is still published under that title. 15 notes.   R. A. Garfinkle

694. Stern, Norton B. A NEW CLUB FOR LOS ANGELES. *Western States Jewish Hist. Q. 1978 10(4): 374-376.* About 40 Jewish men met in Levy's Cafe in Los Angeles, California, on 9 December 1908 to organize the Jewish Progress Club. Its object was to read papers and discuss current literary and scientific topics, especially those pertaining to Judaism. Those who founded and joined the club were a homogeneous group of civic and business leaders.
                                                               B. S. Porter

695. Stern, Norton B. THE ORANGEVALE AND PORTERVILLE, CAL-IFORNIA, JEWISH FARM COLONIES. *Western States Jewish Hist. Q. 1978 10(2): 159-167.* In 1891, David Lubin of Sacramento, California, helped organize The International Society for the Colonization of Russian Jews. Lubin and Harris Weinstock settled 10 families on land they owned at Orangevale, several miles northeast of Sacramento. Philip Nettre Lilienthal established the Porterville settlement in the southeastern San Joaquin Valley. Both colonies failed because of poor land, inadequate capital and equipment, and lack of experience and motivation on the part of the colonists, most of whom had backgrounds in commerce and small business. Based on interviews and published sources; photo, 37 notes.
                                                               B. S. Porter

696. Stern, Norton B. and Kramer, William M. THE POLISH JEW IN POSEN AND IN THE EARLY WEST. *Western States Jewish Hist. Q. 1978 10(4): 327-329.* Polish Jews came early and were the numerically dominant Jewish subethnic group in the West. Their Polish-Jewish culture was often disguised because they came from Prussian-occupied areas, carried Prussian passports, and frequently claimed to be Germans instead of Poles because of the prejudice of Americans. In America, they engaged in the same type of business they had known in the province of Posen—selling dry goods, hardware, farming implements, liquor, and so on. Covers the 1880's.   B. S. Porter

697. Stern, Norton B. and Kramer, William M. A PRE-ISRAELI DIPLO-MAT ON AN AMERICAN MISSION, 1869-1870. *Western States Jewish Hist. Q. 1976 8(3): 232-242.* Rabbi Hayyim Zevi Sneersohn (1834-82) spent several years traveling the world lecturing about the Holy Land with the goal of gaining support for the establishment of a Jewish homeland in Palestine. In 1869 he succeeded in having President Grant send a Jew to work in the American consulate in Jerusalem. In 1870 President Grant sent another Jew as US consul in Rumania. Rabbi Sneersohn wanted Jews in these posts because he believed they would be able to help their fellow Jews in areas of oppression. His lectures were well attended. 29 notes.   R. A. Garfinkle

698.   Stern, Norton B. and Kramer, William M.   THE SAN BERNARDINO
HEBREW AND ENGLISH ACADEMY 1868-1872.   *Western States Jewish
Hist. Q. 1976 8(2): 102-117.* The first Jewish day school in southern California
was opened on 27 May 1868 by the Jewish community in San Bernardino.
Siegmund Bergel served as the teacher for the San Bernardino Hebrew and
English Academy during 1868-72. The subjects included English, Latin, Greek,
Hebrew, and other branches of education. Theatrical productions were given each
year for different Jewish holidays. Bergel was active in civic affairs. He helped
establish the San Bernardino Literary Society and served as its first president. In
1872, he left for his homeland in Germany. He became internationally known for
his work as a Jewish community leader. He died in 1912. Photo, 52 notes.
R. A. Garfinkle

699.   Stern, Norton B.   A SAN FRANCISCO SYNAGOGUE SCANDAL IN
1893.   *Western States Jewish Hist. Q. 1974 6(3): 196-203.* A scandal developed
at Temple Sherith Israel in 1893, when a new rabbi was being installed. The
cantor, Max Rubin, did not want a new rabbi who would start receiving fees for
weddings and funerals, as he had been filling in as reader for over a year and liked
the large sum collected for officiating at various functions. In June, 1893, Rabbi
Jacob Nieto was elected Rabbi of the congregation, and the scandal soon died
down. Primary and secondary sources; 14 notes.   R. A. Garfinkle

700.   Stern, Norton B. and Kramer, William M.   THE SINSHEIMERS OF
SAN LUIS OBISPO.   *Western States Jewish Hist. Q. 1973 6(1): 3-32.* Traces
Aaron Sinsheimer's family from his German ancestors to his children who reside
in California. Aaron Zachary Sinsheimer came to America in 1845, settled in
Vicksburg, Mississippi, and then moved to San Luis Obispo, California, in 1878.
In 1884 the Sinsheimers built an iron front store that is considered one of the
best-preserved structures of its style. Aaron took over the store in 1898 and was
a leading citizen in his day. Includes short biographies of the 10 Sinsheimer
children. 2 illus., 4 photos, 90 notes.   R. A. Garfinkle

701.   Stern, Norton B.   WHEN THE FRANCO-PRUSSIAN WAR CAME
TO LOS ANGELES.   *Western States Jewish Hist. Q. 1977 10(1): 68-73.* On 16
August 1868 a group of Los Angeles Jews formed a branch of the Universal
Jewish Alliance (UJA), an international society whose objectives were the emancipation of all the Israelites, and the redress of all wrongs upon the race all over
the globe. The officers of the Los Angeles branch included men of French, Polish,
and German backgrounds. The UJA dissolved when several of the German- and
French-born members became active in their respective war relief efforts. Bad
feelings culminated in a fist fight in a saloon when Moritz Morris (Prussian) and
Eugene Meyer (French), both naturalized American citizens, took sides with
their former homelands in the Franco-Prussian War. Based on newspapers and
other published sources; 19 notes.   B. S. Porter

702.   Stern, Norton B. and Kramer, William M.   THE WINE TYCOON OF
ANAHEIM.   *Western States Jewish Hist. Q. 1977 9(3): 262-278.* Benjamin
Dreyfus (1824-1886) came to America from Bavaria in the late 1840's, moving
to Los Angeles, California in 1854. He immediately became involved in several
businesses, including a general store, a brewery, and an oil refinery manufacturing
kerosene. In 1858 he moved to Anaheim where he established vineyards and

produced sweet and dry wines. By 1880, he owned vineyards and wineries in Anaheim, San Gabriel, Cucamonga, and Napa, California. Much of the wine was shipped to San Francisco and eastern cities. Dreyfus was an active Democratic Party member, and was elected to the posts of city councilman and mayor in Anaheim. Primary and secondary sources; 3 photos, 68 notes.   B. S. Porter

703.   Stern, Norton B. and Kramer, William M.   AN 1869 JEWISH STANDARD FOR GENTILE BEHAVIOR: A REVIEW ESSAY.   *Western States Jewish Hist. Q. 1977 9(3): 282-285.* On 22 January 1869, the *Los Angeles Daily News* printed a lengthy essay describing the local Jewish community. Modern historians such as Esther Boulton Black in *Rancho Cucamonga and Dona Merced* (Redlands, Calif., 1975) and Leonard Pitt have revised the earlier interpretation of the article—that it was a defense of Jews under verbal attack—and have determined that it was a reproof of native Californios and immigrant Anglos for their shortcomings. The article praised Jews for their sobriety, literacy, charity, chastity, and decorous demeanor. By implication, their gentile neighbors were noted for intemperance, political corruption, financial extravagance, and criminal violence, among other faults. The article stated that the Jews were an example for the gentiles.   B. S. Porter

704.   Stork, Joe and Rose, Sharon.   ZIONISM AND AMERICAN JEWRY. *J. of Palestine Studies [Lebanon] 1974 3(3): 39-57.* Discusses the attitudes of American Jews toward Zionism and the development of those attitudes since the 1920's; Zionism today is accepted by most Americans as equal to Judaism itself.

705.   Strober, Gerald S.   AMERICAN JEWS AND THE PROTESTANT COMMUNITY.   *Midstream 1974 20(7): 47-66.* The 1972 Dallas-based General Assembly of the National Council of Churches illustrates the problem of the Jewish community in presenting its agenda and forestalling anti-Jewish or anti-Israeli actions.   S

706.   Stuhler, Barbara.   FANNY BRIN: WOMAN OF PEACE.   Stuhler, Barbara and Kreuter, Gretchen, ed. *Women of Minnesota: Selected Biographical Essays* (St. Paul: Minnesota Historical Society Press, 1977): 284-300. In 1884, three-month-old Fanny Fligelman came to Minneapolis with her Romanian Jewish parents. A serious student in high school and at the University of Minnesota, Fanny was active in the Minerva Literature Society and was elected to Phi Beta Kappa. She became a teacher, and in 1913 wed Arthur Brin, a successful businessman. Fanny raised a family, became a prominent volunteer activist, and worked for woman suffrage, world peace, democracy, and Jewish heritage. During the 1920's and 30's, she was especially active in the National Council of Jewish Women and served as director of the Minneapolis Woman's Committee for World Disarmament. Stimulated by the Nazi attack on Jews, Fanny became a strong Zionist. As the alternate delegate for the Women's Action Committee for Lasting Peace, Fanny attended the 1945 San Francisco meetings which gave birth to the United Nations. An excellent speaker, Fanny served in many organizations, promoted many causes, took civic responsibilities as serious duties, and worked to better use women and their contributions to improve world affairs. Primary and secondary sources; photo, 44 notes.   A. E. Wiederrecht

707. Stuppy, Laurence J. HENRY H. LISSNER, M.D., LOS ANGELES PHYSICIAN. *Western States Jewish Hist. Q. 1976 8(3): 209-216.* Dr. Henry H. Lissner (1875-1968), San Francisco-born and Oakland-raised, took over his father's pawnshop in Oakland in 1886 along with his two brothers. In 1895, Henry and his brother Meyer moved to Los Angeles to open a branch of the pawnshop. They soon closed the new store when Meyer entered law school and Henry started medical school. Henry opened his medical practice in Los Angeles and became a prominent doctor. He was a pioneer in electrocardiography. He served on the staff of several hospitals and was the chief of staff at Cedars of Lebanon Hospital. Photo, 19 notes.   R. A. Garfinkle

708. Stutz, George M. FIFTY YEARS OF DETROIT JEWISH COMMU-NAL ACTIVITY: A PERSONAL BIOGRAPHICAL MEMOIR. *Michigan Jewish Hist. 1975 15(1): 5-25.*

709. Sultanik, Aaron. MOVE OVER, MARLOWE! *Midstream 1977 23(1): 81-84.* Discusses the influence of Jewish attitudes, wit, and characters in the detective novels of Roger Simon (*The Big Fix*, *Wild Turkey*) and Andrew Bergman (*The Big Kiss-Off of 1944*, *Hollywood and LeVine*), 1970's; the strain of cynicism in their work is a departure from the traditional detective fiction of Raymond Chandler, Ross Macdonald, and Dashiell Hammett.

710. Sutherland, John F. RABBI JOSEPH KRAUSKOPF OF PHILADEL-PHIA: THE URBAN REFORMER RETURNS TO THE LAND. *Am. Jewish Hist. Q. 1978 67(4): 342-362.* Joseph Krauskopf (1858-1923) came to the United States as a 14-year-old. He graduated with the first class of four at Hebrew Union College in 1883 and was Philadelphia's foremost reform rabbi during 1887-1922. He introduced English into both services and the religious school, popularized the Jewish Sundry Services, and drafted the Pittsburgh Platform of 1885. His great concern with social reform led him into close cooperation with Jacob Riis. After a visit with Leo Tolstoy at Yasnaya Polyana, Krauskopf became the driving spirit of the Jewish "back-to-the land" movement and of the National Farm School, today known as the Delaware Valley College of Science and Agriculture, the only private agricultural school in the country. Thoroughly part of America's urban milieu, Krauskopf nevertheless sought to modify it with the agrarian myth, an urban-agrarian ambivalence which still influences American thought and action.   F. Rosenthal

711. Swichkow, Louis J. MEMOIRS OF A MILWAUKEE LABOR ZION-IST. *Michael: On the Hist. of the Jews in the Diaspora [Israel] 1975 3: 125-151.* Summarizes the 159-page Yiddish memoir of Louis Perchonok (1889-1949), a founder and long-time secretary of the Poale Zion movement in Milwaukee, and includes an extract of the original. The memoir contains valuable information on the history of Jewish immigrant life in America and the role of Zionism. Milwau-kee's Socialist Zionists, including Golda Meir in her youth, participated in all aspects of Jewish life and were especially influential during World War I in creating "Ezra Betzar" for the relief of Eastern European Jews, and in democra-tizing the community via popular elections to the American Jewish Congress. Primary and secondary sources; 32 notes.   T. Sassoon

712. Szajkowski, Zosa. THE CONSUL AND THE IMMIGRANT: A CASE OF BUREAUCRATIC BIAS. *Jewish Social Studies 1974 36(1): 3-18.* Examines the tightening restrictions on immigration from Eastern Europe and Germany to the United States in the first few years after the end of World War I. Quotas enabled anti-Semitic diplomatic representatives to apply American immigration restrictions to Jews unequally. Based on primary and secondary sources in English, Yiddish, and Polish; 62 notes.   P. E. Schoenberg

713. Szajkowski, Zosa. DEPORTATION OF JEWISH IMMIGRANTS AND RETURNEES BEFORE WORLD WAR I. *Am. Jewish Hist. Q. 1978 67(4): 291-306.* A series of acts during 1875-1907 effectively restricted free immigration to the United States, even though their confused wording allowed the most varied and contradictory interpretations by officials and the courts. Describes challenges to these interpretations, several by Simon Wolf and his associates. Mentions the plight of forced as well as voluntary returnees, who often were forced to work on cattle boats under the most inhumane conditions. The most unusual feature of Jewish immigration to America was its definitive character: the percentage of Jewish returnees was greatly below that of other ethnic groups. 43 notes.   F. Rosenthal

714. Szajkowski, Zosa. THE *YAHUDI* AND THE IMMIGRANT: A REAPPRAISAL. *Am. Jewish Hist. Q. 1973 63(1): 13-44.* Recent research has shown that the American Jews of German origin—called the *yahudim* by their East-European brethren—undertook positive and meaningful action to assure mass immigration of Russian Jews into the United States in the period before World War I. Distribution of immigrants away from New York, care of women and children, appeals to prevent unjust deportations, and ultimately strenuous efforts to prevent limiting legislation were some of the efforts of the established Jewish organizations and of leaders such as Jacob Schiff, Abram I. Elkus, Max James Kohler, Louis Marschall, and Simon Wolf. Based on contemporary newspapers, archives, and collections of papers; 72 notes.   F. Rosenthal

715. Tabory, Ephraim and Lazerwitz, Bernard. MOTIVATION FOR MIGRATION: A COMPARATIVE STUDY OF AMERICAN AND SOVIET ACADEMIC IMMIGRANTS TO ISRAEL. *Ethnicity 1977 4(2): 91-102.* Comparative analysis of academic Jews migrating to Israel from the United States and the USSR shows that both groups are prompted by negative factors in the larger society. American Jews, however, are measurably more religious and find that pursuit of a truly Jewish lifestyle is easier in Israel. Soviet Jews, because of subtle yet constant discrimination and harassment, are less religious but cling to their Jewish heritage as a form of nationalism. This pattern may also hold true for Jews outside academe, and Soviet Jews may be as willing to migrate to other economically advanced countries as to Israel.   G. A. Hewlett

716. Tenenbaum, Marc H. HOLY YEAR 1975 AND THE JEWISH JUBILEE YEAR. *Lutheran Q. 1974 26(3): 258-268.* Describes the concept of the Jewish Jubilee Year as an aid to those Christians celebrating the holy year of 1975 proclaimed by Pope Paul VI. Derived from the God-given law on Mount Sinai, the Jubilee had four objectives: freeing the slaves with their families, restoring all purchased land to the original owner, releasing the land from cultivation, and educating the people in the knowledge of the Torah. For centuries, Jews observed

the Jubilee every 50 years. It is estimated 1975 is the 20th year of the current Jubilee cycle. Based largely on the Torah; 4 notes. J. A. Kicklighter

717. Thurlow, Richard C. THE POWERS OF DARKNESS: CONSPIR-ACY BELIEF AND POLITICAL STRATEGY. *Patterns of Prejudice [Great Britain]* 1978 12(6): 1-12, 23. The Jewish conspiracy theory, a theme in 20th-century intellectual history, was developed in the "notorious" document *Protocols of the Elders of Zion,* and was embraced by neofascist and rightist political groups in Great Britain and the United States.

718. Toll, William. FRATERNALISM AND COMMUNITY STRUC-TURE ON THE URBAN FRONTIER: THE JEWS OF PORTLAND, ORE-GON: A CASE STUDY. *Pacific Hist. Rev.* 1978 47(3): 369-403. Portland's Jews were residentially dispersed according to class standing, but they clustered in occupations to which they had been confined in Germany and Russia. Extensive trading contacts with relatives and friends in San Francisco and elsewhere produced economic stability in the late 19th and early 20th centuries so that the community retained a higher proportion of its members than most ethnic enclaves and provided remunerative employment for most of its sons and many newcomers. In general, only Jews with capital, contacts, or skills migrated to Portland. Based on manuscript census, city directories, and B'nai B'rith lodge records; map, 11 tables, 51 notes. W. K. Hobson

719. Toll, William. VOLUNTARISM AND MODERNIZATION IN PORTLAND JEWRY: THE B'NAI B'RITH IN THE 1920'S. *Western Hist. Q.* 1979 10(1): 21-38. A case study of how ethnic groups and community development are related, addressing the issues raised by Moses Rischin, John Higham, and Kenneth Roseman. Examines the role of Jews in Portland, Oregon, in the 1920's in the local economy and their specific patterns of institutional adaptation to find out what their particular contributions were to the city's growth. Traces the effects of the particular region in which they settled on their internal patterns of change. Through its B'nai B'rith lodge, Portland Jewry "sorted out its social classes and allowed new spokesmen to coalesce." 3 tables, 37 notes. D. L. Smith

720. Toren, Nina. RETURN TO ZION: CHARACTERISTICS AND MO-TIVATIONS OF RETURNING EMIGRANTS. *Social Forces* 1976 54(3): 546-558. Examines the relationships between certain characteristics and motivations of return migrants from the United States to Israel. Characteristics are those bearing on "success" as measured by level of education and occupation. Motivations are classified by using a push-pull model to explain migratory selection and movement. The data show that return migration from the United States to Israel is nonselective and that remigrants are motivated mainly by the attraction of the country of destination. A subclassification of the push-pull dichotomy reveals that: (1) the decision of the more successful return migrants is primarily influenced by occupational opportunities back home; (2) the less successful are motivated chiefly by patriotic attachment and loyalty to the home country. The predictive value and policy implications of the results of this analysis are indicated. J

721.   Toury, Jacob.   M.E. LEVY'S PLAN FOR A JEWISH COLONY IN FLORIDA: 1825.   *Michael: On the Hist. of the Jews in the Diaspora [Israel] 1975 3: 23-33.* Publishes an 1825 letter addressed to Isaac L. Goldsmid of London by the American Jew, Moses Elias Levy, advocating the foundation of a Jewish colony in Florida, the nucleus of which was apparently to be a theological seminary. Levy was also an outspoken proponent of the abolition of Negro slavery and of Jewish political disabilities in Europe. His religious fervor inspired him to advocate a Bible-based socialism. Opposed to Jewish emancipation in Europe because of its ultimate threat to Jewish existence, Levy was a proud defender of the American "right to be different." Primary and secondary sources; 35 notes.
T. Sassoon

722.   Trice, Robert H.   FOREIGN POLICY INTEREST GROUPS, MASS PUBLIC OPINION AND THE ARAB-ISRAELI DISPUTE.   *Western Pol. Q. 1978 31(2): 238-252.* Considers the roles played by domestic groups and mass public opinion in the American foreign policy process. Interest groups use both direct and indirect strategies in attempts to influence decisions. Earlier studies have concluded that domestic groups generally have very little impact on foreign policy decisions. An essential part of an indirect strategy is to rally mass public support behind the group's policy position. A comparative analysis of the behavior and indirect impact of pro-Israel and pro-Arab groups on American Middle East policy suggests that public opinion may be relatively insensitive to interest group activities on foreign policy issues. These findings raise serious questions concerning the general ability of nongovernmental forces to have any meaningful impact on American foreign policy.   J

723.   Trilling, Diana.   LIONEL TRILLING, A JEW AT COLUMBIA.   *Commentary 1979 67(3): 40-46.* Describes the difficulties Lionel Trilling had to face as a Jew in the early 1930's establishing himself as an English professor at Columbia University.

724.   Trunk, Isaiah.   THE CULTURAL DIMENSION OF THE AMERICAN JEWISH LABOR MOVEMENT.   *Yivo Ann. of Jewish Social Sci. 1976 (16): 342-393.* Divides the cultural history of the American Jewish labor movement into three periods. The first period, 1880's-90's, was characterized by socialism, a desire for educational achievement, and a tendency toward assimilation. The second period, 1900-20's, was caused by a new influx of immigrants coming after the Dreyfus trial and the Kishinev pogrom. As a result, they were disillusioned with socialism and tended toward cultural autonomy, radical nationalism, and Zionist socialism. A growth of the Hebrew and Yiddish press and literature characterized the Jewish labor movement during this period. The last period, extending from the 1930's to the end of World War II, saw a rise of national solidarity through such groups as the Workmen's Circle and the Jewish Labor Committee, which worked against anti-Semitism.   R. J. Wechman

725.   Tsukashima, Ronald Tadao and Montero, Darrel.   THE CONTACT HYPOTHESIS: SOCIAL AND ECONOMIC CONTACT AND GENERATIONAL CHANGES IN THE STUDY OF BLACK ANTI-SEMITISM. *Social Forces 1976 55(1): 149-165.* Studies indicate that respondents experiencing equal-status contact across ethnic lines are more likely to hold tolerant attitudes toward minorities than those not having been exposed to such interaction. The

authors build on the thesis by examining (1) responses of blacks reporting equal-status contact with Jews; (2) effects of equal-status contact compared with other types of reported associations with Jews such as perceived economic mistreatment; and (3) possible trends in the shifting effects of both types of reported contact over time. The findings indicate strong support for the contact hypothesis, particularly when equal-status contact is intimate and occurs in a noninstitutional setting. On the other hand, they show that perceived economic mistreatment is strongly related to heightened antipathy towards Jews. Examines trends in the changing effects of these two types of reported contact on anti-Semitism. The younger generation of blacks exhibits a weaker inverse relationship between intimate, equal-status contact and anti-Semitism than do older cohorts. The positive association between perceived economic mistreatment and the dependent variable increases with each younger generation. These findings suggest that there are generational changes taking place in black-white relations.   J

726. Tuchman, Barbara W.   THE ASSIMILATIONIST DILEMMA: AMBASSADOR MORGENTHAU'S STORY. *Commentary 1977 63(5): 58-62.* In 1914 Henry Morgenthau, Sr., then US Ambassador to Turkey, arranged for financial aid to the Jewish colony in Palestine, enabling it to survive and preserving it for eventual Jewish statehood. Yet in 1918 he resigned as president of the Free Synagogue, when its Rabbi, Stephen S. Wise, led a delegation to the White House to support the Zionist homeland, and in 1921 he wrote an article stating his strong opposition to Zionism. Not until after the Holocaust, when he was in his 80's, did Morgenthau acknowledge that he had misread history. Assimilation into American life was his ideal, assimilation meaning acceptance as Jews, not absorption into Christianity. The Western Democracies did not function according to his ideal and the horrors of the Holocaust turned many assimilationists into supporters of the Jewish State. Based on primary and secondary sources as well as personal recollections.   S. R. Herstein

727. Tuerk, Richard. JACOB RIIS AND THE JEWS. *New-York Hist. Soc. Q. 1979 63(3): 178-201.* The great influx of immigrants during 1875-1920's increased opposition in the United States to immigrants in general and Jews in particular. A result was the post-World War I nativism and the restrictive immigration act of 1924. For some, however, the opposite reaction took place; Jacob Riis, an immigrant himself, was one of these. His most famous work, *How the Other Half Lives,* published in 1890, contained much anti-Semitism, for he believed that Jews from Eastern Europe would never be assimilated. Within a decade he was changing his mind and, after another ten years, much of his prejudice had disappeared. He had begun to accept the idea that people could be different but live in harmony and be "good Americans." Primary sources; illus., 5 photos, 42 notes.   C. L. Grant

728. Twersky, Rebecca. THE FOUNDING OF A JEWISH COMMUNITY: AHAVATH SHALOM OF WEST WARWICK. *Rhode Island Jewish Hist. Notes 1977 7(3): 420-429.* History of the Congregation Ahavath Shalom of West Warwick, Rhode Island, from its inception in 1912 to around 1938.

729. Unrau, William E. JUSTICE AT FORT LARAMIE: THE TRIAL AND TRIBULATIONS OF A GALVANIZED YANKEE. *Arizona and the West 1973 15(2): 107-132.* By 1864, when the manpower needs of the Union

Army became critical, Confederate prisoners ("Galvanized Yankees") were enrolled and deployed to Indian country. The monotony, inhospitable environment, low morale, arbitrary military justice, and indecisive Indian policy debilitated the average western soldier. Emanuel H. Saltiel, alias Sergeant Joseph Isaacs, a British citizen and military officer and an ambitious Galvanized Yankee, was court-martialed on trumped-up charges of mutiny, sedition, and encouraging desertion and disloyalty. He was convicted of "entertaining and promulgating disloyal sentiments." Though he was drummed out of the service at Fort Laramie, Dakota Territory, in May 1866, Saltiel's subsequent business ventures left a spectacular mark on the economy of Colorado Territory. He was recognized as a leading citizen and benefactor of the Jewish community of Denver. 4 illus., 47 notes.

D. L. Smith

730. Urofsky, Melvin I.   AMERICA AND ISRAEL: TRYING TO FIND THE STRAIGHT PATH.   *Reviews in Am. Hist. 1975 3(3): 383-388.* Discusses the evolution, 1945-48, of President Truman's policy on Israel, analyzes the importance of the Zionist cause in the 1948 presidential election, and summarizes the social and theological responses of American Protestantism since the Puritans in this review of Hertzel Fishman's *American Protestantism and a Jewish State* (Detroit, Mich.: Wayne State U. Pr., 1973) and John Snetsinger's *Truman, the Jewish Vote, and the Creation of Israel* (Hoover Institution Studies 39. Stanford, Calif.: Hoover Institution Pr., 1974).

731. Urofsky, Melvin I.   AMERICAN ZIONISTS AND THE BALFOUR DECLARATION.   *Midstream 1978 24(10): 28-34.* The declaration stated that the British government favored and would work for a Jewish homeland in Palestine that would not prejudice the rights of non-Jews; Arthur James Balfour's letter to Lord Rothschild in 1917 confirmed President Woodrow Wilson's approval for the establishment of a Jewish homeland in Palestine.

732. Urofsky, Melvin I.   THE EMERGENCE OF BRANDEIS AS A ZIONIST.   *Midstream 1975 21(1): 42-58.* Describes the work of Louis D. Brandeis (1856-1941) in the American Zionist movement and his efforts to aid Jewish settlements in Palestine during World War I.

S

733. Urofsky, Melvin I.   FIFTY YEARS OF THE JEWISH AGENCY. *Midstream 1979 25(9): 42-46.* Reviews the history of the Jewish Agency for Palestine in Western Europe and the United States since its creation by Chaim Weizmann and Louis Marshall in Zurich in 1929.

734. Urofsky, Melvin I.   STEPHEN WISE: THE LAST OF THE SUPERSTARS.   *Present Tense 1979 6(4): 21-26.* Recounts the deeds and achievements —especially those devoted to Zionism, ecumenism, charity, and efforts to persuade President Franklin Delano Roosevelt to assist in saving the European Jews during World War II—of the Hungarian-born American rabbi, Stephen Samuel Wise (1874-1949).

735. Vanger, Max.   MEMOIRS OF A RUSSIAN IMMIGRANT.   *Am. Jewish Hist. Q. 1973 63(1): 57-88.* The author, a retired businessman, recounts his experiences since his arrival in Canada before World War I. He worked as a shoemaker, junk peddler, cloth cutter, fish merchant, cattle buyer, lumber dealer, shoe store operator, millinery and sweater manufacturer, and finally garage operator and owner in New York City.

F. Rosenthal

736. Varon, Benno Weiser. THE HAUNTING OF MEYER LEVIN. *Midstream 1976 22(7): 7-23.* Discusses why the Jewish literary establishment has ignored the talented author Meyer Levin and gives a brief summary of his work, 1931-76.

737. Viener, Saul. ROSENA HUTZLER LEVY RECALLS THE CIVIL WAR. *Am. Jewish Hist. Q. 1973 62(3): 306-313.* A letter written in 1907 by Rosena Hutzler Levy (1840-1914) to her children recalled the Civil War service of their father, Richard Levy (1828-97). The hitherto unpublished letter is a telling record of the catastrophe which altered so many southern families.
F. Rosenthal

738. Voorsanger, Jacob. THE BEGINNING OF THE FIRST JEWISH HOSPITAL IN THE WEST. *Western States Jewish Hist. Q. 1976 8(2): 99-101.* Reprint of an article first published in the *Emanu-El*, San Francisco, 1 January 1897, announcing the founding in San Francisco of Mount Zion Hospital. The hospital was to use the medical facilities of Julius Rosenstirn. There had been some concern about the necessity of a Jewish hospital, but a trial operation proved successful.
R. A. Garfinkle

739. Voorsanger, Jacob and Stern, Malcolm H., ed. LEON MENDEZ SOLOMONS, 1873-1900. *Western States Jewish Hist. Q. 1978 10(2): 138-145.* Leon Mendez Solomons was born in San Francisco, California. He graduated from the University of California in 1893 with degrees in mathematics and physics, but found his interest turning to the new science of psychology. After earning his Ph.D. in psychology at Harvard University, he accepted a teaching post at the University of Wisconsin. Publication of several research reports enhanced his reputation and led to the offer of a permanent chair at the University of Nebraska. After one semester he became ill and died at the age of 26 from complications following surgery. Quoted from eulogy; 7 notes.
B. S. Porter

740. Voorsanger, Jacob. THE RELIEF WORK IN SAN FRANCISCO. *Western States Jewish Hist. Q. 1976 8(3): 243-250.* In this reprint of an article published in *Out West*, June 1906, the author tells of his role in obtaining food for San Francisco after the earthquake of 1906. He was on Mayor Eugene Schmitz's Food Committee. His job was to locate food and to get it to relief centers. 2 notes.
R. A. Garfinkle

741. Voss, Carl Hermann. THE AMERICAN CHRISTIAN PALESTINE COMMITTEE: THE MID-1940S IN RETROSPECT. *Midstream 1979 25(6): 49-53.* Reviews the efforts of American Christian groups to influence world opinion, and in particular the British government, to establish a homeland for the Jews in what is now Israel.

742. Wacker, R. Fred. AN AMERICAN DILEMMA: THE RACIAL THEORIES OF ROBERT E. PARK AND GUNNAR MYRDAL. *Phylon 1976 37(2): 117-125.* Many of Franz Boas's students were Jewish and helped popularize the idea that there were no biological races; by the 1940's the idea of race had become taboo in many quarters; social scientists preferred to talk about minority groups. In *An American Dilemma,* Gunnar Myrdal attacked the "overly pessimistic" race relations theory of Robert E. Park. Myrdal's major thesis was that "the Negro problem" was one of ideology. "His optimism . . . was

based upon his belief that . . . white Americans felt a dissonance between their democratic ideals and their treatment of Negroes." Park did not believe that America was an idealistic nation. "For Park, California was a symbol of the "last frontier," a region and an environment where races and peoples would . . . intermingle." Park's vision was deeper than Myrdal's. 15 notes.   E. P. Stickney

743. Wald, Alan M.   THE MENORAH GROUP MOVES LEFT. *Jewish Social Studies 1976 38(3-4): 289-320.* A group of Jewish intellectuals clustered around Elliott Ettleson Cohen and worked on *The Menorah Journal* in the 1920's. They generated the development of a Jewish humanism that led to a Jewish cultural renaissance. In the early 1930's, Cohen, Lionel Trilling, George Novack, Herbert Solow and others in the group gravitated toward the Communists and became especially prominent in the National Committee for the Defense of Political Prisoners. By the mid-1930's, most of these individuals broke from the Communists and supported Trotskyist and other radical organizations. Tess Slesinger's novel, *The Unpossessed,* provides a vivid portrait of the attitudes and personality traits of some members of the Menorah Group.   N. Lederer

744. Wald, Alan.   MIKE GOLD AND THE RADICAL LITERARY MOVEMENT OF THE 1930'S.   *Internat. Socialist R. 1973 34(3): 34-37.* Review essay on Michael Folsom's *Mike Gold: A Literary Anthology* (New York: Int. Publ., 1972).   S

745. Waldinger, Albert.   ABRAHAM CAHAN AND PALESTINE. *Jewish Social Studies 1977 39(1-2): 75-92.* As a result of Abraham Cahan's (1860-1951) trip to Palestine in the fall of 1925 he became an ardent advocate of the creation of a Jewish state. Influential in the American Jewish community as the founder and editor of the *Jewish Daily Forward,* a Yiddish-language, Socialist daily newspaper, Cahan sought the support of the American Jewish labor establishment for the creation of a Jewish Palestine after 1925. Based on firsthand observations, his newspaper articles reported favorably on the religious, commercial, and industrial aspects of the Jewish settlements in Palestine, especially emphasizing the contributions of the agricultural communes and the various institutions created by the Histadrut. In revising his attitude toward a Jewish homeland, Cahan proved more flexible than many of his Jewish Socialist colleagues, including members of his editorial board.   N. Lederer

746. Walker, Sheila S.   THE BLACK-JEWISH PARADOX: AMBIVALENCE OF U.S. RACE FEELING.   *Patterns of Prejudice [Great Britain] 1973 7(3): 19-24.* Black intellectuals identify closely with Biblical Hebrews and accept Jewish nationalism as a model. Blacks respond to the economically dominant Jews in the ghettos with an anti-Semitism which is really an antiwhite feeling directed at area whites who happen to be mainly Jewish. Based on personal observation and on secondary sources; 11 notes.   M. W. Szewczyk

747. Wall, Bennett H.   LEON GODCHAUX AND THE GODCHAUX BUSINESS ENTERPRISES.   *Am. Jewish Hist. Q. 1976 66(1): 50-66.* Reconstructs the life and influence of Leon Godchaux (1824-99), New Orleans merchant, plantation owner, sugar refiner, real estate developer, and financier, who proved that hard work, canny business judgment and ingenuity made it possible for a poor immigrant boy to rise rapidly to wealth and importance. Based on papers and clippings of the Godchaux family. 29 notes.   F. Rosenthal

748. Walton, Clyde C. PHILIP DAVID SANG, 1902-1975. *J. of the Illinois State Hist. Soc. 1975 68(5): 429-434.* Despite his extensive business involvement, Philip David Sang found time to demonstrate his life-long interest in the cause of human freedom, and his concerns for education, for the Jewish religion and for the importance of history. He avidly collected manuscripts and other historical materials and donated them to historical societies and libraries. Sang devoted considerable time, effort and money to the growth of the Illinois State Historical Society.   N. Lederer

749. Waltzer, Kenneth. URBAN AMERICA: BOILING POT AND MELTING POT. *Rev. in Am. Hist. 1979 7(2): 241-246.* Review article prompted by Ronald H. Bayor's *Neighbors in Conflict: The Irish, Germans, Jews, and Italians of New York City, 1929-1941* (Baltimore, Md.: The Johns Hopkins U. Pr., 1978).

750. Ward, Dana. KISSINGER: A PSYCHOHISTORY. *Hist. of Childhood Q. 1975 2(3): 287-348.* Basic tensions in Henry A. Kissinger's psyche, traceable to traumatic childhood and adolescent experiences, influence his world view and hence his actions as Secretary of State. Notable among those events were his Jewish childhood near Hitler's Nuremberg and subsequent need to flee to the United States, his father's loss of economic status and importance in the family, and the presence of favored siblings or quasi-siblings. Examines development of the "depressive personality" resulting from these factors. Explains Kissinger's relationships with business and political leaders, his first wife, and other women in terms of ego fulfillment, and relates his decisions of state to his personality development. Based on interviews, newspapers and magazines, and other primary and secondary sources; 187 notes.   R. E. Butchart

751. Warsen, Allen A. THE DETROIT JEWISH DIRECTORY OF 1907 AS A RESEARCH SOURCE. *Michigan Jewish Hist. 1978 18(2): 20-23.* The Detroit Jewish directory listed 2,470 people with their occupations and addresses, reflecting the demographic, vocational, and organizational history of Detroit Jewry.

752. Warsen, Allen A. MORRIS GARVETT—A GREAT COMMUNITY LEADER, 1893-1971. *Michigan Jewish Hist. 1973 13(1): 8-11.* An obituary of Morris Garvett, active in the Detroit Jewish community.   S

753. Warsen, Allen A. THE ODESSA PROGRESSIVE AID SOCIETY OF DETROIT, MICHIGAN. *Michigan Jewish Hist. 1976 16(1): 39-42.* Reports on the operation, activities, and membership of the Odessa Progressive Aid Society, a charitable organization of Jews who assisted sick and disabled members and financially supported various associations, 1915-18.

754. Washburn, Emory. THE JEWS IN LEICESTER, MASSACHUSETTS. *Rhode Island Jewish Hist. Notes 1975 7(1): 34-41.* Discusses three Newport, Rhode Island Jewish families of Portuguese descent: those of Abraham Mendez, Jacob Rodriguez Rivera, and Aaron Lopez, who sought refuge from the invasion of British troops during the American Revolution, 1777-83.

755. Watters, Gary. THE RUSSIAN JEW IN OKLAHOMA: THE MAY BROTHERS. *Chronicles of Oklahoma 1975-76 53(4): 479-491.* Facing increased persecution in tsarist Russia, Hyman Madanic and his son Ben emigrated

to the United States in 1889. After leaving Ellis Island, where their name was changed to Madansky, they took jobs in the sweatshop system of St. Louis' clothing industry. Hard work and frugality brought enough money to bring the rest of the family from Russia in 1893. Soon the family was Americanized and opened its own clothing store in Fairfield, Illinois. In 1908 they moved to the boomtown of Tulsa, Oklahoma, where their business proved successful enough to open branches in nearby towns. Following World War I, they changed their name to the May brothers and their business became widely known. The Great Depression undercut the family fortunes and closed the Tulsa store, but the branches survived. Primary and secondary sources; 3 photos, 21 notes.

M. L. Tate

756. Watters, William R., Jr. THE LONELINESS OF BEING JEWISH: THE CHRISTIAN'S UNDERSTANDING OF ISRAEL. *Religion in Life 1975 44(2): 212-221.*

757. Wax, Bernard. "OUR TOURO SYNAGOGUE." *Rhode Island Jewish Hist. Notes 1977 7(3): 440-441.* Discusses the history and symbolism of the Touro Synagogue in Providence, Rhode Island; discusses Jews in Providence since 1654.

758. Wax, Bernard. RHODE ISLAND MATERIALS IN THE AMERICAN JEWISH HISTORICAL SOCIETY COLLECTIONS. *Rhode Island Jewish Hist. Notes 1975 7(1): 171-174.*

759. Waxman, Chaim I. and Helmreich, William B. RELIGIOUS AND COMMUNAL ELEMENTS OF ETHNICITY: AMERICAN JEWISH COLLEGE STUDENTS AND ISRAEL. *Ethnicity 1977 4(2): 122-132.* Surveys of attitudes among Jewish students in the Northeast show that attitudes on Zionism, Jewishness, and Israel were part of strong and complex self-images based on combinations of Americanism, religiosity, and belief in communalism. Most expressed positive identification with Israel, but few expressed desire to live there. Extent of support of Zionism was based upon its compatibility with their self-professed Americanism (which seemed to consistently outweigh identification with Jewishness). Covers 1973-76.

G. A. Hewlett

760. Weinfeld, Morton. LA QUESTION JUIVE AU QUÉBEC [The Jewish question in Quebec]. *Midstream 1977 23(8): 20-29.* With the victory of René Levesque's Parti Québecois in the Quebec provincial elections in 1976, many Quebec Jews (most of whom are English-speaking) began to fear that the separatist philosophy of the P.Q. would lead to disenfranchisement for non-French residents of Quebec (even those able to speak French).

761. Weinfeld, Morton. A NOTE ON COMPARING CANADIAN AND AMERICAN JEWRY. *J. of Ethnic Studies 1977 5(1): 95-103.* Evaluates the two factors usually cited to account for the greater communal identification of Canadian Jews compared with their American brethren: 1) that the Canadian community is one generation younger or closer to Europe and 2) the Canadian mosaic is more accepting and supportive of ethnic diversity than is the conformity of the American melting pot ethos. Sees the major empirical differences between the two groups as somewhat misleading because of variations in statistical criteria between the United States and Canada. Still, Canadian Jews rate of intermarriage is much lower, day school enrollment far exceeds that in the United States,

retention of Yiddish is stronger in Canada, and religious affiliation of Canadian synagogues leans more to Orthodoxy than does that of American Jews. Canada's new national preoccupation with fostering national sentiment, its official multiculturalism, and its government expenditures to promote ethnic maintenance, which are four times those of the United States explain the greater sense of Jewish identity in Canada. Primary and secondary sources; 3 tables, 13 notes.

G. J. Bobango

762. Weitz, Marvin. AFFIRMATIVE ACTION: A JEWISH DEATH WISH? *Midstream 1979 25(1): 9-17.* Assesses the outcome of affirmative action spawned by the Civil Rights Act of 1964 in light of the Bakke decision; discusses anti-Semitism in the black community and the need to reassess the workings of affirmative action.

763. Weitz, Marvin. THE SHATTERED ALLIANCE BETWEEN THE US BLACKS AND JEWS. *Patterns of Prejudice [Great Britain] 1978 12(3): 11-18.* Economic and social competition during 1940's-70's has resulted in growing tension between American blacks and Jews, which may lead to violent conflict.

764. Werner, Alfred. BEN-ZION, JEWISH PAINTER. *Midstream 1973 19(9): 24-35.* Discusses the career of the Expressionist painter Ben-Zion Weinman (b. 1897). Ben-Zion turned to the visual arts while living in New York in the 1930's. He exhibited as one of The Ten, with Adolph Gottlieb and Mark Rothko, 1936-42. 6 illus. D. D. Cameron

765. Werner, Alfred. GHETTO GRADUATES. *Am. Art J. 1973 5(2): 71-82.* For religious and political reasons, Jewish settlements in Eastern Europe were "devoid of anything artistic." But Jewish immigrants (1880's-1920's) settling in American urban ghettos were free from tradition, and ghetto artists involved themselves fully in revolutionary art trends. Secondary sources; 12 fig., 23 notes. R. M. Frame III

766. Werner, Alfred. THROUGH THE GOLDEN DOOR. *Am. Jewish Arch. 1977 29(2): 95-106.* Between 1905 and 1945, a "Jewish School" of artists and sculptors maintained a discernible presence in the world of American art and especially in New York City. Examines these individuals who shunned the stereotyped paths to Jewish success in America—as doctors or lawyers—and instead contributed their talents for the sake of beauty and expression. J

767. Weyne, Arthur. THE FIRST JEWISH GOVERNOR: MOSES ALEXANDER OF IDAHO. *Western States Jewish Hist. Q. 1976 9(1): 21-42.* Moses Alexander (1853-1932), a Bavarian immigrant to the United States, first entered politics in Chillicothe, Missouri, where he was elected as city councilman and mayor. Stagnant business conditions prompted him to move his dry goods business to Boise, Idaho. After two terms as Boise's mayor, the Democratic Party persuaded him to run for governor in 1914. As a two-term governor (1915-18) Alexander's chief accomplishment was to cut back expenditures. He was also credited with passage of a prohibition law, enactment of a workman's compensation act, creation of a state highway system, and construction of the Arrowrock Dam and the Dalles-Celilo Canal. Critics charged that he used his veto power too frequently. After his second term of office Alexander became an informal elder statesman while remaining active in his merchandizing business. Based on family records and published material; 3 photos, 27 notes. B. S. Porter

768. Whiteman, Maxwell. WESTERN IMPACT ON EAST EUROPEAN JEWS: A PHILADELPHIA FRAGMENT. Miller, Randall M. and Marzik, Thomas D., ed. *Immigrants and Religion in Urban America* (Philadelphia: Temple U. Pr., 1977): 117-137. Jewish clothiers from Eastern Europe who immigrated to the United States in the late 19th century were faced with impossible living and labor conditions. Long working hours, low pay, and especially the necessity of working on the Sabbath brought about the Jewish Tailors and Operators Association, in 1888. Lacking outside support, however, the organization saw its first wage-increase demand suppressed, and workers were warned they would be punished by God for their actions. Anarchists cited this to support their claim that religion was used to "subvert the labor movement." Their campaign became so strong that the union was reestablished in 1890 as the Cloakmakers Union No. 1 and another strike was called. The manufacturers formed the Philadelphia Cloak Manufacturers' Association. The most prominent Philadelphian rabbi, Sabato Morais, emerged as arbitrator. Negotiations progressed until the strikers demanded more and shattered all hopes for settlement. Manufacturers brought in Negro women to work. Three months later, Morais achieved settlement. His success in "rabbinical arbitration" reveals the force of religion in the immigrants' lives; their Judaic roots allowed Morais to build upon common religious concepts and sensibilities. 40 notes.   S. Robitaille

769. Wiegand, Wayne A. THE LAUCHHEIMER CONTROVERSY: A CASE OF GROUP POLITICAL PRESSURE DURING THE TAFT ADMINISTRATION. *Military Affairs 1976 40(2): 54-59.* Demonstrates the effectiveness of political pressure on the Taft administration in the case of the transfer of Colonel Charles Lauchheimer, a Jewish Marine Corps officer, from Washington, D.C. in 1910. After a dispute between the colonel and the Marine Corps Commandant, a court of inquiry concluded that he had been in Washington too long. Lauchheimer was returned in 1912, a victory for his friends, but there is no concrete evidence to prove that he was the victim of anti-Semitism. Based on primary and secondary sources; 11 notes.   A. M. Osur

770. Wieseltier, Leon. PHILOSOPHY, RELIGION AND HARRY WOLFSON. *Commentary 1976 61(4): 57-64.* Harry Austryn Wolfson (1887-1974) occupied the chair in Hebrew Literature and Philosophy at Harvard for more than 30 years and published prodigiously. His works include *The Philosophy of Spinoza* (1934), *Philo: Foundations of Religious Philosophy in Judaism, Christianity, and Islam* (1947), *The Philosophy of the Church Fathers* (1956), and others. His philosophy of history premised the deepest meaning for philosophy in its encounter with religion. The paganism of the ancients and the skepticism of the moderns pales for Wolfson before the marriage of philosophy and religion exemplified by the medievals. For Wolfson, the Jews held central place in medieval culture. Based on Wolfson's works.   S. R. Herstein

771. Wildavsky, Aaron. THE RICHEST BOY IN POLTAVA. *Society 1975 13(1): 48-56.* The author primarily discusses his Jewish father, Sender Wildavsky, who immigrated to Brooklyn, New York, from the USSR about 1921.

772. Williams, John A. THE BOYS FROM SYRACUSE: BLACKS AND JEWS IN THE OLD NEIGHBORHOOD. *Present Tense 1977 4(3): 34-38.* Examines the historical and contemporary relationship between American Jews

and Afro-Americans in Syracuse, New York. Cites author's experiences and those of other residents. Primary and secondary sources; photo, note.
R. B. Mendel

773. Williams, Oscar R., Jr. HISTORICAL IMPRESSIONS OF BLACK-JEWISH RELATIONS PRIOR TO WORLD WAR II. *Negro Hist. Bull. 1977 40(4): 728-731.* Prior to the 1920's, black and Jewish relations were limited to the South, where Jews reacted to blacks like other white southerners. Migration during World War I brought blacks into northern ghettos where they were exploited by Jewish landlords and merchants; this aroused "Black anti-Semitism" which was directed at the exploitation, not at Jewish religious beliefs. At the same time, blacks have held Jews as success models, identifying with their escape from bondage and their rise in status here. By 1940, black and Jewish relations had entered a new era of awareness from which developed cooperation in the area of civil rights. Based on secondary material; 22 notes. R. E. Noble

774. Winchevsky, Morris. ZIHRONOTH [Memoirs]. *Asupoth [Israel] 1965 (9): 71-84.* Memoirs on Jewish personalities, culture, and Hebrew works by Morris Winchevsky (1856-1932), known as the grandfather of Jewish socialism.
B. Lubelski

775. Winn, Karyl. THE SEATTLE JEWISH COMMUNITY. *Pacific Northwest Q. 1979 70(2): 69-74.* Reproduces 10 photographs of Seattle's Jewish citizens and their businesses during the early 20th century. Though Jews constituted less than one percent of the city's population, their influence in civic and commercial affairs surpassed their numbers. M. L. Tate

776. Winograd, Leonard. DOUBLE JEOPARDY: WHAT AN AMERICAN ARMY OFFICER, A JEW, REMEMBERS OF PRISON LIFE IN GERMANY. *Am. Jewish Arch. 1976 28(1): 3-17.* The author, who was a prisoner of war held by the Germans 1944-45, emphasizes the treatment of Jewish prisoners of war.

777. Wisse, Ruth R. *DI YUNGE* AND THE PROBLEM OF JEWISH AESTHETICISM. *Jewish Social Studies 1976 38(3-4): 265-276.* The group of working class Jewish immigrant writers known as *Di Yunge* emerged on the Yiddish literary scene, mainly in New York City, during 1902-13. Their goal of striving toward an aesthetic ideal by emphasizing mood and feeling was at variance with the dominant Yiddish literary tradition of homily, practicalism, and didacticism. To the young men of *Di Yunge,* beauty was the highest ideal; and the means to achieve its actuality were to be sought not only in the Jewish milieu but also within the literary traditions of other cultures. N. Lederer

778. Wisse, Ruth R. and Cotler, Irwin. QUEBEC'S JEWS: CAUGHT IN THE MIDDLE. *Commentary 1977 64(3): 55-59.* With the rise of Quebec's separatist movement and the 1976 *Quebecois* victory, the prevailing French-English tension, formerly a stimulant to Jewish cohesiveness, began to cause uncertainty in the Jewish community. Sympathetic toward French Canadian aspirations, yet fearful of negative repercussions, Jews in Montreal face a crisis of conscience. Should they strive to adapt to the new political situation in order to preserve and nuture their many achievements? Or should they accept their latest difficulty as evidence corroborating the Zionist judgment that the Diaspora will never treat Jews altogether kindly? D. W. Johnson

779. Wolkinson, Benjamin W. LABOR AND THE JEWISH TRADITION —A REAPPRAISAL. *Jewish Social Studies 1978 40(3-4): 231-238.* Responds to Michael S. Kogan's "Liberty and Labor in the Jewish Tradition," *(Ideas, A Journal of Contemporary Jewish Thought,* Spring, 1975). Argues that union efforts to compel workers to join a union or to pay dues as a condition of employment do not conflict with biblical and talmudic principles concerning the rights of workers. Kogan, supported by Rabbi Jakob J. Petuchkowski, also stated that such union demands were opposed by leading Jewish figures in the trade union movement, including Samuel Gompers. Gompers supported voluntarism in the formulation of AFL policies, but he was very concerned about union security. Even Louis D. Brandeis, an opponent of the closed shop, favored preferential employment of union members. The thesis that union security is antagonistic to Jewish law and tradition regarding freedom of choice ignores the fact that throughout Jewish history freedom of choice has been subordinated to the well-being of the group. N. Lederer

780. Wyman, David S. WHY AUSCHWITZ WAS NEVER BOMBED. *Commentary 1978 65(5): 37-46.* Chronicles the numerous requests to the War Department to bomb the rail lines evacuating Hungarian Jews to Auschwitz and the camp itself in 1944. The War Department replied that such air strikes required diversion of air support from more strategic targets and were of doubtful efficacy. The Allies controlled the skies of Europe at the time and, on several occasions, the Air Force bombed installations very near Auschwitz with considerable success, so that it could have struck the camp and its gas chambers. J. Tull

781. Yellowitz, Irwin. AMERICAN JEWISH LABOR: HISTORIOGRAPHICAL PROBLEMS AND PROSPECTS. *Am. Jewish Hist. Q. 1976 65(3): 203-213.* Although the history of American Jewish labor has been a subject of inquiry for over half a century, the major problems in concept and method have not been resolved. The boundaries of American Jewish labor as distinguished from that of the American Jewish labor *movement* should be defined by the influence of Jewish identity and concerns upon leaders and institutions, and the impact of these major figures and their organizations upon the Jewish community. The complex interaction of Jewish, American, trade union, and socialist concerns deserves further study (e.g., Samuel Gompers or Meyer London as Jewish rather than American labor leaders) as well as considerations of events and persons outside New York City. 34 notes. F. Rosenthal

782. Yellowitz, Irwin. MORRIS HILLQUIT: AMERICAN SOCIALISM AND JEWISH CONCERNS. *Am. Jewish Hist. 1978 68(2): 163-188.* Morris Hillquit (1869-1933), an agnostic and an American socialist leader, posed antireligious appeals and worked to neutralize this issue because it tended to drive away potential supporters. Throughout his career Hillquit, often following the advice of his friend Abraham Cahan, had to accept the reality of his ethnic political base in the New York City Jewish ghetto. Evidence from his political campaigns illustrates this thesis. Ethnic identity and concerns were a stronger influence among socialists in the Jewish community in 1930 than in 1900, and Hillquit recognized this. 42 notes. F. Rosenthal

783. Yenish, Joseph. THE ASSOCIATION OF JEWISH LIBRARIES. *Special Lib. 1967 58(10): 707-709.* An offshoot of the Jewish Librarians Association (established in 1946), the Association of Jewish Libraries seeks to promote and improve Jewish libraries, the publication and dissemination of information of aid to Jewish libraries, and the establishment of more Jewish libraries; 1965-67.

784. Zanger, Jules. ON NOT MAKING IT IN AMERICA. *Am. Studies (Lawrence, KS) 1976 17(1): 39-48.* The Jewish mother has become a standard literary stereotype, and a boy turning his back on his mother has symbolized the rejection of a cluster of religious and cultural values. This became a necessary reaction to the Americanization process. American Jewish literature also reveals that behind every Jewish mother is a failed Jewish father. To accept an Americanness, these immigrants frequently had to reject part of their Jewishness. Primary and secondary sources; 6 notes.   J. Andrew

785. Zucker, Bat-Ami. RADICAL JEWISH INTELLECTUALS AND THE NEW DEAL. Artzi, Pinhas, ed. *Bar-Ilan Studies in History* (Ramat-Gan, Israel: Bar-Ilan U. Pr., 1978): 275-283. American socialists, communists and liberals of the 1930's were predominantly non-Jewish, but they contained small pockets of Jewish radicals, who had originated in the 1900's. Argues that the second generation Jews in the 1930's faced an "alienation" crisis because of their transition from poverty to wealth; therefore, many became radicals. But Franklin D. Roosevelt's election campaign of 1932 promised Jews greater social and economic freedom. This made it much easier for Jewish radicals to accept the new Establishment, which they saw as more unified than the Left. Based on newspapers and secondary works; 34 notes.   A. Alcock

786. Zuroff, Efraim. RESCUE PRIORITY AND FUND RAISING AS ISSUES DURING THE HOLOCAUST: A CASE STUDY OF THE RELATIONS BETWEEN THE VA'AD HA-HATZALA AND THE JOINT, 1939-1941. *Am. Jewish Hist. 1979 68(3): 305-326.* The rescue of a group of East European rabbis and students by the Orthodox Jews of America through the Yeshiva Aid Committee (Va'ad Ha-Hatzala) was organized by Rabbi Eliezer Silver of the Union of Orthodox Rabbis. In complex dealings with the Joint Distribution Committee (JDC) the Va'ad, even though it needed the funds contributed by the JDC, maintained its independent stance and engaged in some separate fund raising. By December 1941, approximately 625 rabbis, students, and members of their families had been rescued via Japan and Shanghai. 4 illus., 3 photos, 27 notes.   F. Rosenthal

787. —. [ANTI-SEMITISM AND CHRISTIAN BELIEFS]. *Am. Sociol. R. 1973 38(1): 33-61.*
Middleton, Russell. DO CHRISTIAN BELIEFS CAUSE ANTI-SEMITISM?, *pp. 33-52.*
Glock, Charles Y. and Stark, Rodney. DO CHRISTIAN BELIEFS CAUSE ANTI-SEMITISM?—A COMMENT, *pp. 53-59.*
Middleton, Russell. RESPONSE, *pp, 59-61.*
Middleton examines Glock and Stark's contention that certain Christian religious beliefs are causally related to anti-Semitism, using data from a 1964 national survey. Religious orthodoxy proves to be uncorrelated with anti-Semitism at the zero-order. A path analysis reveals that the relationships in the causal sequence

hypothesized by Glock and Stark are weak. Furthermore, the influence of religious orthodoxy, religious libertarianism, religious particularism, and religious hostility to the historic Jew is not expressed solely through the intervening step of religious hostility to modern Jews; the coefficents for the direct paths to anti-Semitism are in some cases sizable. The five religious belief variables taken together in a simple additive model account for approximately 15 percent of the variance in anti-Semitism. When socio-economic status, a number of other social attributes, and a number of social psychological traits are held constant, however, the five religious belief variables account uniquely for only 2 percent of the variance in anti-Semitism. Even here one must be cautious in inferring a causal relationship, particularly since some of the religious measures may simply reflect a more general anti-Semitic ideology. A revised model is presented which includes socioeconomic status and social psychological variables.   J

788. —. ATTITUDES OF YOUTH TO THE HOLOCAUST. *Yad Vashem News [Israel] 1973 4: 19-22.* Reports on the research of Dr. Hillel Klein and Uriel Last, "Conscious and Emotional Aspects in Attitudes to the Holocaust and its Victims among Jewish Youth in Israel and in the U.S.A." which tested the hypothesis that the experience of the European Holocaust is a basic component of contemporary Jewish and Israeli experience. The differences in responses between US and Israeli youth was attributed to the subject's emphasis in Israel's educational system and the Israeli youths' closer link with Holocaust survivors.
                                                                    J. P. Fox

789. —. A COLLECTION OF CALIFORNIA JEWISH HOMES. *Western States Jewish Hist. Q. 1973 6(1): 43-47.* Photographs of the homes of five prominent California Jews: Jacob Leow, David and Jacob Neustader, Jacob Stern, Edward R. Levy, and Max Meyberg. Includes short biographies of each family. 5 photos.   R. A. Garfinkle

790. Unsigned. CONGREGATIONAL POLITICS IN LOS ANGELES— 1897. *Western States Jewish Hist. Q. 1974 6(2): 120-123.* There was much in-fighting in the B'nai B'rith Congregation in the 1890's over the type of rabbi for their temple, but no one was trying to solve the temple's financial problems. The wealthy members wanted to keep out the poor Jews by raising dues, but the increase in dues would not cover the temple's debts. Reprint of an article in *Emanu-El*, San Francisco, 9 July 1897.   R. A. Garfinkle

791. Unsigned. DATA ON DUTCH JEWRY IN AMERICA. *Michigan Jewish Hist. 1973 13(1): 30-31, (2) 22-31.* Gives the names, origins, occupation, age, and other information on Dutch Jews who immigrated to the United States during 1852-77.   S

792. —. [ECONOMIC OPPORTUNITY AND EASTERN EUROPEAN JEWISH IMMIGRANTS]. *J. of Econ. Hist. 1978 38(1): 235-255.*
Kahan, Arcadius. ECONOMIC OPPORTUNITIES AND SOME PILGRIM'S PROGRESS: JEWISH IMMIGRANTS FROM EASTERN EUROPE IN THE U.S., 1880-1914, *pp. 235-251.* The Jewish immigrants from Eastern Europe during 1890-1914 can be distinguished as three successive cohorts which differed in terms of skills, education and degree of urbanization experienced in the countries of their origin. The Jewish immigrants

were able to take advantage of the economic opportunities in the US for the following reasons: 1) To a large extent their skill endowment was congruent with the demand for labor of certain United States industries; 2) The high concentration of the immigrants in the large cities permitted development of various networks of communication which provided job information and facilitated search; 3) the immigrants' rate of literacy was high relative to other ethnic immigrant groups and their urban background made it easier to adjust to the conditions of an industrializing and urbanizing society. The Jewish immigrants from Eastern Europe were able after 10-15 years of residence in the United States to reach the income level of native-born workers of similar age, education and skill.

Hannon, Joan U. DISCUSSION, *pp. 252-255.*   J

793. —. THE FIRST FUND-RAISERS FOR THE HEBREW UNION COLLEGE IN THE FAR EAST. *Western States Jewish Hist. Q. 1975 8(1): 55-58.* Founded in July 1873 by Rabbi Isaac Mayer Wise, the Union of American Hebrew Congregations set as one of its goals the establishment of a Hebrew college. Rabbi Wise used his Anglo-Hebrew weekly paper, *The Israelite*, to solicit funds for the school. Lists of principal Jews in many western communities were published in the paper. These men collected donations from their communities. Provides the lists for California, Nevada, New Mexico, Utah, and Washington Territory. On 4 October 1875 the first classes of the Hebrew Union College were held. 4 notes.   R. A. Garfinkle

794. —. FIRST SYNAGOGUE AT ALBUQUERQUE: 1900. *Western States Jewish Hist. Q. 1978 11(1): 46-48.* Temple Albert in Albuquerque, New Mexico, was dedicated on 14 September 1900. In a joint ceremony, Pizer Jacobs was installed as the new rabbi. Music and speeches preceded the solemn installation services which were presented to a large audience. Reprinted from *The American Israelite,* Cincinnati, 27 September 1900. Photo, 5 notes.

    B. S. Porter

795. —. A GENTILE REPROVES AN ANTI-SEMITE: FRESNO—1893. *Western States Jewish Hist. Q. 1977 9(4): 299-300.* During a murder trial in Fresno, California, defense lawyer William D. Foote attempted to undermine the testimony of a Jewish prosecution witness by abusing Jews generally. Grove L. Johnson, prosecuting attorney, in offering a rejoinder to Foote's anti-Semitic views, emphasized traditional American religious tolerance and Constitutional rights and privileges. Johnson's speech is quoted at length. 9 notes.

    B. S. Porter

796. Unsigned. HEBREW UNION COLLEGE-JEWISH INSTITUTE OF RELIGION—A CENTENNIAL DOCUMENTARY. *Am. Jewish Arch. 1974 26(2): 103-244.* "Founded in Cincinnati in 1875 the Hebrew Union College was conjoined in later years with New York's Jewish Institute of Religion and subsequently added campuses in Los Angeles and Jerusalem. It is not only the Reform movement's leading seminary for the training of rabbis but also a major center of Jewish intellectual endeavor."   J

797. Unsigned. IMPORTANT HISTORIC DOCUMENTS: REGARDING A STATE MARKER FOR THE LAFAYETTE STREET BETH EL CEMETERY. *Michigan Jewish Hist. 1973 13(1): 21-26.* Publishes letters on securing a historic marker for Beth El cemetery in Detroit, Michigan, the first Jewish cemetery owned and maintained by a Jewish congregation.   S

798. —. AN INTIMATE PORTRAIT OF THE UNION OF AMERICAN HEBREW CONGREGATIONS—A CENTENNIAL DOCUMENTARY. *Am. Jewish Arch. 1973 25(1): 3-116.* The Union of American Hebrew Congregations is the national organization encompassing Reform Jewish congregations. Documents cover the founding in 1873, the famous "trefa" (nonkosher) banquet of 1883, Zionism, Jewish-Christian dialogues, Jewish chaplains for the armed forces, tradition and rituals, the exposure of anti-Semitism in the Soviet Union and racism in the United States, opposition to the Vietnam War and the Jewish Chautauqua Society. Based on the Union's archives; 7 photos, 46 notes.

E. S. Shapiro

799. —. JEWISH AMERICANS. Sowell, Thomas, ed. *Essays and Data on American Ethnic Groups* (Washington, D.C.: Urban Inst. Pr., 1978): 362-373. Statistics on Jewish American family income distribution by number of income earners per family; family income by age, education, and sex of family head; family income by number of income earners, education, and sex of family head; and number of children in the household by woman's education and family income. From National Jewish Population Study, 1969; 3 tables.

K. A. Talley

800. —. JEWS IN EARLY SANTA MONICA: A CENTENNIAL REVIEW. *Western States Jewish Hist. Q. 1975 7(4): 327-350.* Many Los Angeles Jews spent their summers camping out at Santa Monica Canyon before the town was established in 1875. Many of these Jews were the first to purchase lots when the town was laid out by John P. Jones and R. S. Baker in 1875. The Jewish community consisted mostly of vacationers during the summer. The first Jewish religious services were held in 1912 by Los Angeles Rabbi Sigmund Hecht. In 1939, the first permanent Jewish congregation was formed. 16 photos, 56 notes.

R. A. Garfinkle

801. —. LETTERS FROM JACOB H. SCHIFF AND DAVID WOLFF-SON TO BERNARD SCHIRESON, EL CENTRO, CALIFORNIA, 1914. *Western States Jewish Hist. Q. 1977 9(4): 350-353.* Bernard Schireson was a Zionist who operated a wholesale general merchandise business in El Centro, California. Jacob Schiff was a New York philanthropist and major contributor to the Technion, Israel Institute of Technology. In his letter, he offers more money to the project on condition that it be completed. David Wolffson was a pioneer Zionist leader in Germany. His letter tells of ill health and his hopes to recover and return to his home. Reprint of private correspondence; 2 photos, 5 notes.

B. S. Porter

802. —. LIFE IN EARLY AMERICA: THE JEWS IN THE COLONIES. *Early Am. Life 1978 9(1): 20-25.* Throughout the colonies the reception of Jews varied greatly, but during the American Revolution Jews acted like other citizens: some were active revolutionaries, attracted to the Revolution by the Declaration

of Independence, others remained loyal to Britain. It wasn't until 1876 however, that Jewish Americans achieved full protection of the law and legal equal opportunity.

803.   —.   LOS ANGELES B'NAI B'RITH LODGE NO. 487: A 1905 REPORT. *Western States Jewish Hist. Q. 1979 11(2): 167-169.* Los Angeles B'nai B'rith Lodge No. 487 was founded in 1899 with about 40 charter members. By 1905, it had approximately 170 members who enjoyed a new fraternal hall with a lodge room, billiard room, library, kitchen, and lockers. In addition to social events, the lodge devoted much money and energy to benevolent works. Reprinted from *The Jewish Times and Observer,* San Francisco, 17 February 1905.
B. S. Porter

804.   —.   THE MARKS BROTHERS OF LOS ANGELES, A PICTURE STORY. *Western States Jewish Hist. Q. 1979 11(4): 311-317.* Joshua H. Marks (1884-1965) and David X. Marks (1891-1977) were brought to Los Angeles by their parents in 1902. Joshua entered their father's brick business and became a building designer and contractor. Among his better known works are Grauman's Chinese and Egyptian theaters, and the Santa Anita Race Track. He also built several shopping centers, churches, business offices, and movie studios. David entered the insurance business and was active in civic affairs. He helped establish the Los Angeles Civic Light Opera Association, and contributed financially to developments at the University of Southern California, and other educational institutions. Family records and published sources; 7 photos, 8 notes.
B. S. Porter

805.   —.   MEN OF DISTINCTION IN EARLY LOS ANGELES. *Western States Jewish Hist. Q. 1975 7(3): 225-233.* Contains brief biographies of Samuel Norton (1834-1902), Charles Gerson (1839-1907), Isaiah M. Hellman (1831-90), Abraham Baer (1814-82), Samuel Prager (1831-1907), Wolf Kalisher (1826-89), Leopold Harris (1836-1910), David Solomon (1824-?), and Joseph Newmark (1799-1881), 9 photos.   R. A. Garfinkle

806.   —.   [MYER MYERS, SILVERSMITH]. *Am. Art and Antiques 1979 2(3): 50-59.*
Werner, Alfred.   MYER MYERS: SILVERSMITH OF DISTINCTION, *pp. 50-57.* Gives the biography of American silversmith Myer Myers (1723-1795), one of a few Jews among 3,000,000 American colonists in the 18th century, a prominent member of the New York Jewish community and a colleague of Paul Revere whose fine work was largely unappreciated until the beginning of the 20th century.
Feigenbaum, Rita.   CRAFTSMAN OF MANY STYLES, *pp. 58-59.* Describes the varied styles of silversmith Myer Myers who designed pieces for households and churches, and most notably for Jewish rituals in the 18th century.

807.   —.   NELLIE NEWMARK OF LINCOLN, NEBRASKA: A PICTURE STORY. *Western States Jewish Hist. Q. 1979 11(2): 114-118.* Nellie Newmark (1888-1978) was the clerk of the District Court at Lincoln, Nebraska, during 1907-56. She gained a reputation for assisting judges and new attorneys assigned to the court. Primary sources; 5 photos, 3 notes.   B. S. Porter

808. —. THE NEW JEWISH CEMETERY IN EAST LOS ANGELES, 1902. *Western States Jewish Hist. Q. 1978 11(1): 64-68.* Congregation B'nai B'rith (now the Wilshire Boulevard Temple) established the new Home of Peace Cemetery in East Los Angeles in 1902. Oscar Willenberg, the cemetery superintendent, kept a photograph album of scenes from the cemetery, which are presented here. 6 photos, 3 notes.   B. S. Porter

809. —. NEWS FROM THE PORTLAND JEWISH COMMUNITY. *Western States Jewish Hist. Q. 1977 9(3): 235-237.* In 1885, Portland, Oregon, had 1,000 Jewish residents. Religious organizations included two B'nai B'rith lodges, the First Hebrew Benevolent Society, and the Judith Montefiore Society. Rabbi Jacob Bloch headed the Reform Congregation Beth Israel. The congregation, assisted by a leading merchant, Colonel L. Fleischner, undertook to raise funds for construction of a new temple, large enough for the needs of the active and growing Jewish community. Reprint of a report sent from Portland, Oregon, to *The American Israelite,* Cincinnati, Ohio, 8 January 1886; 4 notes.

B. S. Porter

810. —. THE NEWS FROM WOODLAND AND OROVILLE, CALIFORNIA IN 1879. *Western States Jewish Hist. Q. 1979 11(2): 162-166.* Rabbi Aron J. Messing of Congregation Beth Israel in San Francisco traveled to scattered Jewish settlements in California encouraging fellow Jews to organize Hebrew societies and Sabbath schools. Following his visits to Woodland and Oroville, both communities established Hebrew associations and Sabbath schools for their children. Based on reports in *The American Israelite,* Cincinnati, 23 May 1879; photo, 23 notes.   B. S. Porter

811. —. NOTES ON SOL RIPINSKY OF ALASKA IN 1905. *Western States Jewish Hist. Q. 1976 8(4): 370-374.* Reprints a 28 September 1905 article from Cincinnati's *The American Israelite.* Discusses Sol Ripinsky (1850-1927), a merchant, doctor, political advisor, and teacher who lived in the township of Haines Mission in southeastern Alaska for many years. He worked as the United States Commissioner to Alaska and as a teacher for the native Alaskans. He was a character and loved to pull practical jokes. 2 photos, 4 notes.

R. A. Garfinkle

812. —. OAKLAND JEWRY AND THE EARTHQUAKE-FIRE OF 1906. *Western States Jewish Hist. Q. 1977 9(3): 251-252.* When refugees from the fire-stricken, poorer Jewish quarter of San Francisco came to Oakland, the synagogue provided immediate aid. Food and clothing were given to the needy and 350 people were given a place to sleep. For about a week the synagogue fed up to 500 people three times a day. A large part of the expenses were paid by the Jewish Ladies' organization of the synagogue. Reprint of article in *Emanu-El,* San Francisco, 4 May 1906.   B. S. Porter

813. —. THE OLD JEWISH CEMETERY IN CHAVEZ RAVINE, LOS ANGELES: A PICTURE STORY. *Western States Jewish Hist. Q. 1977 9(2): 167-175.* The Hebrew Benevolent Society of Los Angeles established the Home of Peace Cemetery in 1855. A new cemetery was established in 1902. The remains and monuments were transferred to the new location during 1902-10. Based on photos collected by cemetery superintendent Oscar Willenberg, interviews, and published material; 8 photos, 3 notes.   B. S. Porter

814. —. PORTLAND JEWRY COLLECTS FOR RUSSIAN REFUGEES. *Western States Jewish Hist. Q. 1978 10(4): 343-346.* On 4 January 1891 the International Society for the Colonization of Russian Jews was organized with the goal of settling Russian Jewish refugees on land in California or Mexico. A fund raising tour of Oregon and Washington included the city of Portland, Oregon. Meeting in Temple Beth Israel, the Jewish citizens of Portland subscribed $5,000. One of the fund raisers wrote a letter describing the Portland meeting and admonishing the Society's members to help check the influx of Jewish paupers and cheap labor in order to lessen the prejudice against the Russian Jews. Reprints the letter, which was first published in *The Jewish Voice* of St. Louis on 20 February 1891; 5 notes. B. S. Porter

815. —. PROBLEMS OF A NEVADA JEWISH COMMUNITY IN 1875. *Western States Jewish Hist. Q. 1976 8(2): 160-162.* Reprints a letter to the editor of the *American Israelite*, 3 September 1875, in which an anonymous resident of Eureka, Nevada complained that his Jewish community could not afford a good rabbi for the High Holy Days. He complained that many of the men previously hired to be rabbis had been frauds. R. A. Garfinkle

816. —. THE RISE AND FALL OF THE JEWISH COMMUNITY OF AUSTIN, NEVADA. *Western States Jewish Q. 1976 9(1): 87-90.* Reprints letters from Jewish correspondents to Jewish newspapers in San Francisco and New York. In 1864 there were 150 Jews, including three families, who kept the principles of the faith and maintained an active Hebrew Benevolent Association in Austin, Nevada. By 1882, silver mining had declined and so had the town's population. Jews numbered only 11. Religious observance was minimal among both Jews and Christians, although the town was remarkably law-abiding. B. S. Porter

817. —. A SAN BERNARDINO CONFIRMAND'S REPORT: 1891. *Western States Jewish Hist. Q. 1979 11(2): 111-113.* The Henrietta Hebrew Benevolent Society sponsored the first Sunday School in San Bernardino, California, in 1891. Fourteen of the students were confirmed in their faith in a ceremony on 14 June 1891. Reverend Dr. Blum of Los Angeles officiated. Reprint of a letter from *The Sabbath Visitor,* Cincinatti, 31 July 1891; 6 notes. B. S. Porter

818. —. THE SHAFSKY BROTHERS OF FORT BRAGG: A MENDOCINO COUNTY VIGNETTE. *Western States Jewish Hist. Q. 1976 9(1): 49-54.* The Shafsky family, Russian emigrants, came to the United States by way of Canada. Starting as pack peddlers in the lumber camps of northern California, two of the brothers, Abraham Harry and Samuel, opened a general merchandise store in Fort Bragg. The business prospered and is still operated by a son and grandson of Abraham Harry Shafsky. Based on interviews, family records, and published works; 3 photos, 13 notes. B. S. Porter

819. Unsigned. SIGMUND ROTHSCHILD. *Michigan Jewish Hist. 1973 13(2): 16-18.* Gives a biography of Sigmund Rothschild (1838-1907), founder of the Detroit leaf-tobacco house Rothschild & Brother. S

820. —. [STOW AND ANTI-SEMITISM]. *Western States Jewish Hist. Q. 1975 7(4): 312-322.*

Stern, Norton B.   LOS ANGELES JEWRY AND STOW'S ANTI-SEMITISM, *pp. 312-320.* Speaker of the California State Assembly William W. Stow (1824-95) made anti-Semitic remarks during a debate on a Sunday closing law before the legislature. During this debate on 16 March 1855 he showed that he had no sympathy for Jews and that he was ignorant of their role within the state. Within a few days many newspapers throughout the state carried editorials denouncing Stow's remarks.

Shumate, Albert.   OTHER SAN FRANCISCO REACTIONS TO STOW'S REMARKS,   *pp. 321-322.* "This early criticism of the Jewish community in California was quickly refuted. . . ."   R. A. Garfinkle and S

821.   —.   TWO LETTERS FROM THE JEWISH PATRIARCH OF LOS ANGELES.   *Western States Jewish Hist. Q. 1979 11(3): 231-233.* Joseph Newmark (1799-1881), was one of the principal founders of Los Angeles's Congregation B'nai B'rith (1862). In 1881, several months before his death, he wrote these letters to his granddaughter, Caroline, who lived in St. Louis, Missouri. The letters contain news of family members' health and activities. They are published through the courtesy of the addressee's granddaughter; 17 notes.

B. S. Porter

822.   —.   TWO VIEWS OF AN INTERNATIONAL JEWISH COMMU-NITY: BROWNSVILLE, TEXAS AND MATAMOROS, MEXICO.   *Western States Jewish Hist. Q. 1978 10(4): 306-310.* Letters to editors of Jewish newspapers in 1876 and 1882 described the Jews of Brownsville (Texas) and Matamoros, (Tamaulipas, Mexico) as a unified religious community. Matamoros, having the greater number of Jewish families, was the location of religious ceremonies on feast and fast days. Some of the leading merchants in both towns were Jews; they were highly respected citizens who took an interest in civic affairs and contributed to every public and religious institution. Reprints letters to the *American Israelite,* Cincinnati, Ohio, 28 July 1876, and the *Jewish Messenger,* New York, 27 January 1882. 7 notes.   B. S. Porter

823.   —.   A WESTERN PICTURE PARADE.   *Western States Jewish Hist. Q. 1976 8(4): 345-350.* Presents six photos with captions concerning early western Jewish history. Includes: cantor Josef (Yosele) Rosenblatt (1880-1933) with Yiddish actor Elia Tenenholtz (b. 1890) and Rabbi Solomon M. Neches (1893-1957); pioneer Tucson businessman Samuel H. Drachman (1837-1911); professional boxer Joe Choynski fighting Jeff Jeffries; San Bernardino County, California supervisor Isaac R. Brunn (1836-1917); Harris Newmark High School in Los Angeles; and Jewish owned tent stores in Candle City, Kotzebue Sound, Alaska. 6 photos.   R. A. Garfinkle

824.   —.   WORD FROM PORTLAND A CENTURY AGO.   *Western States Jewish Hist. Q. 1979 11(3): 252-254.* Portland, Oregon's, Jewish community recently had received a lecture series by the Reverend Moses May, whose heavy German accent grated on the ears of the Congregation Beth Israel. Social visits between friends and relatives in San Francisco and Portland were frequent. The approaching state elections (3 June 1878) were of great interest because of the nominations of several excellent candidates, including Edward Hirsch, A. Noltner, and Solomon Hirsch. Reprinted from the *Jewish Progress,* San Francisco; 4 notes.   B. S. Porter

825. —. [ZIONISM]. *Am. Jewish Hist. Q. 1974 63(3): 215-243.*
Urofsky, Melvin I. ZIONISM: AN AMERICAN EXPERIENCE, pp. 215-230.
Zionism in America, as it was structured by such men as Louis Brandeis,
developed along unique American lines. Brandeis' assertion that Zionism
and Americanism shared similar values, and his insistence on a pragmatic,
nonideological approach to all problems, were responsible for the success
and acceptance of Zionism by ever larger numbers of Jews.
Feingold, Henry L. DISCUSSANT, pp. 230-238. Disputes Urofsky's thesis
and maintains that concern with matters of organization and fund raising
and the Provisional Executive Committee for General Zionist Affairs' insistence on migration to Palestine, was shared by all west European countries.
Sachar, Howard Morley. DISCUSSANT, pp. 238-243. Supports Urofsky, but
reiterates the watershed significance of the Balfour Declaration which galvanized positive Jewish support. The east European background of most
American Jews since 1900 should also be weighed properly.

F. Rosenthal

826. —. A ZIONIST DISCUSSION IN 1904. *Western States Jewish Hist.
Q. 1977 9(4): 315-318.* Israel Zangwill (1864-1926) was an English Zionist who
advocated settlement in East Africa as a Jewish homeland instead of the apparently unattainable Palestine. Colonel Henry I. Kowalsky (1858-1914), a former
US Army officer and prominent San Francisco lawyer, stated that a good Jew
ought to aid the fulfillment of the Lord's promise by working for a Jewish state.
Kowalsky argued that America should be the Jews' homeland, and that Jews were
equal and integral members of the American community and owed loyalty and
patriotism. Based on a report in the *Jewish Times and Observer,* San Francisco;
3 notes.

B. S. Porter

827. —. 50 YEARS OF THE *AMERICAN MERCURY. Patterns of Prejudice [Great Britain] 1974 8(2): 27-29.* Discusses anti-Semitism and the doctrine
of white supremacy in *American Mercury* magazine, 1924-74, and the attitudes
of founder Henry Louis Mencken.

SUBJECT INDEX

Subject Profile Index (ABC-SPIndex) carries both generic and specific index terms. Begin a search at the general term but also look under more specific or related terms.

Each string of index descriptors is intended to present a profile of a given article; however, no particular relationship between any two terms in the profile is implied. Terms within the profile are listed alphabetically after the leading term. The variety of punctuation and capitalization reflects production methods and has no intrinsic meaning; e.g., there is no difference in meaning between "History, study of" and "History (study of)."

Cities, towns, and counties are listed following their respective states or provinces; e.g., "Ohio (Columbus)." Terms beginning with an arabic numeral are listed after the letter Z. The chronology of the bibliographic entry follows the subject index descriptors. In the chronology, "c" stands for "century"; e.g., "19c" means "19th century."

Note that "United States" is not used as a leading index term; if no country is mentioned, the index entry refers to the United States alone. When an entry refers to both Canada and the United States, both "Canada" and "USA" appear in the string of index descriptors, but "USA" is not a leading term.

The last number in the index string, in italics, refers to the bibliographic entry number.

A

Academic Freedom. Hebrew Union College. Judaism, Reform. Kohler, Kaufmann. Ohio (Cincinnati). Zionism. 1903-07. *484*

Acculturation. Canada. Ethnicity. USA. 1961-74. *761*

—. Clothing industry. May brothers. Oklahoma (Tulsa). Retail Trade. 1889-1970. *755*

—. Farms. New Jersey (Farmdale). Settlement. 1919-70's. *116*

—. Immigrants. New York City. Yiddishe Arbeiten Universitett. 1921-39. *161*

—. Immigrants. Novels. 1900-17. *156*

—. Italian Americans. Pennsylvania (Pittsburgh). Slavic Americans. Women. 1900-45. *368*

—. Jewish Theological Seminary. Kaplan, Mordecai M. New York City. Theology. 1920's. *615*

Adler, Lewis. Business. California (Sonoma). 1840's-96. *3*

Adler, Samuel. Judaism. Morality. New York City. Theology. ca 1829-91. *231*

Admissions Policies. *DeFunis* v. *Odegaard* (US, 1974). Discrimination (reverse). Law schools. Washington. 1970's. *33*

Admissions (quotas). Colleges and Universities. *DeFunis* v. *Odegaard* (US, 1974). Jews (Sephardic). Washington, University of. 1974. *72*

Advertisements. American Revolution. Business. Newspapers. Salomon, Haym. 1777-85. *309*

Advertising. California. *Ketubot* (contract). Marriage certificates. San Francisco *Weekly Gleaner* (newspaper). 1850-61. *398*

Aestheticism. *Di Yunge* (group). Literature. New York City. 1902-13. *777*

Affirmative action. Anti-Semitism. Bakke, Allan. Negroes. *Regents of the University of California* v. *Allan Bakke* (US, 1978). 1964-78. *762*

—. Discrimination. 1973. *146*

—. Discrimination. Health, Education, and Welfare Department. Negroes. 1973. *247*

—. Ethnicity. Religiosity. 1960's-70's. *128*

Agricultural Cooperatives. Immigration. New Jersey (Alliance, Woodbine). Rosenthal, Herman. Russian Americans. Socialism. 1880-92. *268*

Agriculture. Bank of A. Levy. California (Ventura County). French Americans. Levy, Achille. 1871-1905. *354*

—. California. Hamburg, Sam. Israel. 1898-1976. *221*

—. Farmers. Jewish Agriculturists' Aid Society of America. Levy, Abraham R. North Dakota (central). Reminiscences. Settlement. Slavic Americans. 1903. *400*

—. Happyville Colony. South Carolina. 1900-08. *630*

—. Judaism. Krauskopf, Joseph. Reform. 1880's-1923. *710*

—. Prairie Provinces. Settlement. 1884-1920's. *529*

Air Warfare. Auschwitz. Concentration Camps. Military Strategy. World War II. 1944-45. *780*

Alaska. Business. Gold Rushes. Reminiscences. Rozenstain, Yael. 1900-44. *575*

—. Business. Reminiscences. Ripinsky, Sol. 1867-1909. *530*

—. Fur trading. Gold rushes. Nome Hebrew Benevolent Society. 1867-1916. *205*

—. Immigration Policy. Nazism. Persecution. 1930-40. *467*

Alaska (Haines Mission). Ripinsky, Sol. Teachers. 1850-1905. *811*

Alberta (Calgary). Immigration. 1974. *395*

Aleichem, Shalom. Detroit Progressive Literary and Dramatic Club. Michigan (Detroit). 1915. *198*

Alexander, Moses. Democratic Party. Governors. Idaho. Retail Trade. 1914-32. *767*

Alienation. Intellectuals. Journalism. Rosenfeld, Isaac. Social analysis. 1917-55. *635*

—. Intellectuals. Leftism. New Deal. Roosevelt, Franklin D. 1930's. *785*

—. Judaism. Liberalism. Utah (Salt Lake City). 1974. *195*

Allen, Woody. Comedians. Humor. Rickles, Don. Steinberg, David. Stereotypes. 1960's-70's. *508*

Alliance Israelite Universelle. Montana (Helena). Philanthropy. 1868. *682*

Bible. American history. Imber, Naphtali Herz *(The Fall of Jerusalem: Reflecting upon the Present Condition of America)*. Myths and Symbols. Populism. 1856-1909. *185*
Bibliographies. 1960-75. *130*
—. 1960-75. *131*
—. 1960-74. *132*
—. 1960-79. *310*
—. 1974-75. *311*
—. 1960-76. *312*
—. 1960-73. *313*
—. 16c-1978. *314*
—. 1960-78. *315*
—. Anthologies. Literature. 1950's-70's. *80*
—. Authors. Collectors and Collecting. Deinard, Ephraim. Newspapers. Zionism. 1846-1930. *308*
—. Fiction. Immigration. 1867-1920. *338*
—. Israel. Noah, Mordecai Manuel. 1785-1851. 1930's-76. *316*
—. *Jewish Social Studies* (periodical). 1964-78. *202*
—. Judaism (Reform). 1883-1973. *670*
Bibliotheca Rosenthaliana. Book Collecting. Felsenthal, Bernard. Illinois (Chicago). Letters. Netherlands (Amsterdam). Roest, Meyer. Rosenthal, George. 1868-96. *91*
Bicentennial poem. Historians. Judaism. Pennsylvania (Lancaster County). Shain, Samson Aaron (tribute). 1906-76. *628*
Black, Esther Boulton. Behavior. California. *Los Angeles Daily News* (newspaper). Pitt, Leonard. 1869. *703*
Bloch, Ernest. California. Music. San Francisco Conservatory of Music. 1922-30. *509*
B'nai B'rith. California (Los Angeles). 1905. *803*
—. Modernization. Oregon (Portland). Social Change. Voluntary Associations. 1920's. *719*
B'nai B'rith Congregation. California (Los Angeles). Finance. Political Factionalism. Rabbis. 1897. *790*
B'nai B'rith (Judah Touro Lodge No. 998). Rhode Island (Newport). 1924-74. *373*
B'nai B'rith Messenger (newspaper). California (Los Angeles). Newspapers. 1895-1929. *693*
B'nai B'rith (Paradise Lodge No. 237). California (San Bernadino). Choynski, Isidor N. 1875-1975. *471*
Bombing attack. Civil rights. Informers. Jewish Defense League. Legal defenses. Seigel, Sheldon. 1972-73. *104*
Book Collecting. Bibliotheca Rosenthaliana. Felsenthal, Bernard. Illinois (Chicago). Letters. Netherlands (Amsterdam). Roest, Meyer. Rosenthal, George. 1868-96. *91*
—. Judaism. Kohut, George Alexander. Yale University Library (Kohut Collection). 1901-33. *77*
Books. Language. Libraries, public. New York City. Readership. Yiddish Language. 1963-72. *143*
Bowman, Isaiah. Attitudes. Europe, Eastern. League of Nations. Letters. Royse, Morton W. 1927. *411*
Boxerman, William I. Anti-Semitism. Coughlin, Charles Edward. Jewish Community Council. Michigan (Detroit). Radio. 1939. *645*
Boxing. California (San Francisco). Choynski, Joe. ca 1884-1904. *364*
Boy Scouts of America. Rhode Island. 1910-76. *289*
Boycott. American Jewish Committee. American Jewish Congress. Anti-Defamation League of B'nai B'rith. Arab-Israeli conflict. Legislation. 1975-77. *434*

Boycotts. American Olympic Committee. Anti-Semitism. Brundage, Avery. "Fair Play for American Athletes" (pamphlet). Germany (Berlin). Olympic Games. 1935-36. *372*
—. Anti-Nazi Movements. Fram, Leon. League for Human Rights. Michigan (Detroit). Reminiscences. 1930's-40's. *169*
Brandeis, Alfred. Anti-Semitism. Brandeis, Louis D. Letters. Michigan (Detroit). 1914. *535*
Brandeis, Louis. Americanism. Provisional Executive Committee for General Zionist Affairs. Zionism. 1900-74. *825*
—. Cleveland Conference. Mack, Julian. Weizmann, Chaim. Zionist Organization of America. 1921. *479*
Brandeis, Louis D. Anti-Semitism. Brandeis, Alfred. Letters. Michigan (Detroit). 1914. *535*
—. Frankfurter, Felix. New Deal. Politics. Roosevelt, Franklin D. World War I. 1917-33. *102*
—. Freund, Paul A. Law. Reminiscences. Supreme Court. 1932-33. *175*
—. Gompers, Samuel. Judaism. Kogan, Michael S. Labor Unions and Organizations. 1880's-1975. *779*
—. Kallen, Horace M. Zionism. 1912-15. *606*
—. Palestine. Settlements. Zionism. ca 1877-1918. *732*
—. Politics. Zionism. 1912-16. *189*
—. Weizmann, Chaim. Zionist Conference (London, 1920). 1920. *585*
—. Zionism. 1910. *182*
Brandeis University. Educators. Massachusetts (Waltham). Students. 1948-79. *567*
Braude, William G. Rabbis. Reminiscences. Wolfson, Harry. 1932-54. *63*
Brin, Fanny Fligelman. Minnesota (Minneapolis). Peace. Women. 1913-60's. *706*
Brooks, Juanita. Settlement. Utah. Watters, Leon L. 1864-65. 1952-73. *680*
Brown University. Belkin, Samuel. Reminiscences. Rhode Island (Providence). 1932-35. *64*
Brundage, Avery. American Olympic Committee. Anti-Semitism. Boycotts. "Fair Play for American Athletes" (pamphlet). Germany (Berlin). Olympic Games. 1935-36. *372*
Buildings. Grand Opera House. Judah, Abraham. Missouri (Kansas City). Theater. 1883-1926. *92*
Buildings (iron front). California (San Luis Obispo). Sinsheimer, Aaron Zachary (and family). 1878-1956. *700*
Bureau of Social Morals. Hertz, Rosie. Law Enforcement. New York City. Prostitution. 1912-13. *226*
Business. Adler, Lewis. California (Sonoma). 1840's-96. *3*
—. Advertisements. American Revolution. Newspapers. Salomon, Haym. 1777-85. *309*
—. Alaska. Gold Rushes. Reminiscences. Rozenstain, Yael. 1900-44. *575*
—. Alaska. Reminiscences. Ripinsky, Sol. 1867-1909. *530*
—. Banking. California (Ventura County). Levy, Achille. 1853-1936. *359*
—. California (Anaheim). Democratic Party. Dreyfus, Benjamin. Winemaking. 1854-86. *702*
—. California (Fort Bragg). Russia. Shafsky family. 1889-1976. *818*
—. California (Los Angeles). Housing. Middle Classes. Social Mobility. 1880's. *188*
—. California (San Diego). City Government. Mannasse, Joseph Samuel. Schiller, Marcus. 1853-97. *326*
—. California (San Francisco; San Bruno Avenue). Esther Hellman Settlement House. Neighborhoods. 1901-68. *391*

California (Ventura County). Agriculture. Bank of A. Levy. French Americans. Levy, Achille. 1871-1905. *354*
—. Banking. Business. Levy, Achille. 1853-1936. *359*
Calish, Edward Nathan. Virginia (Richmond). Zionism. 1891-1945. *44*
Canada. 1977. *260*
—. Acculturation. Ethnicity. USA. 1961-74. *761*
—. Anti-Semitism. Integration. Legislation. Nazism. 1930's. *50*
—. Anti-Semitism. Nazism. 1963-79. *332*
—. Communist Party. Gershman, Joshua. Labor Unions and Organizations. Reminiscences. 1913-77. *1*
—. Deserters. USA. Vietnam War. 1969-73. *141*
—. Education. Immigration. Reminiscences. Segal, Beryl. USA. 1900-70's. *616*
—. France. Great Britain. Poverty. Uruguay. 1975. *179*
—. Galveston Plan. Immigration. Schiff, Jacob H. USA. 1907-14. *48*
Canada (Western). Anti-Semitism. 1942-72. *137*
Capitalism. Arizona. Frontier and Pioneer Life. Wormser, Michael. 19c. *216*
Carigal, Hakham Raphael Haim Isaac. Rabbis. Rhode Island (Newport). 1771-77. *492*
Catholic Church. Drinan, Robert. Elections (congressional). Massachusetts. 1970-76. *394*
—. Family. Judaism. Private Schools. 1960's-70's. *279*
Cavaignac, Louis. Mann, A. Dudley. Switzerland. Treaties. 1850-55. *455*
Cave, Daniel. California (Los Angeles, San Diego). Dentistry. Freemasons. Leadership. 1873-1936. *355*
Cedars of Lebanon Hospital. California (Los Angeles). Hospitals. Schlesinger, Jacob. 1901-30. *256*
Cemeteries. California (Los Angeles). Congregation B'nai B'rith. Home of Peace Cemetery. 1902. *808*
—. California (Los Angeles; Chavez Ravine). Hebrew Benevolent Society of Los Angeles. Home of Peace Jewish Cemetery. Photographs. 1855-1910. *813*
—. California (San Francisco). First Hebrew Benevolent Society. Funerals. Johnson, Henry D. 1849-50. *679*
—. Congregation Beth El. Historic markers. Letters. Michigan (Detroit). 1850-1971. *797*
—. Saskatchewan. 1975. *379*
Census. California (Los Angeles). Clothing. Retail Trade. 1870's. *685*
Charities. California. Disaster relief. Economic aid. Nieto, Jacob. San Francisco Earthquake and Fire. 1906. *476*
—. California (Los Angeles). Chicago fire. 1871. *688*
—. California (Los Angeles). Civic associations. Lazard, Solomon. 1826-1916. *378*
—. California (San Francisco). Cholera. Neustadt, Samuel I. 1850. *677*
—. Galveston Plan of 1907. Immigrants. Industrial Removal Office. Migration, Internal. New York City. 1890-1914. *545*
—. Hannah Schloss Old Timers. Michigan (Detroit). 1903-73. *236*
—. Jewish Welfare Federation of Detroit. Michigan. 1926. *119*
—. Michigan (Detroit). Odessa Progressive Aid Society. 1915-18. *753*
—. Michigan (Detroit). Reminiscences. Simons, Leonard N. 1901-75. *646*
—. Nebraska (Omaha). Political Leadership. Refugees. Settlement. 1820-1937. *191*

Chicago fire. California (Los Angeles). Charities. 1871. *688*
Chickens. California (Petaluma). Farmers. Socialists. 1900-77. *70*
Child Welfare. California (Los Angeles). Jewish Orphans' Home of Southern California. 1907-09. *428*
—. Foster homes. Immigrants. New York City. Working class. 1900-05. *546*
Childhood. California (Pomona). Cole, Sylvan. People's Store. Reminiscences. Retail Trade. 1886-1901. *93*
Children. Council of Jewish Women. Neighborhood House. Oregon (Portland). Women. 1895-1905. *55*
—. Immigrants. Manitoba (Winnipeg). Public schools. 1900-20. *625*
—. Judaism (Orthodox). New York City (Brooklyn; Boro Park). Parents. Social Status. 1973. *437*
Cholera. California (San Francisco). Charities. Neustadt, Samuel I. 1850. *677*
Chomsky, Noam. Israel. Liberalism. Self-alienation. 1975. *74*
Choynski, Harriet. California (San Francisco). Letters. 1850-72. *78*
Choynski, Isidor N. B'nai B'rith (Paradise Lodge No. 237). California (San Bernardino). 1875-1975. *471*
Choynski, Isidor Nathan. California, southern. Cities. Journalism. Travel (accounts). 1881. *654*
Choynski, Joe. Boxing. California (San Francisco). ca 1884-1904. *364*
Christianity. Anti-Semitism. 1964. *787*
—. Conversion. Daland, William C. Friedlaender, Herman. New York City. *Peculiar People* (newspaper). 1880's-90's. *631*
—. Israel. 1975. *756*
—. Judaism. Niebuhr, Reinhold. 1930-60. *528*
—. Judaism. Women. 17c-1978. *303*
—. King-Crane Report. Palestine. Zionism (opposition to). 1919. *351*
Christians. Anti-Semitism. Genocide. Toynbee, Arnold. World War II. ca 1940-1975. *415*
—. Genocide. Theology. World War II. 1945-74. *118*
—. Marriage, Interfaith. 1962-79. *648*
Church schools. Documents. Education. Finance. Public Policy. Religion in the Public Schools. 1961-71. *90*
—. Education. Hasidim (Lubavitch). Judaism. Quebec (Montreal). 1969-71. *626*
Cincinnati Union Bethel. Ohio. Settlement houses. Social reform. 1838-1903. *140*
Cities. California, southern. Choynski, Isidor Nathan. Journalism. Travel (accounts). 1881. *654*
—. Family. Immigration. Italian Americans. Rhode Island. 1880-1940. *661*
—. Poor. 1967-77. *644*
City Government. Business. California (San Diego). Mannasse, Joseph Samuel. Schiller, Marcus. 1853-97. *326*
City Life. Autobiography. California (San Francisco). Newmark, Helen. 1840-1900. *474*
—. California (Julian, San Diego, Temucula). Levi, Adolph. Levi, Simon. 1850-1943. *612*
—. Immigration. Manitoba (Winnipeg). 1874-82. *20*
City Politics. Koehl, Matt. National Socialist White People's Party. Nazism. Wisconsin (Milwaukee). 1974-76. *501*
Civic associations. California (Los Angeles). Charities. Lazard, Solomon. 1826-1916. *378*

Civic leaders. Business. Filene, Edward A. Massachusetts (Boston). Philanthropy. 1860-1937. *133*
Civil rights. Bombing attack. Informers. Jewish Defense League. Legal defenses. Seigel, Sheldon. 1972-73. *104*
—. Colonization. Europe. Florida. Levy, Moses Elias. 1825. *721*
—. Education. Intermarriage. Israel. 1950's-70's. *170*
—. Ethnicity. Riis, Jacob. Social Organization. 1870-1914. *177*
—. Liberals. Minorities in Politics. New York City. Social reform. 1963-70's. *271*
Civil rights movement. South. 1954-70. *108*
Civil War. Levy, Richard. Levy, Rosena Hutzler. Reminiscences. South or Southern States. 1860-65. *737*
—. Polish Americans. Social organizations. 1860-65. *393*
Civil Wars. Press. Spain. 1934-39. *653*
Clar, Reva. Ballet. California (San Francisco). Hirsch-Arnold Ballet School. Pavlova, Anna. Reminiscences. 1924. *83*
Class consciousness. Cohn, Fannia. International Ladies' Garment Workers' Union. Newman, Pauline. Pesotta, Rose. Women. 1900-35. *337*
Cleaver, Eldridge. Attitudes. 1968-70's. *69*
Clerks. Courts. Nebraska (Lincoln). Newmark, Nellie. 1888-1978. *807*
Cleveland Conference. Brandeis, Louis. Mack, Julian. Weizmann, Chaim. Zionist Organization of America. 1921. *479*
Cloakmakers Union No. 1. Anarchism. Jewish Tailors and Operators Association. Labor Unions and Organizations. Morais, Sabato. Pennsylvania (Philadelphia). Strikes. 1880's-90's. *768*
Clothing. California (Los Angeles). Census. Retail Trade. 1870's. *685*
—. California (San Francisco). German Americans. Strauss, Levi. 1850-1970's. *504*
—. Department stores. Marketing. Neiman-Marcus Co. Texas (Dallas). 1900-17. *248*
—. Outlet Company Store. Retail Trade. Rhode Island (Providence). Samuels, Joseph. Samuels, Leon. 1894-1974. *291*
Clothing industry. Acculturation. May brothers. Oklahoma (Tulsa). Retail Trade. 1889-1970. *755*
Cohen, Morris R. Colleges and Universities. New York, City University of. Philosophy. Teaching. 1912-38. *285*
Cohn, Fannia. Class consciousness. International Ladies' Garment Workers' Union. Newman, Pauline. Pesotta, Rose. Women. 1900-35. *337*
Cohn, Isaac. California (San Bernardino). Cohn, Wolff. Cole, Dick. Murder. 1862. *674*
Cohn, Wolff. California (San Bernardino). Cohn, Isaac. Cole, Dick. Murder. 1862. *674*
Cole, Dick. California (San Bernardino). Cohn, Isaac. Cohn, Wolff. Murder. 1862. *674*
Cole, Sylvan. California (Pomona). Childhood. People's Store. Reminiscences. Retail Trade. 1886-1901. *93*
Collections. American Jewish Historical Society. Rhode Island. 1692-1975. *758*
Collectors and Collecting. Authors. Bibliographies. Deinard, Ephraim. Newspapers. Zionism. 1846-1930. *308*
Colleges and Universities. Admissions (quotas). *DeFunis* v. *Odegaard* (US, 1974). Jews (Sephardic). Washington, University of. 1974. *72*
—. Anti-Semitism. Columbia University. Trilling, Lionel. 1930's. *723*

—. Attitudes. Northwestern University. Students. Yale University. 1968-69. *500*
—. California (San Francisco). California, University of, Berkeley. Journalism. Lawyers. Newmark, Nathan. 1853-1928. *361*
—. Cohen, Morris R. New York, City University of. Philosophy. Teaching. 1912-38. *285*
—. Curricula. Ethnic studies. Literature. Malamud, Bernard. Roth, Henry. 20c. *298*
—. Curricula. Jewish studies. 1960's-74. *10*
—. Ethnicity. Jewish studies. 1967-77. *643*
—. Faculty. 1973. *650*
—. Hebrew Union College. Jewish Institute of Religion. Religious Education. 1875-1974. *796*
—. Hebrew Union College. Ohio (Cincinnati). Wise, Isaac M. 1870's-1900. *97*
—. Hillel Foundation. 1923-78. *642*
—. Jewish Studies. 1974. *125*
—. Literature. Negroes. Stereotypes. Students. 1933-69. *225*
—. Psychology. Solomons, Leon Mendez. 1873-1900. *739*
Colman, Blanche. Colman, Nathan. Frontier and Pioneer Life. South Dakota (Deadwood). 1877-1977. *7*
Colman, Nathan. Colman, Blanche. Frontier and Pioneer Life. South Dakota (Deadwood). 1877-1977. *7*
Colonization. Civil Rights. Europe. Florida. Levy, Moses Elias. 1825. *721*
—. Palestine. Zionism. 1908-34. *596*
Colorado. Farmers. Ranches. 1880's-1977. *94*
—. Lobbyists. Mears, Otto. Republican Party. State Politics. 1876-89. *321*
Colorado (Denver). Authors. Physicians. Social work. Spivak, Charles. ca 1880-1927. *287*
—. Beth Ha Medrosh Hagodol Synagogue. Judaism (Orthodox). Kauvar, Charles E. H. Progressivism. 1902-71. *580*
—. Beth Ha Medrosh Hagodol Synagogue. Judaism (Orthodox). Kauvar, Charles E. H. Zionism. 1902-71. *579*
—. Germany. *Intermountain Jewish News* (newspaper). Nazism. 1932-39. *581*
—. Immigration. Shwayder family. 1865-1916. *47*
Colorado (San Juan Mountains). Mears, Otto. Mines. Tollroads. 1881-87. *322*
Columbia University. Anti-Semitism. Colleges and Universities. Trilling, Lionel. 1930's. *723*
—. Anti-Semitism. Educators. Hook, Sidney. New York City. Reminiscences. Trilling, Lionel. 1920's-70's. *284*
Columbian Council. National Council of Jewish Women. Pennsylvania (Pittsburgh). Women. 18c-20c. *621*
Comedians. Allen, Woody. Humor. Rickles, Don. Steinberg, David. Stereotypes. 1960's-70's. *508*
Commerce. American Revolution. Georgia (Savannah). Memoirs. Sheftall, Levi. 1739-1809. *669*
—. New England. Peddlers and Peddling. Travel. 18c-19c. *334*
Communism. Folsom, Michael. Gold, Mike. Literature. 1914-37. *744*
—. Intellectuals. Menorah Group. 1930's. *743*
Communist Party. Canada. Gershman, Joshua. Labor Unions and Organizations. Reminiscences. 1913-77. *1*
—. Judaism. Literature. New York City. Roth, Henry (interview). 1906-77. *566*
Community affairs. California (Escondido). Grape Day. Politics. Steiner, Sigmund. 1886-1912. *594*
Comparative History. Genocide. History Teaching. Indians. Negroes. Racism. 20c. *218*

Concentration Camps. Air Warfare. Auschwitz. Military Strategy. World War II. 1944-45. *780*

—. Genocide. Germany. Press. World War II. 1939-42. *240*

Conductors. Klasmer, Benjamin. Maryland (Baltimore). Music. 1909-49. *87*

Confederate States of America. Benjamin, Judah. 1861-68. *367*

—. Business. Levy, Jonas Phillips. Merchant marine. North Carolina (Wilmington). 1830's-60's. *527*

Confirmation. California (San Bernardino). Henrietta Hebrew Benevolent Society. Judaism. Religious Education. 1891. *817*

Conflict and Conflict Resolution. Bayor, Ronald H. (review article). German Americans. Irish Americans. Italian Americans. New York City. 1929-41. 1978. *749*

Congregation Ahavath Shalom. Judaism. Rhode Island (West Warwick). 1912-38. *728*

Congregation Beth El. Cemeteries. Historic markers. Letters. Michigan (Detroit). 1850-1971. *797*

—. Michigan (Detroit). 1859-61. *121*

Congregation Beth Israel. California (Oroville, Woodland). Messing, Aron J. Travel. 1879. *810*

Congregation Bickur Cholim. Beth Olam Cemetery. California (San Jose). 1850-1900. *339*

Congregation B'nai B'rith. California (Los Angeles). Cemeteries. Home of Peace Cemetery. 1902. *808*

—. California (Los Angeles). Letters. Newmark, Joseph. Rabbis. 1881. *821*

Congregation Kol Ami. Judaism. Utah (Salt Lake City). 1964-76. *587*

Congregation Sharey Tzedick. Judaism (Orthodox). Utah (Salt Lake City). 1916-48. *589*

Congregation Shearith Israel. Netherlands. New York. Pinto, Joseph Jesurun. Travel. 1759-82. *595*

Congregation Sons of Zion. Finesilver, Moses Ziskind. Judaism. Rabbis. Rhode Island (Providence). 1880-83. *330*

Congress. Anti-Semitism. Displaced Persons Act (US, 1948). Germans. Immigration. World War II. 1945-48. *107*

—. Arab States. Foreign Policy. Israel. 1973-74. *184*

—. California (San Francisco). Kahn, Julius. Political Leadership. Public Policy. Republican Party. 1898-1924. *57*

—. Industry. Lobbying. Middle East policy. Military. Zionism. 1974. *477*

—. International Ladies' Garment Workers Union. Labor Unions and Organizations. London, Meyer. Social insurance movement. Socialism. 1914-22. *214*

Conley, James. Frank, Leo (trial). Georgia (Atlanta). Negroes. Press. 1913-15. *401*

Connecticut (Norwich). 1851-1975. *213*

Conservatism. 1969-79. *160*

—. 1960-74. *551*

—. Foreign policy. Liberalism. 1969-79. *390*

—. New York City. Politics. Radicals and Radicalism. 1900's-20's. *153*

Conspiracy theory. Anti-Semitism. Great Britain. Intellectual History. *Protocols of the Elders of Zion* (document). 20c. *717*

Construction. Copper Mines and Mining. Investments. Newhouse, Samuel. Utah (Salt Lake City). Weir, Thomas. 1879-1930. *588*

Conversion. Christianity. Daland, William C. Friedlaender, Herman. New York City. *Peculiar People* (newspaper). 1880's-90's. *631*

Converts. Assimilation. Ontario (Toronto). Presbyterian Church. 1912-18. *242*

—. California (Santa Cruz). Judaism. Schlutius, Emma. 1877. *163*

Copper Mines and Mining. Arizona. California. Newman, John B. (Black Jack). Real estate. 1880's-1920's. *672*

—. Construction. Investments. Newhouse, Samuel. Utah (Salt Lake City). Weir, Thomas. 1879-1930. *588*

Corporations. Family. Lilienthal family pact. New York. 1814-1904. *687*

Coughlin, Charles Edward. Anti-Semitism. Boxerman, William I. Jewish Community Council. Michigan (Detroit). Radio. 1939. *645*

Council of Jewish Women. Children. Neighborhood House. Oregon (Portland). Women. 1895-1905. *55*

Counter Culture. Cabala. Mysticism. Rationalism. Traditionalism. 1940's-70's. *539*

—. Ethnicity. Students. 1960's-70's. *204*

Courts. Clerks. Nebraska (Lincoln). Newmark, Nellie. 1888-1978. *807*

Courts Martial and Courts of Inquiry. Galvanized Yankees. Indian Wars. Saltiel, Emanuel H. (pseud. of Joseph Isaacs). 1866. *729*

Crane, Stephen. Cahan, Abraham. Fiction. Romanticism. Slums. 1890's. *155*

Crime and Criminals (white-collar). 1969-78. *101*

Cuddihy, John Murray (review article). Intellectuals. 1974. *9*

Culture. California (Los Angeles). Historic preservation. Lummis, Charles F. Newmark, Harris. Newmark, Marco. Newmark, Maurice. Southwest Museum. 1859-1930. *224*

Curricula. Colleges and Universities. Ethnic studies. Literature. Malamud, Bernard. Roth, Henry. 20c. *298*

—. Colleges and universities. Jewish studies. 1960's-74. *10*

—. Hebrew Union College. Jewish history. Ohio (Cincinnati). Seminaries. Wise, Isaac Mayer. 1817-90's. *448*

—. Hebrew Union College. Judaism. Ohio (Cincinnati). 1942-45. *576*

—. Higher Education. Jewish studies. 1972-74. *162*

Cynicism. Bergman, Andrew. Novels, detective. Simon, Roger. 1970's. *709*

D

Daily Life. Illinois (Chicago). Women. 20c. *668*

—. Interethnic relations. New York. Religion. Schools. 18c. *99*

—. Oregon (Portland). 1878. *824*

—. Siegel, Richard. Strassfeld, Michael. Strassfeld, Sharon. 1973. *657*

Daland, William C. Christianity. Conversion. Friedlaender, Herman. New York City. *Peculiar People* (newspaper). 1880's-90's. *631*

D'Ancona, David Arnold. Anti-Semitism. California (San Francisco). Letters-to-the-editor. Newspapers. Pixley, Frank M. 1883. *98*

Davidson, Herman. California (Stockton). Judaism. Opera. Rabbis. Russian Americans. 1846-1911. *82*

Davidson, Israel. Letters. Literary History. Zinberg, Israel. 1925-37. *307*

Davidson, Sue. Howe, Fanny Quincy. Pinzer, Maimie. Rosen, Ruth. Social Classes. Women (review article). 1910-22. 1977. *571*

Defense budget. Foreign Policy. Israel. Liberals. Senate. 1975. *420*

DeFunis v. *Odegaard* (US, 1974). Admissions Policies. Discrimination (reverse). Law schools. Washington. 1970's. *33*

Editorials. Anti-Semitism. Dreyfus, Alfred. France. Press. Public opinion. Trials. 1895-1906. *151*

Editors and Editing. California (Los Angeles). German Americans. Jacoby, Conrad. *Sud-California Post* (newspaper). 1874-1914. *67*

Education. Americanization. Jewish Family and Children's Service. Michigan (Detroit). Voluntary Associations. 1876-1976. *392*

—. Assimilation. Labor Unions and Organizations. Socialism. 1880's-1945. *724*

—. Canada. Immigration. Reminiscences. Segal, Beryl. USA. 1900-70's. *616*

—. Church Schools. Hasidim (Lubavitch). Judaism. Quebec (Montreal). 1969-71. *626*

—. Civil rights. Intermarriage. Israel. 1950's-70's. *170*

—. Economic opportunity. Employment. Immigrants. Urbanization. 1880-1914. *792*

—. Family. Income. 1969. *799*

—. Immigrants. Pennsylvania (Pittsburgh). 1862-1932. *620*

—. Levy, William (speech). Negroes. Northwest Texas Colored Citizens College. Social Mobility. Texas (Sherman). 1890. *403*

—. Rhode Island (Providence). 1854-1946. *618*

Education, Finance. Church schools. Documents. Public Policy. Religion in the Public Schools. 1961-71. *90*

Educational associations. Immigrants. Libraries. New York City. Newspapers. 1880-1914. *35*

Educators. Anti-Semitism. Columbia University. Hook, Sidney. New York City. Reminiscences. Trilling, Lionel. 1920's-70's. *284*

—. Brandeis University. Massachusetts (Waltham). Students. 1948-79. *567*

Ehrlich, Abraham. Georgia (Valdosta). Kaul, Bernard. 1866-90. *607*

Einhorn, David. History. Millenarianism. 1830-79. *235*

Einstein, Albert. Art. Intellectuals. Religion. ca 1900-55. *282*

—. Institute for Advanced Study. New Jersey (Princeton). 1933-55. *31*

—. Nuclear arms. Pacifism. Zionism. 1939-55. *150*

—. Zionism. 1911-55. *228*

Elections. Democratic Party. 1950's-70's. *159*

Elections (congressional). Catholic Church. Drinan, Robert. Massachusetts. 1970-76. *394*

Elections (mayoral). Aloe, Louis Patrick. Anti-Semitism. Missouri (St. Louis). Progressivism. 1910-25. *58*

Elections, provincial. Parti Québécois. Quebec. Separatist Movements. 1976. *760*

Eliot, T. S. Anti-Semitism. Literature. Pound, Ezra. Roth, Philip. 20c. *139*

Elites. Anti-Semitism. Freedom of speech. Mencken, H. L. Public opinion. 1917-41. *28*

—. Intellectuals. 1945-78. *498*

—. Social Classes. 20c. *583*

Elkin, Mendel. Immigrants. Yivo Library. 1918-63. *427*

Emancipation. Assimilation. Jewish studies. 18c-1974. *329*

—. Ghettos. Negroes. 15c-20c. *371*

Emanu-El (newspaper). Anti-Semitism. California (San Francisco). Immigrants. Slavic Americans. Voorsanger, Jacob (views). 1905. *556*

Emigrants. USSR. 1974. *68*

Emigration. Anti-Semitism. Famine. Foreign Relations. Russia. 1891-92. *664*

—. Hawaii. 1850-1913. *206*

—. Israel. 1970's. *720*

—. Jackson, Henry M. Legislation. Most-Favored-Nation status. USSR. 1972-74. *554*

—. Morocco. Quebec (Montreal). 1960's-70's. *323*

—. Russia. 1881-1914. *375*

Emigres. Genocide. Kremer, Charles H. Rumanian Americans. Trifa, Valerian. World War II. 1941-74. *425*

Employment. Assimilation. Immigration. Israel. 1967-70's. *197*

—. Economic opportunity. Education. Immigrants. Urbanization. 1880-1914. *792*

—. Immigration. New York City. Social Organization. 1970's. *376*

Energy crisis. Anti-Semitism. Public opinion. 1970's. *423*

Engle, Paul. Attitudes. Iowa (Cedar Rapids). Reminiscences. 1900-60. *134*

Entrepreneurs. California (Temecula Valley). Indians. Jackson, Helen Hunt. Wolf, Louis. 1852-87. *686*

Equal Opportunity. American Revolution. 1760's-1876. *802*

Eris, Alfred. Israel. New York City. Reminiscences. Six-Day War. 1967. *138*

Esther Hellman Settlement House. Business. California (San Francisco; San Bruno Avenue). Neighborhoods. 1901-68. *391*

Ethnic Groups. Illinois (Chicago). Protestants. 1960's-70's. *388*

—. Jewish History Project. Methodology. Ohio (Columbus). Oral history. 1920-70. *516*

Ethnic Relations. Illinois (Chicago). Polish Americans. 20c. *407*

Ethnic studies. Colleges and Universities. Curricula. Literature. Malamud, Bernard. Roth, Henry. 20c. *298*

Ethnic unity. Rav Tzair (Chaim Tchenowitz). 1974. *79*

Ethnicity. Acculturation. Canada. USA. 1961-74. *761*

—. Affirmative action. Religiosity. 1960's-70's. *128*

—. American Dream. Literature. 20c. *181*

—. Anti-Semitism. Liberals. Negroes. 1969. *73*

—. Attitudes. Israel. Northeastern or North Atlantic States. Students. Zionism. 1973-76. *759*

—. California (San Francisco). Synagogue. 1848-1900. *365*

—. Civil Rights. Riis, Jacob. Social Organization. 1870-1914. *177*

—. Colleges and universities. Jewish studies. 1967-77. *643*

—. Counter culture. Students. 1960's-70's. *204*

—. Deinard, Samuel N. Minnesota (Minneapolis). 1915-21. *519*

—. Identity. Religion. 1800-1975. *325*

—. Immigration. Niger, Shmuel. Slavic Americans. 1920-33. *485*

—. Jews, Sephardic. 1967-75. *385*

—. Lumbee Indians. Negroes. South Carolina (Robeson County). Stereotypes. 1967-68. *53*

—. Maryland, University of. Parents. Religion. Students. 1949-71. *386*

—. Religion. 1975. *659*

—. Social Organization. 1772-1977. *38*

Europe. American Jewish Committee. Factionalism. Jewish Agency for Palestine. Palestine. World Zionist Organization. Zionist Organization of America. 1923-29. *482*

—. Art. Stereotypes. 1870-1976. *23*

—. Civil Rights. Colonization. Florida. Levy, Moses Elias. 1825. *721*

G

Jacoby, Conrad. California (Los Angeles). Editors and Editing. German Americans. *Sud-California Post* (newspaper). 1874-1914. *67*

Jewish Agency for Palestine. American Jewish Committee. Europe. Factionalism. Palestine. World Zionist Organization. Zionist Organization of America. 1923-29. *482*

—. Europe, Western. Zionism. 1929-79. *733*

Jewish Agriculturists' Aid Society of America. Agriculture. Farmers. Levy, Abraham R. North Dakota (central). Reminiscences. Settlement. Slavic Americans. 1903. *400*

Jewish Committee for Personal Service in State Institutions. California. Mental hospitals. Meyer, Martin A. Prisons. Psychiatric social histories. Shirpser, Elsie. 1920-60. *456*

Jewish Community Council. Anti-Semitism. Boxerman, William I. Coughlin, Charles Edward. Michigan (Detroit). Radio. 1939. *645*

Jewish Community Council of Metropolitan Detroit. Michigan (Detroit). 1935-37. *345*

Jewish Daily Forward (newspaper). Cahan, Abraham. Palestine. Socialism. Zionism. 1925. *745*

Jewish Defense League. Bombing attack. Civil rights. Informers. Legal defenses. Seigel, Sheldon. 1972-73. *104*

—. Foreign Relations. Kahane, Meir. USSR. ca 1950's-75. *341*

—. Kahane, Meir. Zionism. 1950's-75. *342*

Jewish Family and Children's Service. Americanization. Education. Michigan (Detroit). Voluntary Associations. 1876-1976. *392*

Jewish Historical Society of Michigan (annual meeting). Historical societies. Michigan. 1973. *122*

Jewish history. Curricula. Hebrew Union College. Ohio (Cincinnati). Seminaries. Wise, Isaac Mayer. 1817-90's. *448*

Jewish History Project. Ethnic Groups. Methodology. Ohio (Columbus). Oral history. 1920-70. *516*

—. Ohio (Columbus). ca 1974. *513*

Jewish Institute of Religion. Colleges and Universities. Hebrew Union College. Religious Education. 1875-1974. *796*

Jewish Jubilee Year. Social Customs. ca 3000 BC-1975. *716*

Jewish Observer (periodical). Judaism, Orthodox. *Tradition* (periodical). 1880-1974. *651*

Jewish Orphan's Home. California (Huntington Park, Los Angeles). Frey, Sigmund. Social work. 1870's-1930. *26*

Jewish Orphans' Home of Southern California. California (Los Angeles). Child Welfare. 1907-09. *428*

Jewish Progress Club. California (Los Angeles). Voluntary Associations. 1908. *694*

Jewish Social Studies (periodical). 1939-78. *32*

—. Bibliographies. 1964-78. *202*

Jewish Spectator (periodical). California. Intellectuals. New York. Weiss-Rosmarin, Trude. 1930-78. *199*

Jewish Student Movement. Massachusetts (Boston). Radicals and Radicalism. Social Change. Youth Movements. 1960-75. *568*

Jewish studies. Assimilation. Emancipation. 18c-1974. *329*

—. Colleges and Universities. 1974. *125*

—. Colleges and universities. Curricula. 1960's-74. *10*

—. Colleges and universities. Ethnicity. 1967-77. *643*

—. Curricula. Higher Education. 1972-74. *162*

—. Hebrew University (Institute of Contemporary Jewry). Israel (Jerusalem). 1972-74. *100*

—. Higher Education. 1972-74. *660*

—. Higher Education. Philosophy. 1972-74. *167*

—. Higher Education. Political Science. 1972-74. *126*

—. Higher Education. Religious studies. 1972-74. *469*

Jewish studies (Sephardic). 1972-74. *142*

Jewish Tailors and Operators Association. Anarchism. Cloakmakers Union No. 1. Labor Unions and Organizations. Morais, Sabato. Pennsylvania (Philadelphia). Strikes. 1880's-90's. *768*

Jewish Theological Seminary. Acculturation. Kaplan, Mordecai M. New York City. Theology. 1920's. *615*

—. Fund raising. Mergers. New York City. Religious Education. Yeshiva College. 1925-28. *510*

Jewish tradition. National Characteristics. Theology. Yiddish tradition. 19c-20c. *652*

Jewish War Veterans of the United States. Madison, Harry T. Michigan (Detroit). Veterans. 1938-50's. *542*

Jewish Welfare Federation of Detroit. Charities. Michigan. 1926. *119*

Jews (Sephardic). Admissions (quotas). Colleges and Universities. *DeFunis* v. *Odegaard* (US, 1974). Washington, University of. 1974. *72*

—. American Revolution. Massachusetts (Leicester). Rhode Island (Newport). 1777-83. *754*

—. Behar, Leon. Theater. Washington (Seattle). 1920's-1930's. *13*

—. California. Pioneers. 1850-1900. *683*

—. Ethnicity. 1967-75. *385*

—. Immigration. Persecution. Portugal. 1654-1978. *413*

—. Immigration. Washington (Seattle). 1906-24. *12*

Joel, Joseph. Reminiscences. Social Customs. Virginia (Richmond). 1884-92. *43*

Johnson, Grove L. Anti-Semitism. California (Fresno). Foote, William D. Trials. 1893. *795*

Johnson, Henry D. California (San Francisco). Cemeteries. First Hebrew Benevolent Society. Funerals. 1849-50. *679*

Joint Distribution Committee. Fund raising. Genocide. Judaism (Orthodox). Rescue work. World War II. Yeshiva Aid Committee. 1939-41. *786*

Jones, Arthur. National Socialist White People's Party. Nominations for Office. Petition signing. Primaries (mayoral). Wisconsin (Milwaukee). 1976. *51*

Journalism. Alienation. Intellectuals. Rosenfeld, Isaac. Social analysis. 1917-55. *635*

—. California (San Francisco). California, University of, Berkeley. Colleges and Universities. Lawyers. Newmark, Nathan. 1853-1928. *361*

—. California, southern. Choynski, Isidor Nathan. Cities. Travel (accounts). 1881. *654*

—. Goldfaden, Abraham. Language. New York City. *Nuyorker Yidishe Ilustrirte Tsaytung* (newspaper). Theater. Yiddish Language. 1875-88. *215*

Judah, Abraham. Buildings. Grand Opera House. Missouri (Kansas City). Theater. 1883-1926. *92*

Judaism. Adler, Samuel. Morality. New York City. Theology. ca 1829-91. *231*

—. Agriculture. Krauskopf, Joseph. Reform. 1880's-1923. *710*

—. Alienation. Liberalism. Utah (Salt Lake City). 1974. *195*

K

Lilienthal, Max. *Hebrew Sabbath School Visitor* (periodical). Religious education. ca 1840-82. *444*

Lilienthal, Philip Nettre. California (Orangevale, Porterville). Lubin, David. Settlement. Weinstock, Harris. 1890's. *695*

Lipsitch, I. Irving. Immigration. New York City (Ellis Island). United Hebrew Charities. 1891-1910. *515*

Lissner, Henry H. California (Los Angeles). Physicians. 1895-1968. *707*

Literary criticism. Roth, Philip (*Portnoy's Complaint*). 1969-76. *54*

Literary History. Davidson, Israel. Letters. Zinberg, Israel. 1925-37. *307*

Literary mafia. Kostelanetz, Richard (review article). 1970's. *19*

Literature. Aestheticism. *Di Yunge* (group). New York City. 1902-13. *777*

—. American dream. Bellow, Saul (*Henderson The Rain King*). Technology. 1965. *540*

—. American Dream. Ethnicity. 20c. *181*

—. Anthologies. Bibliographies. 1950's-70's. *80*

—. Anti-Semitism. Drama. Stereotypes. 1830's-1920's. *111*

—. Anti-Semitism. Eliot, T. S. Pound, Ezra. Roth, Philip. 20c. *139*

—. Anti-Semitism. Stereotypes. 1880's-90's. *112*

—. Assimilation. ca 1900-20. *784*

—. Attitudes. Tyler, Royall. ca 1777-1826. *76*

—. Autobiography. 1975. *553*

—. Autobiography. Kazin, Alfred. National Characteristics. New York City (Brooklyn). 1940-76. *117*

—. Bellow, Saul (*Mr. Sammler's Planet*). Mailer, Norman (*Armies of the Night*). Political Theory. 1975. *344*

—. Colleges and Universities. Curricula. Ethnic studies. Malamud, Bernard. Roth, Henry. 20c. *298*

—. Colleges and Universities. Negroes. Stereotypes. Students. 1933-69. *225*

—. Communism. Folsom, Michael. Gold, Mike. 1914-37. *744*

—. Communist Party. Judaism. New York City. Roth, Henry (interview). 1906-77. *566*

—. Ghetto culture. Negroes. 20c. *601*

—. Harap, Louis (review article). 1775-1914. 1974. *599*

—. Immigrants. Values. 19c-20c. *640*

—. Levin, Meyer. 1931-76. *736*

—. Negroes. 1975. *578*

—. New York City. *Shriften* (periodical). Yiddish Language. 1912-26. *246*

—. Poland. Singer, Isaac Bashevis (interview). Singer, Israel Joshua. 20c. *647*

—. Stereotypes. 1900-77. *637*

Littauer, Lucius Nathan. Glove factory. House of Representatives. New York. Philanthropy. Politics. 1859-1944. *59*

Littmann, Max. Fort Phil Kearney. Indian Wars. Wagon Box Fight (1867). Wyoming. 1865-1921. *333*

Lobbying. American Israel Public Affairs Committee. Foreign Policy. Israel. 1922-76. *29*

—. American Jewish Committee. Foreign relations. Immigration Policy. Russia. 1915-17. *222*

—. Anti-Semitism. Lauchheimer, Charles. Marines. Taft, William H. (administration). 1910-12. *769*

—. Congress. Industry. Middle East policy. Military. Zionism. 1974. *477*

—. District of Columbia. Feuer, Leon I. Public opinion. Reminiscences. Zionism. 1940's. *152*

—. Foreign policy. Presidents. Zionism. 1912-73. *340*

—. German Americans. Immigration. Russian Americans. 1880-1924. *714*

Lobbyists. Colorado. Mears, Otto. Republican Party. State Politics. 1876-89. *321*

Local History. Rhode Island Jewish Historical Association. 1951-74. *219*

Loewenthal, Henry. Georgia (Macon). Judaism. Leeser, Isaac. Letters. Rabbis. 1854-70. *352*

London, Meyer. Congress. International Ladies' Garment Workers Union. Labor Unions and Organizations. Social insurance movement. Socialism. 1914-22. *214*

Los Angeles Daily News (newspaper). Behavior. Black, Esther Boulton. California. Pitt, Leonard. 1869. *703*

Louisiana (New Orleans). Business. Godchaux, Leon. 19c. *747*

Lubin, David. California (Orangevale, Porterville). Lilienthal, Philip Nettre. Settlement. Weinstock, Harris. 1890's. *695*

—. California (Sacramento). Letters. Zionism. 1918. *419*

Lumbee Indians. Ethnicity. Negroes. South Carolina (Robeson County). Stereotypes. 1967-68. *53*

Lummis, Charles F. California (Los Angeles). Culture. Historic preservation. Newmark, Harris. Newmark, Marco. Newmark, Maurice. Southwest Museum. 1859-1930. *224*

Lynching. California. Frank, Leo. Georgia. Progressivism. Trials. 1913-15. *263*

Lyons, Henry A. California. Heydenfeldt, Solomon. Supreme courts, state. 1850's. *464*

M

Mack, Julian. Brandeis, Louis. Cleveland Conference. Weizmann, Chaim. Zionist Organization of America. 1921. *479*

Madison, Harry T. Jewish War Veterans of the United States. Michigan (Detroit). Veterans. 1938-50's. *542*

Magnes, Judah L. Hebrew University (Jerusalem). Palestine. Zionism. 1900-25. *194*

Mailer, Norman (*Armies of the Night*). Bellow, Saul (*Mr. Sammler's Planet*). Literature. Political Theory. 1975. *344*

Malamud, Bernard. Colleges and Universities. Curricula. Ethnic studies. Literature. Roth, Henry. 20c. *298*

Malamud, Bernard (*The Tenants*). Novels. 1971. *414*

Malkiel, Theresa Serber. Labor Unions and Organizations. New York City. Socialist Party. Women. 1900's-14. *453*

Manitoba. Physicians. 19c. *441*

Manitoba (Winnipeg). Children. Immigrants. Public schools. 1900-20. *625*

—. City Life. Immigration. 1874-82. *20*

—. Pioneers. 1860's-1975. *24*

Mann, A. Dudley. Cavaignac, Louis. Switzerland. Treaties. 1850-55. *455*

Mannasse, Joseph Samuel. Business. California (San Diego). City Government. Schiller, Marcus. 1853-97. *326*

Margolin, Arnold. Independence Movements. Ukrainian Americans. 1900-56. *412*

Marines. Anti-Semitism. Lauchheimer, Charles. Lobbying. Taft, William H. (administration). 1910-12. *769*

Marketing. Clothing. Department stores. Neiman-Marcus Co. Texas (Dallas). 1900-17. *248*

—. Fashion. Neiman-Marcus Co. Texas (Dallas). 1880-1970. *85*

—. Congregation Sons of Zion. Finesilver, Moses Ziskind. Judaism. Rhode Island (Providence). 1880-83. *330*

—. Franklin, Leo M. Nebraska (Omaha). Temple Israel. 1892-99. *123*

—. Georgia (Macon). Judaism. Leeser, Isaac. Letters. Loewenthal, Henry. 1854-70. *352*

—. Hebrew Union College. Letters. Stolz, Joseph. Wise, Isaac Mayer. 1882-1900. *449*

—. Hecht, Sigmund. Judaism. New York. Wisconsin (Milwaukee). 1877-1911. *362*

—. Judaism. Letters. Prager, Abraham J. Wise, Isaac Mayer. 1854-1900. *684*

—. Kerman, Julius C. Memoirs. Palestine. World War I. 1913-71. *335*

—. North Dakota (Grand Forks). Papermaster, Benjamin. 1890-1934. *481*

Race Relations. Anti-Semitism. Negroes. 1970. *725*

—. Authors. Negroes. 1956-70. *404*

—. Economic Conditions. Negroes. Social Organization. 1940's-70's. *763*

—. Intellectuals. Negroes. 1970's. *746*

—. Kaplan, Kivie (obituary). NAACP. Negroes. 1975. *278*

—. Negroes. 1960-74. *592*

—. Negroes. 1800-1940. *773*

—. Negroes. New York City. Paris, Moshe. 1979. *591*

—. Negroes. New York (Syracuse). 1787-1977. *772*

—. Negroes. Politics. Social Conditions. 1930's-79. *505*

Race theories. Myrdal, Gunnar. Park, Robert E. 1940's. *742*

Racism. *American Mercury* (periodical). Anti-Semitism. Mencken, H. L. 1924-74. *827*

—. Comparative History. Genocide. History Teaching. Indians. Negroes. 20c. *218*

—. Discrimination. Negroes. 1890-1915. *164*

Radicalism. Theology. 1914-75. *114*

Radicals and Radicalism. Conservatism. New York City. Politics. 1900's-20's. *153*

—. Group-fantasy. Social Psychology. 1840-1975. *572*

—. Jewish Student Movement. Massachusetts (Boston). Social Change. Youth Movements. 1960-75. *568*

Radio. Anti-Semitism. Boxerman, William I. Coughlin, Charles Edward. Jewish Community Council. Michigan (Detroit). 1939. *645*

Ranches. Colorado. Farmers. 1880's-1977. *94*

Rappoport, Angelo S. Ben-Amos, Dan. Folklore (review article). Mintz, Jerome R. 1937-72. *251*

Rationalism. Cabala. Counter Culture. Mysticism. Traditionalism. 1940's-70's. *539*

Rav Tzair (Chaim Tchenowitz). Ethnic unity. 1974. *79*

Readership. Books. Language. Libraries, public. New York City. Yiddish Language. 1963-72. *143*

Real estate. Arizona. California. Copper Mines and Mining. Newman, John B. (Black Jack). 1880's-1920's. *672*

—. Investments. Marks, Anna. Mining. Utah (Eureka City). 1880-1900. *590*

Reese, Michael. Attitudes. California (San Francisco). 1850-78. *366*

Reform. Agriculture. Judaism. Krauskopf, Joseph. 1880's-1923. *710*

—. Filene, Edward A. Industrial democracy. Massachusetts (Boston). 1890-1937. *440*

—. Kallen, Horace M. Zionism. 1887-1921. *603*

Reform (movements). Metropolitan Protective Association. New Mexico (Santa Fe). New York City. Spiegelberg, Flora Langermann. 1875-1943. *387*

Refugees. 1938-39. *229*

—. Armies. Germany. Military Occupation. 1946. *109*

—. California (Oakland). Disaster relief. San Francisco Earthquake and Fire. Synagogues. 1906. *812*

—. Charities. Nebraska (Omaha). Political Leadership. Settlement. 1820-1937. *191*

—. Diplomacy. Évian Conference. Resettlement. 1938-39. *429*

—. Documents. Europe. McDonald, James G. Resettlement. World War II. 1938-43. *148*

—.. Documents. Immigration Policy. Morgenthau, Henry, Jr. State Department. Treasury Department. World War II. 1942-44. *430*

—. Friedman, Saul S. (review article). Genocide. Public Policy. Roosevelt, Franklin D. (administration). World War II. 1938-45. 1973. *537*

—. Fund raising. International Society for the Colonization of Russian Jews. Oregon (Portland). 1891. *814*

—. Genocide. Germany. Immigration Policy. Roosevelt, Franklin D. (administration). 1933-45. *144*

—. Germany. Relief organizations. World War II. 1933-45. *192*

—. McDonald, James. Roosevelt, Franklin D. (administration). State Department. 1933-40's. *193*

Regents of the University of California v. *Allan Bakke* (US, 1978). Affirmative action. Anti-Semitism. Bakke, Allan. Negroes. 1964-78. *762*

Rehine, Zalma. Maryland (Baltimore). 19c. *559*

Relief organizations. Germany. Refugees. World War II. 1933-45. *192*

Religion. Art. Einstein, Albert. Intellectuals. ca 1900-55. *282*

—. Daily Life. Interethnic relations. New York. Schools. 18c. *99*

—. Ethnicity. 1975. *659*

—. Ethnicity. Identity. 1800-1975. *325*

—. Ethnicity. Maryland, University of. Parents. Students. 1949-71. *386*

—. Geographic Mobility. 1952-71. *472*

—. Israel. Secularization. Self-perception. 1957-77. *369*

—. Judaism. Medieval culture. Philosophy of history. Wolfson, Harry Austryn. 6c-16c. 1910-74. *770*

—. Protest movements. Vietnam War. Youth. 1960's. *666*

Religion in the Public Schools. Church schools. Documents. Education. Finance. Public Policy. 1961-71. *90*

Religiosity. Affirmative action. Ethnicity. 1960's-70's. *128*

Religious Education. California (San Bernardino). Confirmation. Henrietta Hebrew Benevolent Society. Judaism. 1891. *817*

—. Colleges and Universities. Hebrew Union College. Jewish Institute of Religion. 1875-1974. *796*

—. Fund raising. Jewish Theological Seminary. Mergers. New York City. Yeshiva College. 1925-28. *510*

—. *Hebrew Sabbath School Visitor* (periodical). Lilienthal, Max. ca 1840-82. *444*

—. Judaism. Michigan (Detroit). Sholom Aleichem Institute. 1926-71. *555*

Religious freedom. Georgia. Judaism. 1733-90. *459*

Religious Liberty. Letters. Rhode Island (Newport). Seixas, Moses. Washington, George. 1790. 1974. *439*
Religious studies. Higher Education. Jewish studies. 1972-74. *469.*
—. Judaism. Tradition. 20c. *470*
Reminiscences. Agriculture. Farmers. Jewish Agriculturists' Aid Society of America. Levy, Abraham R. North Dakota (central). Settlement. Slavic Americans. 1903. *400*
—. Alaska. Business. Gold Rushes. Rozenstain, Yael. 1900-44. *575*
—. Alaska. Business. Ripinsky, Sol. 1867-1909. *530*
—. Anti-Nazi Movements. Boycotts. Fram, Leon. League for Human Rights. Michigan (Detroit). 1930's-40's. *169*
—. Anti-Semitism. Columbia University. Educators. Hook, Sidney. New York City. Trilling, Lionel. 1920's-70's. *284*
—. Assimilation. California (Los Angeles). Sichel, Carolyn Meyberg. 1902-31. *639*
—. Attitudes. Engle, Paul. Iowa (Cedar Rapids). 1900-60. *134*
—. Ballet. California (San Francisco). Clar, Reva. Hirsch-Arnold Ballet School. Pavlova, Anna. 1924. *83*
—. Belkin, Samuel. Brown University. Rhode Island (Providence). 1932-35. *64*
—. Brandeis, Louis D. Freund, Paul A. Law. Supreme Court. 1932-33. *175*
—. Braude, William G. Rabbis. Wolfson, Harry. 1932-54. *63*
—. California. Franklin, Harvey B. Rabbis. 1916-57. *172*
—. California (Los Angeles). Films. Myers, Carmel. 1902-30. *465*
—. California (Los Angeles). Mesmer, Joseph. Newmark, Joseph. 1824-1947. *446*
—. California (Pomona). Childhood. Cole, Sylvan. People's Store. Retail Trade. 1886-1901. *93*
—. California (San Francisco). France. Immigrants. Meyer, Eugene. 1842-60. *447*
—. Canada. Communist Party. Gershman, Joshua. Labor Unions and Organizations. 1913-77. *1*
—. Canada. Education. Immigration. Segal, Beryl. USA. 1900-70's. *616*
—. Charities. Michigan (Detroit). Simons, Leonard N. 1901-75. *646*
—. Civil War. Levy, Richard. Levy, Rosena Hutzler. South or Southern States. 1860-65. *737*
—. District of Columbia. Feuer, Leon I. Lobbying. Public opinion. Zionism. 1940's. *152*
—. Eris, Alfred. Israel. New York City. Six-Day War. 1967. *138*
—. Feuer, Lewis S. Scholarship. Teaching. Wolfson, Harry Austryn. ca 1900-74. *154*
—. Germany. Prisoners of war. Winograd, Leonard. World War II. 1944-45. *776*
—. Hentoff, Nat. Massachusetts (Boston; Roxbury). Neighborhoods. 1930's. *267*
—. Hertzberg, Arthur. Judaism. 1940's-79. *273*
—. Hexter, Maurice B. Ohio (Cincinnati). Social Work. United Jewish Charities. 1910's. *277*
—. Joel, Joseph. Social Customs. Virginia (Richmond). 1884-92. *43*
—. Kalter, Bella Briansky. Ontario (Ansonville). Rural Settlements. 1929-40. *318*
Republican Party. California (San Francisco). Congress. Kahn, Julius. Political Leadership. Public Policy. 1898-1924. *57*
—. Colorado. Lobbyists. Mears, Otto. State Politics. 1876-89. *321*

Rescue work. Fund raising. Genocide. Joint Distribution Committee. Judaism (Orthodox). World War II. Yeshiva Aid Committee. 1939-41. *786*
Resettlement. Diplomacy. Évian Conference. Refugees. 1938-39. *429*
—. Documents. Europe. McDonald, James G. Refugees. World War II. 1938-43. *148*
Residential patterns. Generations. Language. Rhode Island. Yiddish Language. 1910-70. *223*
Resnik, Bezalel Nathan. Business. Memoirs. Rhode Island (Providence). 1891-1971. *523*
Resorts. California (Santa Monica). 1875-1939. *800*
Retail Trade. Acculturation. Clothing industry. May brothers. Oklahoma (Tulsa). 1889-1970. *755*
—. Alexander, Moses. Democratic Party. Governors. Idaho. 1914-32. *767*
—. Auerbach's Department Store. California. Utah (Salt Lake City). 1857-1977. *586*
—. California (Los Angeles). Census. Clothing. 1870's. *685*
—. California (Pomona). Childhood. Cole, Sylvan. People's Store. Reminiscences. 1886-1901. *93*
—. Clothing. Outlet Company Store. Rhode Island (Providence). Samuels, Joseph. Samuels, Leon. 1894-1974. *291*
—. Durkheimer family. Olympia beer. Oregon. 1862-1978. *210*
—. Edison Brothers Company. Georgia. Shoe stores. 1910's-1940's. *56*
—. Immigration. Polish Americans. Western States. 1880's. *696*
—. Westward Movement. 1848-20c. *397*
Revolution. Levy, Jonas P. Merchant Marine. Mexican War. Peru. 1823-48. *525*
Rhode Island. American Jewish Historical Society. Collections. 1692-1975. *758*
—. American Revolution. Great Britain. Touro, Isaac. 1782. *405*
—. Boy Scouts of America. 1910-76. *289*
—. Cities. Family. Immigration. Italian Americans. 1880-1940. *661*
—. Generations. Language. Residential patterns. Yiddish Language. 1910-70. *223*
—. Orphanages. 1909-42. *450*
—. Voluntary Associations. Women. ca 1877-1975. *292*
Rhode Island Jewish Historical Association. Local History. 1951-76. *219*
Rhode Island (Newport). American Revolution. 1763-76. *418*
—. American Revolution. Jews, Sephardic. Massachusetts (Leicester). 1777-83. *754*
—. Ararat (colony). New York. Noah, Mordecai Manuel. 1813-21. *220*
—. Architecture. Bevis Marks Synagogue. Great Britain (London). Harrison, Peter. Touro Synagogue. 1670-1775. *602*
—. B'nai B'rith (Judah Touro Lodge No. 998). 1924-74. *373*
—. Carigal, Hakham Raphael Haim Isaac. Rabbis. 1771-77. *492*
—. Demonstrations. Touro Synagogue. 1893-1902. *374*
—. Freemasons (King David's Lodge). Washington, George. 1780-90. *548*
—. Letters. Religious Liberty. Seixas, Moses. Washington, George. 1790. 1974. *439*
—. Merchants. 1740-90. *320*
—. Touro Synagogue. 1902. *71*
—. Touro Synagogue. 1658-1963. *406*
Rhode Island (Providence). 1900-12. *290*
—. Belkin, Samuel. Brown University. Reminiscences. 1932-35. *64*

Sang, Philip David (obituary). Illinois State Historical Society. 1902-75. *748*

Saskatchewan. Cemeteries. 1975. *379*

—. Galt, Alexander. Kaplun, Alter (family). Settlement. 1880's-90's. *21*

Schaeffer, Susan Fromberg. Authors. Family. Mothers. Olsen, Tillie. Stereotypes. Yezierska, Anzia. 20c. *454*

Schiff, Jacob. California (El Centro). Letters. Schireson, Bernard. Wolffson, David. Zionism. 1914. *801*

Schiff, Jacob H. Canada. Galveston Plan. Immigration. USA. 1907-14. *48*

Schiller, Marcus. Business. California (San Diego). City Government. Mannasse, Joseph Samuel. 1853-97. *326*

Schireson, Bernard. California (El Centro). Letters. Schiff, Jacob. Wolffson, David. Zionism. 1914. *801*

Schlesinger, Jacob. California (Los Angeles). Cedars of Lebanon Hospital. Hospitals. 1901-30. *256*

Schlutius, Emma. California (Santa Cruz). Converts. Judaism. 1877. *163*

Scholars. Immigration. Israel. USSR. 1960's-70's. *715*

Scholarship. Feuer, Lewis S. Reminiscences. Teaching. Wolfson, Harry Austryn. ca 1900-74. *154*

—. Historiography. 1948-76. *253*

—. New York City. Yidisher Visnshaftlekher Institut. 1920-76. *200*

Schools. Daily Life. Interethnic relations. New York. Religion. 18c. *99*

Schreiber, Emanuel. California (Los Angeles). Judaism (Reform). Rabbis. 1881-1932. *356*

Schwartz, Benedict. Assimilation. Duelling. Feinberg, Siegmund. Texas. 1857. *317*

Scientists. Immigrants. Israel. USSR. 1930's. 1970's. *507*

Sculpture. Art. New York City. 1905-45. *766*

Sears, Roebuck and Company. Philanthropy. Rosenwald, Julius. 19c-20c. *27*

Secret Societies. Kallen, Horace M. *Parushim.* Zionism. 1913-1920. *605*

Secularization. Israel. Religion. Self-perception. 1957-77. *369*

Segal, Beryl. Canada. Education. Immigration. Reminiscences. USA. 1900-70's. *616*

Seigel, Sheldon. Bombing attack. Civil rights. Informers. Jewish Defense League. Legal defenses. 1972-73. *104*

Seixas, Gershom Mendes. Noah, Mordecai Manuel. Zionism. 1800-47. *584*

Seixas, Moses. Letters. Religious Liberty. Rhode Island (Newport). Washington, George. 1790. 1974. *439*

Self-alienation. Chomsky, Noam. Israel. Liberalism. 1975. *74*

Self-identity. Assimilation. Social Organization. 1954-74. *324*

Self-perception. Israel. Religion. Secularization. 1957-77. *369*

—. Social studies. Teaching. Textbooks. 1880-1920. 1945-65. *614*

Seminaries. Curricula. Hebrew Union College. Jewish history. Ohio (Cincinnati). Wise, Isaac Mayer. 1817-90's. *448*

Senate. Defense budget. Foreign Policy. Israel. Liberals. 1975. *420*

Separatist Movements. Elections, provincial. Parti Québécois. Quebec. 1976. *760*

—. French Canadians. Quebec. Social Conditions. 1976-77. *778*

Sephardic Hebrew Center. California (Los Angeles). Greek Americans. Immigration. 1900-74. *258*

Sermons. California (San Francisco). Franklin, Lewis Abraham. 1850. *173*

Settlement. Acculturation. Farms. New Jersey (Farmdale). 1919-70's. *116*

—. Agriculture. Farmers. Jewish Agriculturists' Aid Society of America. Levy, Abraham R. North Dakota (central). Reminiscences. Slavic Americans. 1903. *400*

—. Agriculture. Prairie Provinces. 1884-1920's. *529*

—. Brooks, Juanita. Utah. Watters, Leon L. 1864-65. 1952-73. *680*

—. California (Orangevale, Porterville). Lilienthal, Philip Nettre. Lubin, David. Weinstock, Harris. 1890's. *695*

—. Charities. Nebraska (Omaha). Political Leadership. Refugees. 1820-1937. *191*

—. Galt, Alexander. Kaplun, Alter (family). Saskatchewan. 1880's-90's. *21*

—. Geographic mobility. Georgia (Atlanta). Immigrants. 1870-96. *276*

—. German Americans. Polish Americans. Western states. 1820-70. *689*

—. Immigrants. Minnesota (St. Paul; Lower West Side). ca 1860-1920. *488*

—. Lederer, Henry. Michigan (Lansing). 1850-1918. *300*

—. Michigan (Kalkaska County). 1870's-90's. *16*

Settlement houses. Cincinnati Union Bethel. Ohio. Social reform. 1838-1903. *140*

Settlements. Brandeis, Louis D. Palestine. Zionism. ca 1877-1918. *732*

Sex roles. Immigrants. Women. 1880's-1979. *301*

Shafsky family. Business. California (Fort Bragg). Russia. 1889-1976. *818*

Shain, Samson Aaron (tribute). Bicentennial poem. Historians. Judaism. Pennsylvania (Lancaster County). 1906-76. *628*

Sheftall (family). American Revolution. Georgia (Savannah). 1730-1800. *460*

Sheftall, Levi. American Revolution. Commerce. Georgia (Savannah). Memoirs. 1739-1809. *669*

Shirpser, Elsie. California. Jewish Committee for Personal Service in State Institutions. Mental hospitals. Meyer, Martin A. Prisons. Psychiatric social histories. 1920-60. *456*

Shoe stores. Edison Brothers Company. Georgia. Retail Trade. 1910's-1940's. *56*

Sholom Aleichem Institute. Judaism. Michigan (Detroit). Religious Education. 1926-71. *555*

Shriften (periodical). Literature. New York City. Yiddish Language. 1912-26. *246*

Shwayder family. Colorado (Denver). Immigration. 1865-1916. *47*

Sichel, Carolyn Meyberg. Assimilation. California (Los Angeles). Reminiscences. 1902-31. *639*

Siegel, Richard. Daily Life. Strassfeld, Michael. Strassfeld, Sharon. 1973. *657*

Silver mining. Hebrew Benevolent Association. Letters. Nevada (Austin). 1864-82. *816*

Silversmithing. Myers, Myer. 1723-95. *806*

Simon, Joseph. Pennsylvania (Lancaster County). 1715-1804. *89*

Simon, Roger. Bergman, Andrew. Cynicism. Novels, detective. 1970's. *709*

Simons, Leonard N. Charities. Michigan (Detroit). Reminiscences. 1901-75. *646*

Singer, Isaac Bashevis (interview). Literature. Poland. Singer, Israel Joshua. 20c. *647*

Singer, Israel Joshua. Literature. Poland. Singer, Isaac Bashevis (interview). 20c. *647*

Singles, adult. Social Organization. 1970's. *499*

Sinsheimer, Aaron Zachary (and family). Buildings (iron front). California (San Luis Obispo). 1878-1956. *700*

U

V

W

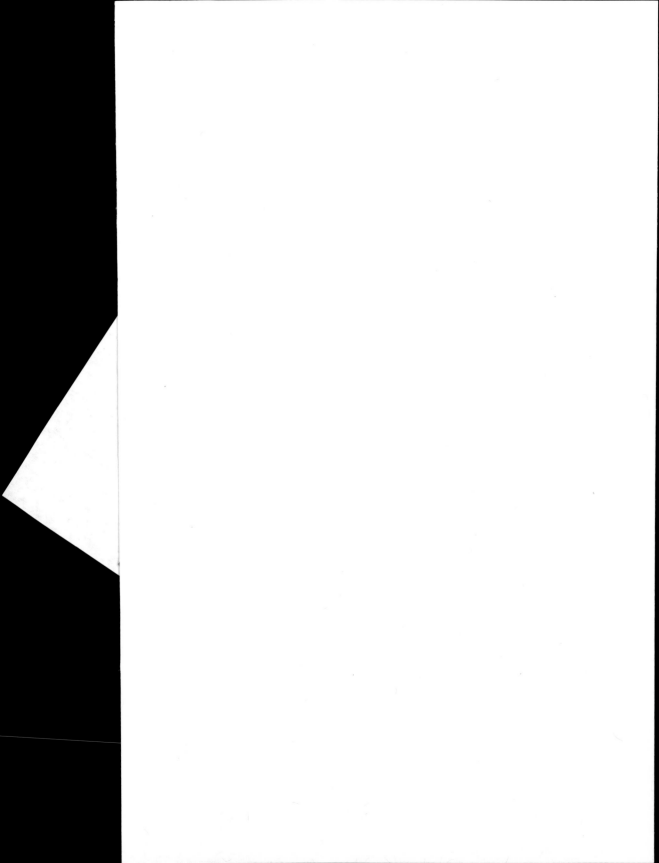

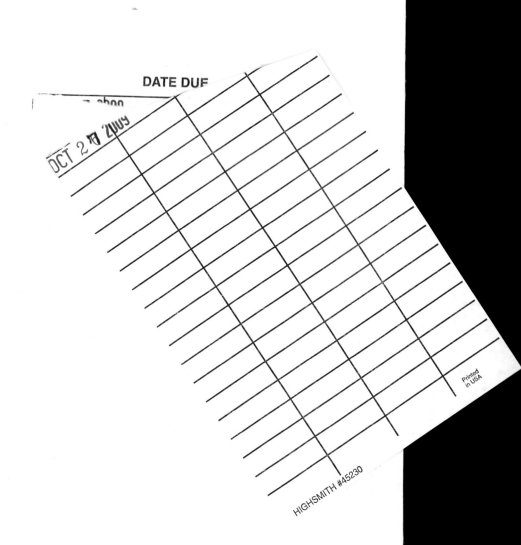

DATE DUE

OCT 2 7 2009

HIGHSMITH #45230

Printed in USA